The Edinburgh Companion to Scottish Women's Writing

Edinburgh Companions to Scottish Literature

Series Editors: Ian Brown and Thomas Owen Clancy

Titles in the series include:

Visit the Edinburgh Companions to Scottish Literature website at www.euppublishing.com/series/ecsl

The Edinburgh Companion to Scottish Women's Writing

Edited by Glenda Norquay

EDINBURGH
University Press

© in this edition Edinburgh University Press, 2012
© in the individual contributions is retained by the authors

Edinburgh University Press Ltd
22 George Square, Edinburgh EH8 9LF

www.euppublishing.com

Typeset in 10.5/12.5 Adobe Goudy
by Servis Filmsetting Ltd, Stockport, Cheshire, and
printed and bound in Great Britain by
CPI Group (UK) Ltd, Croydon, CR0 4YY

A CIP record for this book is available from the British Library

ISBN 978 0 7486 4432 2 (hardback)
ISBN 978 0 7486 4431 5 (paperback)
ISBN 978 0 7486 4445 2 (webready PDF)
ISBN 978 0 7486 6480 1 (epub)
ISBN 978 0 7486 6479 5 (Amazon ebook)

The right of the contributors
to be identified as author of this work
has been asserted in accordance with
the Copyright, Designs and Patents Act 1988.

Contents

Series Editors' Preface

The fourth tranche of the *Companion* series marks in its own way the underlying themes of the series as whole: Scottish literature is multivalent, multilingual and vibrant. Each volume also reflects the series ethos: to challenge, set new perspectives and work towards defining differences of canon in Scottish literature. Such definition of difference must always be sensitive and each volume in the 2012 tranche shows not only the confidence of up-to-date, leading-edge scholarship, but the flexibility of nuanced thought that has developed in Scottish literary studies in recent years. A tranche which balances a volume on women's writing with volumes on two major male writers subverts, even on the most superficial reading, any version of an older tradition which depended on a canon based on 'great' writers, mostly, if not exclusively, male. In approaching Scott and Hogg, contributors have demonstrated fresh thinking and recontextualised their work, opening them to new insights and enjoyment, while the authors in the volume on *Women's Writing* reinterpret and reorganise the very structures of thought through which we experience the writing explored.

Scott, often in the past taken to represent a stuffy old-fashioned male-dominated literary canon, is revisited, reassessed and brought to our minds anew. One is reminded of the remark of the great European scholar Martin Esslin to one of the series editors that Scott was the greatest artist in any art form of the nineteenth century. Such a statement may embody the generalising attitudes of an older generation, but Esslin's argument was based not just on Scott's range and innovations, but on the importance of his influence on his successors, not just in literature but in other arts. Hogg, meantime, has often previously suffered by comparison with Scott, misunderstood and misread in ways that the *Hogg* volume makes clear as it demystifies past perceptions and opens new vistas on his work's scope. The *Scottish Women's Writing* volume completes a trio of innovative *Companions* in its range of disparate viewpoints. Avoiding easy categories or theories, these demonstrate with rigour and vigour that, though in some genres, like drama, women's writing has had a difficult time historically, it has, not least in the Gaelic tradition, always played a crucial role. The volume rightly and lucidly inter-rogates any system of classification that obscures this insight. The 2012 tranche as a whole continues the *Companion* series project of reviewing and renewing the way we read and enjoy the rich diversity of Scottish literature.

Ian Brown
Thomas Owen Clancy

Acknowledgements

The General Editors of the Companion Series, Ian Brown and Thomas Clancy, have been supportive presences. Ian Brown in particular shared expertise, experience and canny advice. Jackie Jones at Edinburgh University Press made useful interventions in the early stages and Aileen Christianson provided a listening ear and a critical eye. I am grateful, as always, to the support of colleagues at Liverpool John Moores University.

Gaelic adviser

The advice and expertise of Michel Byrne has been invaluable in compiling this volume. His has been the steering hand in the chapters which address Gaelic culture and his performance in this role was characterised by the consistency of his insights, sensitivity and attention to detail.

Introduction

Glenda Norquay

When Mary Brunton writes in her journal, 'Welcome, mine own rugged Scotland', she romantically inscribes but distances herself from the nation; Scotland is both hers and craggily, masculinely different.[1] To escape into the liberating 'Seaward Toon', the allocuter in Marion Angus's poem of that name must engage freely with the world around her, rather than making 'ilka ruint stane a wound'.[2] The 'sherp chert tongues of grannies', depicted in Kathleen Jamie's poem 'Arraheids', rest in Scotland's museums, having lain 'fur generations in the land/like wicked cherms': their flinty presence both speaks and holds secrets.[3] When Cassie, in Janice Galloway's *Foreign Parts* visits the French château of Chenonceau and sees grafitti scratched into the wall by the Scots guard of Mary Stuart, she has to address the challenging significance for her of the image HAME.[4] Articulating the dynamic between women, nation and creativity seems to demand such stony confrontations. Yet from this tension the richness of their writing flourishes. Women's writing in Scotland is a story both of bold declarations of self and of the, at times, secret and strategic infiltration of walled areas of literary production. This volume looks at a range of writing by women in Scotland but also examines the contexts in which their literature was produced and its impact on our wider understanding of Scottish literary history. Its chronological spread traces the shifting but shared themes of a significant body of work.

In Volume 3 of the *Edinburgh History of Scottish Literature* historian Richard Finlay notes that: 'Of all the great changes that have affected Scottish society, perhaps the greatest has been within the personal realm of family life and between men and women.'[5] In the first volume of the same series Cairns Craig suggests that the 'recovery' since the 1970s of the works of women writers 'had a disproportionate impact on both the richness of Scotland's literary resources and the overall understanding of its literary history'.[6] Given these significant social changes and the success of recovery work in the field of women's writing, several questions arise. Do we need another study of Scottish women's writing? In the twenty-first century, if literary history has already been reshaped, is there still a value in literary segregation? With the publication of work by a range of Scottish women writers since the 1980s, the appearance of several histories of writing by women as well as a number of critical studies that explore gender dynamics – in terms of both femininity and masculinity – the answer might appear to be no. Conversely, if there is a need, is it because Scotland, as some critics have suggested, lags behind other national literatures in its understanding of writing and gender?[7]

This volume is as much an exploration of these questions as an answer to them. It does not represent itself as an act of recovery: many of the writers mentioned here are now relatively established within the Scottish canon, although perhaps not at its centre. Nor does it seek to address only material which foregrounds issues around gender: engagements with gender now feature much more significantly in Scottish literary criticism.[8] What this collection does move towards is a deeper understanding of the role of gender in the formations of Scottish literature and how women writers might be situated within wider literary patterns. In examining writing by women it thinks about the ways in which women might be have been drawn to, or forced into, areas of literary production – private writing, domestic fiction, genre fiction – or struggled to find their place within dominant, and dominantly masculine, forms such as the periodical press and drama. It also examines the extent to which adding women's writing to the mix might reshape our understanding of key moments – such as the Scottish Renaissance – or cultural formations – such as oral tradition. Rather than recovering women from the margins, this volume takes the opportunity to look at their writing as a means of reconfiguring our understanding of Scottish literature. In so doing it gives evidence of the life flaring through individual women writers but also provides some surprises for our sense of a Scottish canon.

Gifford and McMillan's *A History of Scottish Women's Writing* represented the first major attempt to address the absence of a recognised history and canon of women's writing for Scottish literature: its importance in defining a field of work cannot be overestimated and it remains a key reference point for many of the essays here.[9] Published in 1997, it predates, however, a devolved Scotland and significant advances in the study of gender and cultural production. While some topics and contributors are shared with the *Companion* collection, Gifford and McMillan's essays serve primarily as acts of recovery rather than reconceptualisations of literary paradigms. Subsequent studies of twentieth-century writing such as Anderson and Christianson's *Scottish Women's Fiction: 1920s to 1960s: Journeys into being* (2000) and Christianson and Lumsden's *Contemporary Scottish Women Writers* (2000), again maintain a focus on individual writers, although both are important in identifying a range of shared concerns across the texts they cover.[10] Other significant earlier engagements with gender in a Scottish context include Christopher

Whyte's *Gendering the Nation* (1995), an early and challenging intervention in our understanding of the relationship between gender, sexuality and
nationalism although again it focuses on case studies of individual writers.[11]
The *Edinburgh History of Scottish Literature* weaves the work of women writers
into its impressive coverage: there are references to Anna Gordon and a
chapter on Sìleas na Ceapaich in Volume 1; chapters on the emergence of
privacy, on Joanna Baillie and on travel writing in Volume 2; and in the
third volume chapters on Edwin and Willa Muir and on Muriel Spark and
significant attention to women writers in its chapter on children's fiction. In
terms of engaging directly with the politics of gender, however, the necessarily wide-ranging chapter on 'Aspects of Gender, the Novel and Drama'
by Suzanne Hagemann is the most important in raising wider questions and
suggesting rich directions for further analysis.

Other recent studies of Scottish literature – Petrie (2004); Riach (2005);
Sassi (2005) – have a narrower chronological spread and engage more
directly with issues of national identity.[12] Berthold Schoene's ambitious
Edinburgh Companion to Contemporary Scottish Literature (2007) significantly
extends the range of writers and topics to be considered under the label,
including work of a Scottish diaspora, popular fiction, cinema and storytelling.[13] The drive of that volume is, however, still towards coverage. The
Companion to Scottish Women's Writing engages with the freshness of critical
approaches represented by Schoene but offers more focused thematic groupings and, of course, a broader chronological spread overall. This collection is
structured by its thematic concerns but its chronological drive suggests those
points at which these thematic explorations are most usefully addressed. The
reader is able to follow through a range of issues but also to gain a sense of
historical developments within women's writing in Scotland.

When Gifford and McMillan produced their *History of Scottish Women's
Writing* in 1997 they also asked the question: does women's writing need
to be in a separate volume? At that point they came up with the response
that 'even if the only justification that can be offered for separatism is that
it carves out more space to talk about women's writing then that seems good
enough to be going on with'.[14] They argued furthermore that their collection was a response both to the absence of women from Scottish histories
of writing and to the exclusion of Scottish women from general histories
and anthologies of women's writing. Since then, some things have moved
on, not least the literature itself. In their Introduction to the first volume of
the *Edinburgh History of Scottish Literature* the editors suggest that while the
approach to Scottish literature in the 1980s was very much driven by the
need to 'show and tell', the period since then has seen new and more complex
groupings emerge. One approach that has had a more significant impact than
almost anything else, as Craig notes in his second introductory chapter to

the same volume, was that driven by the inspiration of feminist criticism.[15] Feminist criticism itself has, of course, multiplied into plurality and debate around 'post-feminism', moving from the early calls for 'neglected' women writers to be reassessed and themes of gender within literature re-examined, to an interest in the challenging of gender binaries through 'écriture féminine' and notions of performativity.[16] More recent work on emotion and affect has led to significant re-evaluations of aesthetic formulations while continuing research in the dynamics of print culture has refreshed interest in women as readers and creators in non-canonical forms while also signalling the materiality of literary production.[17] In the *Companion*, individual essays reflect the range of these developments through its consideration of particular historical moments and thematic concerns but the volume itself, with its focus on writing rather than individuals or texts, also offers new mappings of the literary landscape.

One key aspect of this reconfiguration is an attention to Gaelic culture. A paradox of feminist criticism in Scotland has been, Craig notes, that '[f]rom earliest major anthologies in the late eighteenth century, poetry by women had been at the heart of the coalescing canon of Gaelic literature', but their significance remained a 'blind spot' in histories of Scottish women's writing such as Gifford and McMillan.[18] Working with a recognition that we have moved beyond both 'recovery' and 'showing and telling', this *Companion* foregrounds women's place in Gaelic culture in an early chapter by Anne Frater and Michel Byrne on 'Gaelic Poetry and Song', but also acknowledges that women's creative output in Gaelic needs to be considered within a context beyond that of 'two cultures'. In a discussion extended by Sarah Dunnigan and Suzanne Gilbert in their chapters on 'Spirituality' and on 'Orality and the Ballad Tradition', Anne Frater and Michel Byrne address conceptual and critical questions raised by Gaelic culture and by creative traditions in which the accessibility of material and understanding of its transmission pose their own challenges. Acknowledging the complexity of available information on women's lives in Gaelic society, they explore their cultural contributions through analysis of both the creative outputs of high-born women in Gaelic society and of working women. For noblewomen working with the Classical Gaelic tradition, their assumption of masculinised bardic roles and deployment of high generic conventions was in itself transgressive. For others it was their subject matter that crossed boundaries; Sìleas na Ceapaich exploring, even with a conservative morality, sexuality, Màiri nighean Alasdair Ruaidh, working outside the confines of forms deemed acceptable for women. The lives of working woman are also shown to have contributed to the expansion of both the culture and our understanding of its dynamics, in their vernacular engagements with daily occupations, from waulking the tweed to childcare, through which they could find wider social and political articulation. Gaelic culture remains an arena in which the paradoxes of women's cultural contribution will sustain further research.

If the process of recovering women's writing, however, has been so significant, and if women are now more fully represented on the literary map of Scotland, the question remains as to why they should be considered in a separate volume within the *Companion* series. The answer resides in two responses. First, there is general agreement that Scottish literature was relatively late in its deployment of feminist critical approaches to understanding a body of writing. Hagemann suggests that 'in Scottish criticism [feminism] did not happen until the early 1990s', citing as explanation the demands of focusing of the quest for Scottishness in what she terms 'a small-nation syndrome';[19] Caroline Gonda, in 1995, quoted novelist Ali Smith asserting that 'Scottish women's writing has only really been given a place . . . in the last ten years.'[20] Dramatic genres act as an exemplar of just such a phenomenon.

In earlier centuries there have been such women playwrights as Catherine Trotter (1679–1749), Jean Mar(i)shall (*fl.* 1765–89) and Joanna Baillie (1762–1851), but only the first had her work presented on main stages, the latter two tending to write closet drama. Even in the twentieth century, although Agnes Adam wrote one-act plays prolifically for the amateur companies of the Scottish Community Drama Association founded in 1926, until the sensational impact of Ena Lamont Stewart, writing for Glasgow Unity Theatre in the 1940s, women's playwriting was underplayed and neglected on the professional stage. And famously and sadly, she herself was largely ignored as a playwright in subsequent decades until the Scottish Society of Playwrights presented two of her one-act plays in their 1975 Netherbow season and *Men Should Weep* was revived in 7:84's 1982 Clydebuilt season. The widespread recognition of Stewart as a major dramatist in fact happened only recently with productions of *Men Should Weep* by both the Royal National Theatre (2010) and the National Theatre of Scotland (2011). Yet since the 1970s, with forerunners like Ada F. Kay and Joan Ure, a new wave of women playwrights has emerged. A veritable cascade of women's writing talent has flooded the Scottish stage and been performed abroad. Liz Lochhead, Sue Glover, Sharman Macdonald and Jackie Kay are only four that might be mentioned: their work is addressed carefully and prominently in both the *Edinburgh History* and the *Edinburgh Companion to Scottish Drama* (2011). Yet it is striking not just that, until the last few decades, there was no substantial critical attention given to the women playwrights there were, but that, until the recent surge, women playwrights were remarkable largely by their absence from the Scottish stage.

There is, therefore, still work to be done in reshaping our understanding of Scottish literary patterns through a cognizance of women's role. While the *Edinburgh History of Scottish Literature* contained 'more writing by women than any previous histories', and attempted to bring into prominence genres in which women have excelled, there is still a proportional (and historically determined) imbalance in their representation. The publication of *The Biographical Dictionary of Scottish Women* in 2006 revealed further the extent of their creative activities.[21] So the task of profiling women in literary histories retains importance, in terms of representation itself, even if it inevitably involves what Sonya Stephens describes in her introduction to *A History of Women's Writing in France* (2000) as both a sense of vertigo and a necessary myopia, the former created by the range and scale of women's literature and the latter as a pragmatic necessity of producing a historical account.[22]

With this new confidence in women's literary production, brought about in part by publications such as *The History of Scottish Women's Writing*, a new and more positive approach to women's writing is made possible. As early as 1991 Liz Lochhead forcefully articulated what such a strategy might avoid:

> O.K. Three points about being a women writer in Scotland. One: your gender is not a 'problem'. Two: you don't really need 'role models' [. . .] Three: you don't have to 'write positively about women' or create 'heroines'.[23]

This statement by Lochhead chimes in with the observation by Meg Bateman with regard to women poets in Gaelic that Michel Byrne discusses in Chapter 2: 'For writers of a minority language, culture is of greater significance than gender.' Byrne goes on (p. 33) to discuss possible broader implications of Bateman's remark about gender and Gaelic women poets. Nevertheless, the idea that women writers 'struggled' because of their gender, and painfully blazed trails for others to follow, all with the aim of articulating the female nature of their experience, lingers on. The essays in this collection show that while women such as Margaret Oliphant or Naomi Mitchison may have felt marginalised from the literary societies of their time, and writers such as Catherine Carswell and Willa Muir may have searched for new ways to articulate female desire, they also forged ways of writing that challenged – and were often misunderstood, therefore ignored by – the societies in which they worked. As this volume shows, while conventional publication and critical recognition may have been elusive or, as with Jane Welsh Carlyle or Mary Somerville, not even an aim, women wrote, and wrote on their own terms.

Things have also moved on in the conceptualising of literary history since 1997 when Gifford and McMillan acknowledged the 'instability and potential impossibility of the subject'. The editors of the *Cambridge Companion to American Women's Writing*, Dale Bauer and Philip Gould, suggest that they are aiming to challenge the 'seamlessness of cultural contexts' by questioning key concepts such as 'the domestic' and 'sentimentality', thus re-examining the crucial premises for critical study and allowing 'instability' to be an integral part of the project.[24] The ground-breaking *Edinburgh History of Scottish Literature* itself shows the range and diversity of Scottish writing without seeking to impose a unifying framework. But if, as Brown et al. assert, Scottish literature 'inflects genre in a manner distinctively its own', so writing by Scottish women still benefits by being situated within literary approaches inflected by an awareness of gender.[25] Just as the influential collection of essays by Abrams et al., *Gender in Scottish History* sought to 'gender the agenda', integrating women's experience into the dominant narratives of Scotland,[26] this *Companion* seeks to redefine dominant literary narratives through attention both to women writers and to the patterns of their writing. It deploys gender as a point of entry into an examination of: different areas of literary experience – determinants of genre; the masculinisation or feminisation of literary forms; issues of critical neglect; questions of readership – and through its tension of chronology and theme brings together women writers in different configurations, and in relationships perhaps occluded until now, which will give a new perspective on both the writers and their contexts.

In the process many insights and some surprises emerge. One striking feature is the pervasiveness of Margaret Oliphant. Taken by Helen Sutherland as a case study for women's negotiations of the nineteenth-century periodical press, Oliphant is also dominant in Macdonald's discussion of supernatural writing, a significant presence in Christianson's analysis of private writing and features in Carol Anderson's discussion of travel writing. This suggests not only the prolific nature of Oliphant's output but also her importance as a key reference point in nineteenth-century writing, presenting a significant challenge to our literary maps. If, as Pam Perkins argues, a woman like Alison Cockburn has all too often been obscured by Scott's shadow, Oliphant's prolific output has, paradoxically, relegated her to a minor position within Scottish nineteenth-century fiction. Here she emerges as significant force in a number of areas. In her chapter 'Janet Hamilton: Working-class Memoirist and Cultural Commentator', Florence Boos echoes Sutherland on Oliphant in showing the impact of one women writing beyond the limitations of her time. Janet Hamilton transcended both class and gender to acquire a resonant and powerful voice, articulating opinions on a range of subjects. While, as with Oliphant, her contributions may not be explicitly feminist in tone, her presence and range of writing again show a woman as a formidable exponent of ideas and a time in which both her class and gender might have worked against her. Hamilton, like Oliphant, forces us to reassess our maps of the nineteenth-century Scottish canon.

A smaller, but more interestingly geographical, reconfiguration is suggested in chapters by Margery Palmer McCulloch and Anderson in which both, for different reasons, claim Catherine Carswell's *The Camomile* as a great Glasgow novel. As McCulloch observes in 'Interwar Literature', acknowledging the novel's significance in this way pre-empts and challenges Duncan Thaw's complaint in *Lanark* that Glasgow as a city has no imaginative existence.[27] Although previous delineations of the city in literature may have presented a limited locale for male subjectivity, Carswell's novel creates an urban world in which Glasgow's streets offer as much of an entry into explorations of female identity as Virginia Woolf's London provided in the same period.

A second feature to emerge is the consistent demand created by women's writing to reinvestigate literary categories and aesthetic constructs. Gilbert, for example, in a chapter on 'Orality and the Ballad Tradition', demonstrates how female orality both conceptually reinforced and, in more practical terms, undermined Romantic concepts of the voice. Her chapter not only argues for ballad culture's influence on later women writers, an argument reinforced by Brown's analysis of twentieth-century poetry, but also demands that we rethink easy assumptions about the relationship between the continuity of literary tradition and the specificity of performance. In examining what spiritual writing affords women, both individually and within communities, Dunnigan in 'Spirituality' shows that the mystic, whether deployed in spiritual activism, used as a source of eroticism or brought to bear on life-writing, was a dominant imaginative patterning of their work. Her chapter, with its emphasis on points of affinity and difference in a range of writings, suggests that an area of expression often generally understood in gendered terms deserves recognition of the complexity within. Reconsidering the place of women in Scottish Enlightenment adds to understanding of its distinctive nature in terms of its 'mixed intellectual sociability'. Again questioning aesthetic and generic categories, Perkins shows the merging of 'sociable conversation' into 'sophisticated literary play', revealing the sociable and conversable in an arena in which women's contribution was significant. Like Aileen Christianson who, in 'Private Writing' also questions distinctions between public and private, she suggests that the relative silence of Scottish women in published work during this period is not representative of their contribution to intellectual culture. Christianson too addresses issues of literary value in her argument for seeing nineteenth-century women writers as more sophisticated both in their negotiation of distinctions between public and private writing and in their awareness of literary genre, artistic choice and the work of revision even in their 'private' writing.

If these chapters demand a reconsideration of literary categories, they also reveal the extent to which women writers consciously negotiate genre boundaries. The complexity and sophistication of these manoeuvrings is the third striking feature of this collection. By re-situating the domestic fiction of Brunton and Ferrier within socio-political debate over national identity, McIntosh in 'Domestic Fiction' indicates the wider potential offered by the genre of romance, while Glenda Norquay's chapter on 'Genre Fiction' shows twentieth- and twenty-first-century writers working within 'popular' and formulaic genres, turning their characteristics to their own advantage by making repetition and the serial nature of genre writing integral to the more challenging questions posed by their work. In 'Margaret Oliphant and the Nineteenth-century Periodical Press' Sutherland demonstrates the advantages an apparently masculinised area of literary production could give to the woman writer: the authority of a male voice and the disguise of a house style. Working within this context Oliphant nevertheless created a space in which she could voice her own concerns as a woman writer. Kirsty Macdonald, in 'Writing the Supernatural', equally shows the power women writers gained through using the paradigm of supernatural: again it is Oliphant who walks the delicate line between creative deployment of the semiotic and retreat into madness.

If women are seen in this volume as working within, adapting or challenging both generic and social conventions, their other important engagement with boundaries is played out in their emotional and political relationships with national spaces. In 'Domestic Fiction' Ainsley McIntosh shows Mary Brunton structuring her fictions around the cultural discontinuities of Scotland, contrasting Highland and Lowland life in ways which question the viability and desirability of a homogeneous national identity. In their detailed explorations of the dynamics in that long-standing association of the Highlands with emotion and affect, Brunton and Susan Ferrier, show an acute understanding of competing cultural discourses around landscape, national identity and power.

If landscape operates as a marker of national difference for Ferrier, with later writers the representation of space, whether real or fictional, becomes the locus for questioning perceptions of home, rootedness and dwelling. As Anderson shows in her chapter on 'Writing Spaces', Nan Shepherd, Violet Jacob and Catherine Carswell use the matrices of rural life, small town and city to map out questions of subjectivity. The idea of decentring, present in this chapter, appears with more political implications in chapters by McCulloch and Eleanor Bell. McCulloch's chapter claims the significance of Carswell, Lorna Moon, Mitchison and Muir within the interwar years, contributing in important ways to the Scottish Renaissance but offering a more nuanced articulation of national identity than their male counterparts. In 'Experiment and Nation in the 1960s' Bell shows how even a writer with the authority (and, by the 1960s, experience) of Naomi Mitchison could feel sidelined, restricted to the margins of debate in a real world celebration of Scottish cultural politics. Bell goes on to show the strategies of survival in this context adopted by other writers have led them to increasingly formal experimentation or turned them from Scotland itself. Monica Germanà's and

Norquay's chapters offer a more positive analysis of contemporary women's writing, showing the vibrancy and diversity of recent work but also reinforce the sense of strategic manoeuvring of genre and literary form that has been employed to effect this. Indeed Germanà suggests, in 'Contemporary Fiction' that the idea of the decentred self and a resistance to stable roots has become one of the most productive forces in contemporary women's fiction, a perspective reinforced by Macdonald's discussion of contemporary writers and the idea of liminality.

In poetry, as Rhona Brown's chapter on 'Twentieth-century Poetry' charts in its comparative analysis of Marion Angus, Liz Lochhead and Kathleen Jamie, the twentieth century also saw an increasingly complicated tension between home and away. Through analysis of their language, the influence of traditional forms and the ballads in particular, and their handling of memory, Brown argues that all three writers work on the boundaries of the general and specific and through this both challenge and validate the implications of their own Scottishness. That paradoxical resistance to fixity combined with a detailed attention to the particular emerges as one of the major contributions of contemporary women's writing in Scotland, evidenced in the work of Janice Galloway, A. L. Kennedy, Ali Smith, Jackie Kay and Leila Aboulela.

This *Companion* volume too is poised between the general and particular: it brings together a range of writing produced by women who are Scottish. Yet rather than suggesting that an individual writer's sex is the most significant aspect of their work or the gendering of identity necessarily the dominant concern of their writing, it shows that nation and gender are among the coordinates through which writing by women in Scotland can be situated. In both the literature considered and the critical approaches of each chapter it is this attention to the specific, to the details of difference, which becomes a shared and unifying concern.

CHAPTER ONE

Spirituality

Sarah M. Dunnigan

When Lilias Skene, a late seventeenth-century Quaker from Aberdeenshire, confesses that '[t]hough all the capacity, theory, and eloquence of men were in one person, he could not draw or describe Christ's love and the believer's happiness in him in all its lineaments',[1] she sums up the paradox facing the writer of any spiritual experience: how to put the inexpressible into words. Skene's reflection on how '[t]hat which is infinite is of too great extent for finite reach'[2] informs any attempt to circumscribe or define spiritual writing; 'spirituality' is a diverse and nebulous term describing emotional experience, devotional practice, or a system of belief which may conform to or resist orthodox or institutional practice. Within the early modern Scottish context, expressions of 'spirituality' emerge in the wake of the reformation of the Roman Catholic church, the moral and spiritual movement that gathered momentum in Scotland in the late 1550s and 1560s from the Protestant evangelising revolution of northern and central Europe. After the reformed Parliament in 1560 sanctioned a new Confession of Faith, Catholicism became the faith of recusants in most areas in the Highlands and Western Isles while varieties of the Protestant religion proliferated in subsequent decades, often – as in the Covenanting movement – as a consequence of dissent from royal and parliamentary-sanctioned religious practice.

Throughout this period of tumultuous religious change, women's surviving written articulations of faith chart experiences of spiritual practice and belief which refract not just these changing ideologies but the ways in which religion both accommodated and excluded women socially and politically. This chapter explores women's writing from different religious communities in order to understand the points of affinity as well as the obvious differences that (often violently) divide them. It does not suggest that simply by virtue of their femininity the expression of spirituality is shared but examines aspects of the relationship between religious sensibility and writerly expression that too rigid a focus on precise doctrinal areas of conflict might obscure. The chapter is thematically and conceptually shaped rather than focusing on single authors to permit the greatest variety of spiritual voices to be heard.

Early modern female spirituality emerges as a complex phenomenon, emotional and political in import, impinging on questions of voice and selfhood,
agency and desire.

While evidence of a 'feminised' spirituality can be seen in the Marian lyrics
and female saints' lives of Celtic and later medieval Scottish vernacular cultures, as well as in the account of the life of St Margaret (c.1046–93),[3] there
are few substantial surviving written expressions of faith by women prior
to the Reformation, with the exception of female lyrics from the Classical
Gaelic tradition.[4] Accordingly, this chapter focuses on writing from the
period c.1560–c.1700; although its scope cannot be comprehensive, it draws
on spiritual voices which are more familiar such as those of Mary Stuart
Queen of Scots (1542–87), exiled and executed Catholic queen; Elizabeth
Melville (fl. 1599–1631), Lady Colville of Culross;[5] the Gaelic poet Sìleas
na Ceapaich (c.1660–c.1729);[6] and some less well known, such as those
heard in the writings of Skene, and of Katharine Collace (c.1635–97), Helen
Alexander (d.1729), and Elizabeth Blackadder (1659/60–1732).[7] Many
do not write in obviously 'literary' genres, while their common circulation
through private manuscript and exchange makes us examine our assumptions about how, and for whom, these visionaries and witnesses articulated
their experience.[8] That they did so at all means that any perception about a
monolithic hostility to women and the feminine on theological and ethical
grounds within Catholic and Reformed religions (partly on account of 'the
transgressions of Eva the first Woman'),[9] should be qualified by these vivid,
intense survivals of what Collace calls 'soul-work'.

Voice and Selfhood

Spiritual writing composed in the first person is often assumed to be transparent: the voice seeking to portray divine 'truth' is often judged as a truthful representation. 'Personal' experience – such as Sìleas's loss of both her husband
and daughter Anna, and her own apparent illness – may be presented as the
'inspiration' for religious experience, burdening her with 'the gift of suffering pain' ('Glòir thoir do Mhac Muire/ Thug 'e ghibht domh gun d'fhuiling
mi leòn'/ (Give glory to the Son of Mary who gave me the gift of suffering
pain)).[10] In a lyric colloquy with Death, Sìleas's speaker is warned that in
time 'Nì na daolagan dìot fàrdach'/ (worms will make you their home), but
she finds refuge in God: 'Rinn E rium ro-mhóran caoimhneis/ 'S thug E air
an Aog bhith sàmhach'/ (He was extremely kind to me and bade Death be at
peace).[11] Yet in spite, or perhaps because, of such apparent transparency, the
devotional 'self' is carefully shaped. In Mary, Queen of Scots' sonnets spirituels
the extent to which she composes in a 'sovereign' voice is unclear: these are
lyrics of atonement and spiritual divestiture.[12] If read as the supplications of

a fallen, earthly queen to the 'pre sovereign' who judges her, and therefore about the fragility of power itself, whether political or moral, these poems seem intensely personal: poetic acts which grant Mary cathartic or expiatory power. Yet Mary, as an imprisoned Catholic queen, was vigilant of wider representation both by herself and those factions which sought to vilify or glorify her. Her poems about spiritual fortitude published in the *Consolationes*, by the imprisoned Bishop of Ross, John Leslie, widely circulated in Catholic Europe, awarded her 'pitié' for 'longue souffrance'.[13]

Elizabeth Melville raises further questions about the relationship between creativity and voice or 'reputation'. Her religiosity was 'publicly' witnessed at prayer meetings, and praised by other writers;[14] this acknowledged 'authority' may have granted legitimacy to her major published work, *Ane Godlie Dreame*. First printed with the ascription, 'compylit in Scottish meter be M. M. gentelvvoman in Culros, at the requeist of her friends', the extent to which the *Dreame* is 'her' narrative, or explicitly voiced by a female narrator, is debatable.[15] Through the dreamer's communion with Christ and the journey from hell to paradise on which both embark, Melville inscribes her poem within a visionary, allegorical mode of deep literary roots. The dreamer is necessarily a figure of empathic vulnerability, the narrative an easily comprehended story of sin and redemption. The deliverance granted to the *Dreame*'s narrator strengthens 'her' voice not just spiritually but rhetorically so that the poem culminates in exhortation and command: the penitent's voice becomes the preacher's. This may mirror the authority Melville carried within her own spiritual community; or perhaps poetry itself provided a kind of covert rhetorical protection for such devotional and doctrinal expression. If what we see in Mary and Melville is deft manipulation, rather than simply transparent reflection, of selfhood, then life-writing offers a further fascinating illustration of how the encounter between the individual and the divine is mediated by 'voice'.

Life-writing is distinct within the different expressive modes of evangelical piety, although not unique to Scottish seventeenth-century religious reformed culture (accounts of personal 'witnessing' or visionary meditations are found in the medieval mystical tradition too). These largely prose meditations provided a popular means by which the inner life could be examined: a searching model or 'proof' of sanctity, they were circulated or printed in order to instruct, inspire, console, offering an empathic model of spiritual identification.[16] As the number of surviving texts ascribed to women attests, female lives were considered exemplary. Katharine Collace was a schoolmistress from Edinburgh, who taught sewing, 'living in the time of persecution'.[17] In her *Memoirs or Spiritual Exercises* published posthumously in 1735, she creates a narrative of her life, retrospectively constructing experience into relatable segments or 'portions' offered to the reader for similar meditative contemplation. Her initiation into the spiritual life begins when young ('the fourteenth year of my age'); in such narratives, the originary moment of conversion is crucial – foundational in crystallising the moral and spiritual fragility ('backsliding') which inevitably haunts these writers.[18] The journey towards God is necessarily beset by difficulties. Collace's memoir character-istically exemplifies a kind of experiential force in depicting women's lives: the pain of childbirth, the death of children. She describes how the loss of a child, apparently smothered by her wet-nurse, made for 'the breaking of my peace and health. [. . .] a hell arose in my conscience for blood-guiltiness, and sin against light'.[19] In these narratives, the self is laid bare and judged, subject to internal and external scrutiny; Collace is 'made a wonder to many'.[20] As in the narrative of the medieval English mystic, Margery Kempe, these women encounter antagonism or generate hostility: 'a sore blow from a Christian acquaintance and neighbour' compels Collace to move.[21] As Mullan observes, '[t]he striving for holiness exposes the problem of ego in the community'.[22] The quotidian and mundane intrude into these narratives, exemplifying the inchoate nature of the spiritual life lived 'in the world'.

Ultimately, even the most painful or anxious of experiences for Collace (such as her sister's illness) are necessary and justified. In the context of the divine providential plan, there is purpose and meaning to personal suffering. Assured by God of 'the good days'[23] which are imminent, Collace orders and configures her own life within a broader apocalyptic framework of the conflict between God and the devil while Sìleas's speaker eagerly awaits the reunion with the dead on Là Luain (Doomsday).

The Erotics of the Sacred

The desire to know God, to enter into union with the divine, is often figu-ratively expressed by these women through the most intimate and intense of relationships: that of a lover and beloved. Although culturally strange to us, the eroticisation of the sacred is the source of some of the most highly charged poetic and prose writing, with established scriptural precedent in the biblical Song of Solomon. Its relationship between the soul and Christ, conceived as a language of sensual longing and praise, offered a verbal and conceptual model of devotion that found particular affinity with medieval mystical devotion. In the theological climate of the later thirteenth century, the notion of a more 'personal' relationship with the divine, mediated pri-marily through emotion and experience rather than through intellectual or abstract doctrine, fostered what is now often referred to as 'affective piety'. The immediacy and intensity of spiritual eroticism in early modern Scottish women's writing echoes this earlier mystical practice, though expressed in the wholly different doctrinal context of Protestant piety. Its retention of the 'theological role of the affections' meant that subjective experiences of the divine were valued as demonstrating how the Holy Spirit 'illuminated the hearts of the elect'.[24] Strikingly, the writer who might have been the most sympathetic exponent of affective piety, Mary Stuart, rarely eroticises her relationship with God and Christ: God is a fierce lord and master, fearfully obeyed rather than tenderly adored, and she rarely turns to the gentler lovingness of the Virgin Mary.

This lack of eroticisation may be a result of Mary's self-censorship in the wake of the Casket sonnets controversy (which made the expression of queenly desire dangerous) but the interplay between the realms of the sacred and secular is fruitful for other writers. In Aithbhreac inghean Coirceadail's (fl. 1460) formal lament for the death of her husband, Niall Óg of Gigha, the symbol of the rosary, while liturgically fulfilling the speaker's grieving rituals, is a sensuous reminder of loss: 'A phaidrín do dhúisg mo dhéar,/ ionmhain méar do bhitheadh ort'/ (O rosary that woke my tears/ beloved the finger that on you did lie).[25] Melville's reworking of Christopher Marlowe's secular love song, 'Come live with me and be my love', startlingly transposes the profane into the spiritual when Christ's invitation to love him prompts fierce self-denunciation: 'Thy heart is mine I bought it deir/ Then send it not a whooring here';[26] the beauty of spiritual love is realised only by intense focus on its inversion. Elsewhere, Melville's supplicant speaks of the difficulty of knowing Christ as a lover laments an absent beloved. Here, the parallel with the rejected lover of Petrarchan tradition alters the lyric's psychological and rhetorical dynamics: 'What wonder though I ever mourne/ My sweetest sun will not returne/ Who once did shyne so clear/ Since he alace did first depart/ Who can inflame this frozen heart?'[27] The conventional gendered relationship of erotic poetry – whereby a male lover addresses a female beloved – is reversed. As if licensed by scriptural precedent (the Song of Solomon is a clear source of its sensual lyricism), Melville further 'feminises' the poem's spirituality in personifying the soul as 'shee' who 'lakes that Lord of love'.[28] When Skene describes her redemptive '[u]nion with Jesus Christ',[29] she does so through a paradigm drawn from romance or myth: '[. . .] to be brought from a dunghill, from bondage and slavery and innumerable fears, to be a princess, to give love and to receive love of the most pleasant and glorious object in earth or heaven'.[30] It is the humanity of 'the man Christ, Emanuel, God-man' and yet his uniqueness ('I have found him speak as never man spoke')[31] which transforms him into an intimate yet unfathomable object of love.

The identification of Christ as lover helps 'familiarise' or 'personalise' the divine into a series of relationships which defines these women's lives. When Skene 'told [her] husband that the Lord was dealing thus bountifully with me', her relationship with Christ assumes an equal, if not superior, role to that marital bond; indeed, in 'exceeding these earthly relations', the bond means he serves as 'an all-sufficient father, husband, shepherd'.[32] Although Christ may be a husband whose demands are exacting, the role of earthly wife and the bonds of secular marriage are almost gladly renounced or negated. The contract and ritual of this new spiritual marriage is often emphasised: Melville commands that Christ, her 'spous most sweit/ receave my spirit/ With kisis of thy mouth'.[33] Significantly, the conceptualisation of the signing of the National Covenant in Edinburgh in 1638 as a nuptial contract allows Elizabeth Blackadder to imagine her deathbed journey towards God as an imminent marriage, a personal covenant: 'though the cry should be at midnight, "Behold the bridegroom cometh, I may be ready to meet him [. . .]".'[34]

This mystical sublimation of the sacred into the secular impinges on the ways in which the experience of the divine is portrayed. In evoking the generosity of divine love, images of satiety are often sought, as in the appetitive force of this verse from Melville's psalm:

Quhill that I taist
That heavenlie feast
I nevir can be full,
Bot evir murne
Till thou returne
My hungrie saull to fill.[35]

The appeal of these amatory metaphors is partly that they offer a concrete, comprehensible parallel to incomprehensible emotions and experiences; erotic devotion is readily embodied. In Collace's memoir, the divine is felt tangibly and sensorily: '[. . .] I had constant communion with Christ, wherein all my spiritual senses were satisfied. I saw, I felt, I heard his voice, I favoured his "name as ointment poured forth", I tasted that he was gracious. [. . .] I saw no beauty in anything but him.'[36] This intense communion seems to have been experienced physically by Collace but she glosses over this episode: 'I met with a extraordinary confirmation of his love, that I incline not to mention, the sense thereof had almost broken my body [. . .]'.[37] The affective intensity of this particular experiencing of God, in what may have been a frightening fainting episode, was not usually tolerated by mainstream Presbyterianism. Such physical apprehensions of the divine are powerful: public yet private, violent yet tender. The physical pain which many of these Scottish female visionaries record in their diaries and testimonies is deeply rooted in far earlier ecstatic and mystical traditions which, in Western Christianity, is bound up with the notion of *imitatio Christi*: as Christ received wounds on the cross and died for humanity's sinfulness, so the believer mirrors that act through experiencing bodily pain herself.

This corporeal re-enactment of Christ's redemptive agony is the most extreme realisation of this vein of affective piety, cutting across doctrinal traditions as its presence in both Mary's and Sìleas's Catholic writing, and in evangelical prose and poetry, attests. Made safe through God's love and protection, Melville's supplicant is immune to the violence inflicted on her by 'rebels' and 'tyrants': 'Nay, man may pairt me from my parts, my parts/ Disjoynt my joints and funder all/ And stryk me dead with dreadfull dearts, with dearts/ And ret my flesh in peeces small'.[38] This may allude to contemporary persecution of resisting Presbyterians but also recalls the suffering martyrdom of female saints; as in her more famous *Dreame*, the visionary of 'Loves Lament' is a 'heroine' who resists and transcends adversity through divine love.

Languages of the Spirit

Skene's anxiety about how the 'finite' resources of language can articulate the 'infinite' nature of the divine generates a particular need for self-justification in early women writers for whom notions of authorship and creativity are especially complex in the context of spiritual literature. Throughout her writing, Melville reflects on her role and the function of her words: at times, her authorial agency is stressed ('quhill I have dayis/ to peve thy prais'); on other occasions, she is 'merely' a mediator of God's 'worthie word' who solicits inspiration from her muse, 'the holie spirit': 'direct my pen and lat me not offend'.[39] Inhabiting this paradoxical position of both elevation and self-abnegation, she is often ' constrain'd to ceas/ and say no more';[40] in other words, to fall silent. Spiritual writing is condemned to an imperfection or inadequacy which some writers profess more acutely than others. This anxiety is especially heightened when the writing is imaginative, or fictional, in nature. When Katherine Hamilton prays that God 'keep for ever on the thoughts of the imagination of my heart', David Mullan notes that this strikingly does not bear the negative associations of the 'Biblical use of the term "imagination"', which arguably led 'to the Puritan/evangelical rejection of literary works of imagination also'.[41] Narrating a particularly fearful vision of the devil who appeared in her 'chamber' as a 'great black dog', however, Elizabeth Blackadder touchingly confesses that she was 'always (while young) of a very timorous nature, and afraid of apparitions or spirits', prone to 'inventing stories like romances, which never had any foundation other than my own fancy and imagination'.[42] This throws into relief how few of these writers could theologically view their works as 'imaginative': to do so would incur the risk of sacrilege against the true Word of God.

Yet throughout these texts there is a recognisable imaginative patterning at work. They give narrative and poetic shape to religious experience and emotion: in Melville's case, she uses the Protestant psalm tradition as a lyric model and, as Mary Stuart had done decades earlier, deploys the metrical and grammatical intricacies of the sonnet form as a taut, structured means of spiritual exploration. They devise a language by which to define such experience with evident care, precision and deliberateness. The dense scriptural allusiveness of the memoirists mirrors the Protestant belief in the absolute authority of the Word. This extraordinary passage from Skene, for example, condenses multiple citations from, and allusions to, the Song of Solomon, the gospel of Luke, the books of Jonah, Isaiah, Jeremiah, Ezekiel:

> What are the trees of the wood to the apple tree? The bramble to the vine? A night gourd to 'the shadow of a great rock in a weary land'? The brooks of Teman that run dry in summer to rivers of water in a dry and thirsty land? What are broken cisterns to the fountain of living waters? What is the flower of the grass that fades to the noble plant of renown, who is the Eternal? To tell what this object of love is, is a theme above the theory of angels.[43]

The overall effect is of an intensely lyrical sermon; so frequently do these memoirists allude to sermons and scriptural readings as well as recitations of the Psalms which they have either heard or made that their own texts might be considered extensions or recreations of them. This is not to diminish the extent to which these women forge an independent spiritual voice, for they do; but they often refer to, and therefore implicitly suggest, the influence of other religious works such as those by minister Samuel Rutherford (c.1600–61), a Presbyterian agitator and radical Covenanter whose writings were enormously influential.[44] In that respect, this body of writing is deeply intertextual, drawing on a shared pool of imagistic and metaphorical allusions, mostly biblical in origin (the Church militant; darkness/light; sacrificial blood; images of fecundity, nourishing, feeding). In recasting these sources within their own work, writers enter into a process of reimagining that attests the extent and nature of their own spiritual and emotional response to scriptural language. The consequent arresting lyricism is a measure not just of the sensitivity of that response but of the way in which these women – as in Melville's virtuosic stanzaic rendering of the opening of Genesis or Sìleas's radiant vision of Christ, 'Na crùintean air a cheann-sa/ A' lasadh mar na daoimein;/ 'S an t-ùrlar tha fo chosaibh/ Mar chriosdal geal a' soillseadh'/ (The crowns upon His head glistening like diamonds, and the floor beneath His feet shining like brilliant crystal)[45] – are conscious of how their words serve God and strive to reflect divinely creative power.

Protest, Politics, and Persecution

For almost all these women, spirituality was not just a matter of private, reflective practice but entailed being 'out in the world', a kind of spiritual activism. Throughout the seventeenth century, women in the Gàidhealtachd offered vital protection and patronage for the causes of both persecuted Catholicism and early evangelising Protestantism.[46] For others, activism took the form of 'effectual calling', being chosen, in Skene's words, as 'an elect vessel'.[47] In the case of women who attended the illegal conventicles held by Covenanting ministers exiled by Act of Council in 1662, this entailed election, or commitment, to the threat of persecution and repressive and violent governmental action. Ironically, a sense of divinely sanctioned safety and protection informs these memoirists' accounts of dealings with 'the enemies of God'. Helen Alexander describes how she was imprisoned in 1682, having given shelter to one Andrew Guillon who had been involved in the assassination of Archbishop Sharp three years earlier. The measured rhetorical prose of her memoir mirrors the stoical fortitude with which she resisted her interrogators: 'And one of the men said, Ye have the chancellor and other great men to go before; and I answered and said, I have a greater judge to go before, the judge of all the earth'.[48] In effect, her text becomes a re-enactment of her near-martyrdom, dramatising her verbal skills under cross-examination: 'Sir William Patterson asked if the bishop's death were murder, and if the king's authority was lawful. I answered, "They should not ask these things at women."'[49] That this is a tendentious or biased account of proceedings is probable – self-representation is notoriously partial – but that may entirely be Alexander's point. No manuscript copy of her *Life* survives, and it was published by descendants of her family in 1869; Mullan conjectures that '[I]t may more appropriately be read as oral history',[50] suggesting its power as a quasi-legendary witness to her courage.

Alexander's pragmatic religious and political dissent is mirrored in the vein of criticism of contemporary politics and ecclesiastical practices which runs through other texts. The Collace sisters both express their dismay at 'hearing the curates'[51] (conformist Presbyterian ministers), though the conventicles and field preachings which offered an alternative were often condemned as 'disorderly meetings', unfit for any 'young woman unmarryed'.[52] For refusing to swear the Oath of Allegiance and for her attendance at conventicles, Skene was instructed to 'depart this kingdom'; her memoirs powerfully record her resistance to conformist preaching: 'It was a dead sound to me', a 'polluted ordinance'.[53] For Melville, poetry itself became a tool of political resistance and emblem of religious sympathies as shown in sonnets dedicated to John Welsh (1568/9–1622), charismatic Reformed minister and preacher imprisoned at Blackness Castle in 1605 after expressing support for the meeting of the church's general assembly outlawed by divine prerogative, and to Andrew Melville (1545–1622), Presbyterian leader and theologian accused of treason for his hostility to royally sanctioned episcopacy and sent into exile.[54]

The surviving written legacy of these radical Presbyterian women uncovers the networks of political and religious resistance in which they played significant roles, both pragmatic and writerly. Their God is the castigator of 'proud tirrants' and 'kings', the liberator of the 'puir opprest'.[55] And yet the prominence of female spiritual voices from Protestant traditions in the surviving corpus outwith the Gaelic tradition only makes us aware of those other voices that are silenced or oppressed. An executed queen is the starkest emblem of such persecution, though her femininity arguably enriched the politically charged spiritualisation of her death in the martyrologies. Only Sìleas's verse provides a sustained and powerful example of a resistant Catholic female piety (politically manifest in her Jacobitism) through plangent and exhortatory hymns. Her Marian poem, which recounts Christ's life in order to end with praise of Mary's tender vigilance, may have been taught by priests to female parishioners:[56]

> Aig fheabhas rinn thu a ghléidheadh,
> Dol leis a latha 's a dh'oidhche,
> Aig fheabhas rinn thu air feitheamh,
>   'S e do bheatha, Mhoire Mhaighdean.
> (Because thou didst maintain Him so well, going with Him by night and day;
>   because thou didst attend so well to Him, Hail to thee, Virgin Mary!)[57]

The account of the way in which Helen Alexander artfully represented her trial finds two salutary counterpoints, a reminder of the coerciveness of orthodox spirituality. The first relates to the 'genre' of the confession and conversion testimony, printed in order to function as an exemplary model: the 'confession' ascribed to Helen Livingstone (née Hay) (d. 1627), countess of Linlithgow and former tutor to James VI's daughters, in which she recants the lifelong Catholicism which resulted in her being charged with excommunication. Here the question of voice underpinning so many of these female devotional texts is darkly layered: ostensibly a first-person narrative, its apparent (and needful) 'authenticity' is undercut by the probability that Livingston never spoke or wrote such words, contrived in order to make the conversion of such an 'obstinate and profest Papist'[58] more convincing.

Such rhetorical ventriloquism is also exemplified by the extant legal testimonies of women who were executed for witchcraft. The series of witch-hunt panics culminating in the period between 1590 and 1680 were driven by interlocking political and religious reasons, including intolerance of popular folk belief, hostility towards Catholic practices that became associated with occultism, and 'male fears about female sexuality',[59] heightened by the supposed demonic communions of these female witches. In the written depositions of criminal trials in which women are charged with various offences, their mediated voices describe and defend their so-called malfeasance: Agnes

Sampsoune, to whom the devil appeared after her husband's death, parodies the Lord's Prayer; Isobel Gowdie saw spirits and visions, including 'the man of the Midle-earth'; Alesoun Peirson was charged 'for hanting and repairing with the gude nychtbouris [fairies] and the Queen of Elfame'.[60] These records are ghostly witnesses to a kind of spirituality, which neither church nor state could tolerate, a poignant reminder of the ways in which political and religious institutions throughout this long period both accommodated and exiled women. Some extreme or charismatic varieties of spirituality proved especially hospitable to women while other 'deviations' or transgressions could not be sanctioned. Yet the 'soul-work' associated with both lives on in these different spiritual stories.

CHAPTER TWO

Gaelic Poetry and Song

Anne Frater and Michel Byrne

1 Late medieval and pre-modern

Anne Frater

It is all too easy to make sweeping generalisations about the role of women in Gaelic Scotland, especially in the period before the breakdown of the clan system in the eighteenth century. In many ways they were subjugated, treated as lesser humans or mere chattels, but in other ways they could hold positions of respect in a male-dominated society. Class was also an issue, with women of the lower classes to some extent enjoying greater personal freedom than their higher-born sisters.[1] Formal education was denied them until a piece-meal introduction after the Statutes of Iona in 1609 (which prescribed female schooling only for the eldest daughters of gentlemen with over 60 head of cattle and no sons),[2] but this did not at all mean that they were ignorant or uneducated. Surrounded by the oral history and literature of their clan and culture, they absorbed information, stories and songs with which to stock their unwritten libraries.

On studying the poetry reported to be, or presumed to be, produced by women during this period in Gaelic, we can gain insights into how they saw themselves, as well as how they were perceived by the society in which they lived, even though such insights are themselves subject to the constraints, accretions and deletions inherent in oral transmission. It is interesting to note that most of the few 'rule-breakers', the women who strayed into the quasi-sacred realms of the professional poets by composing verse in the bardic style, were from the upper echelons of Gaelic society. One could argue that this is evidence that a noblewoman, far from being regarded as 'on a level with slaves, infants or lunatics'[3] had a higher social status than the professional bards – she was, after all, one of the people on whom the bards relied for their livelihood, so they may, however grudgingly, have tolerated such encroachments into their fiercely guarded territory.

Beginning with the two women who have poems in Classical Gaelic, that is the Scoto-Irish literary dialect of the late medieval period, ascribed to them: Aithbhreac inghean Corcadail was the widow of Niall Óg MacNeil (d. c.1470), the constable of Castle Sween in Knapdale, while the female poets identified as the most likely to be 'Iseabal Ní Mheic Cailéin' were royal Stewarts: the wife (d. 1510) of Mac Cailéin, first Earl of Argyll (d. 1493) and possibly also their daughter. These were noblewomen accustomed to hearing Classical verse being recited: they would have learnt to appreciate the finer points of such verse and the rules which it followed, so why then should it be any surprise that they attempted to emulate the same style in their own compositions? Nonetheless, by doing so they were breaking a societal taboo, as bardic poetry was not only a hereditary profession, where entrance to the order was dependent on lineage, but also a strictly male preserve. We have evidence of several amateurs who attempted to copy the Classical style, but Aithbhreac and Iseabal are the only women among their number.

Aithbhreac is doubly 'guilty' in that she uses her poetic talents to compose an elegy to her dead husband.[4] Women were expected to compose laments, and to keen the dead, but such a formal bardic elegy is outwith the bounds of what they were permitted to create. 'Iseabal Ní Mheic Cailéin' uses her skills to follow the contemporary European fashion for courtly verse which had reached Gaelic Scotland via Ireland, and the two poems in this style which are ascribed to her are short and effective examples of the genre.[5] She is the only female poet featured in Ó Rathile's predominantly Irish anthology of 'courtly love' poetry Dánta Grádha,[6] an indication, surely, of how rare it was for a woman to compose in this style.[7] However, the third poem ascribed to Iseabal is a bawdy, earthy composition describing the genital attributes of her household priest.[8] If the ascription to her is taken at face value (which the mischievous and misogynist nature of much of the material included, like this, in the Book of the Dean of Lismore should possibly guard us against), the poem's bawdiness and clerical lampooning sit very comfortably with the 'playful, subversive spirit animating the poetic contributions of lay amateurs to [the Book]'[9] (who include the Earl of Argyll himself and Campbell of Glenorchy). As a member of the most powerful Gaelic family in Scotland at the time, 'Iseabal' could dabble in metres and subject matter which other, lesser, women would not have dared to use, her adventurism encouraged by the particular cultural ethos of the pre-Flodden Campbell courts.

Later female poets, while not using the Classical Gaelic language of the trained bards, did, nonetheless, use the imagery and structures of bardic poetry in their own vernacular compositions. Chief among these was Màiri nighean Alasdair Ruaidh (Mary Macleod, c.1615–1705), although it has to be said that there is little in her poetry which marks it out as the work of a woman, so closely does she follow the bardic pattern. Unlike her Mull near-contemporary, Mairghread nighean Lachlainn (Margaret Maclean, c.1660–1751?), whose most famous work, Gaoir nam Ban Muileach ('The wail of the women of Mull'),[10] is an obviously female perspective on the downfall of the Clan MacLean, Màiri nighean Alasdair Ruaidh tends to focus on the martial and hunting prowess of Sir Norman Macleod of Berneray, on his ancestry and power, using much of the stock imagery of Classical verse. Mary seems to have been an unusual woman: she did not marry in a society where this would have been the norm; she defied her chief by continuing to compose poetry after he had expressly forbidden her from doing so; she was exiled from Macleod lands for a time, probably for political reasons, and yet she was obviously held in high esteem by the Macleod family, being buried inside St Clement's Church in Rodel in Harris, the burial place of the chiefs of Macleod. Unsurprisingly, her verse reveals very little about Mary herself: one of the songs attributed to her is a waulking song,[11] suggesting that she probably participated in waulking the tweed, and another,[12] celebrating the gift of a snuff mill from a son of Sir Norman Macleod, tells us that she had a snuff habit; but apart from that there is a dearth of personal information in her songs. There are stories about her which hint that she may have been a kinswoman, rather than just a clanswoman, of the Macleod chiefs she praises,[13] but there is no reference to that in her poems. We are told in a mid-nineteenth century source that in one of her poems, sadly no longer extant,[14] she claimed to have nursed five chiefs of the clan, although this is more likely to have referred to the five sons of Sir Norman.

The poems of Mairghread nighean Lachlainn are more evidently from a female perspective, although she too sticks closely to the classical panegyric model in much of her work.[15] Where she diverges from this is where her talent shines through: *Gaoir nam Ban Muileach* is a lament for a clan and a way of life as much as for a lost leader, and her description of the distress of the people, especially the women and children, of Mull is exceptionally powerful.

However, it is not until the poetry of Sìleas na Ceapaich (Giles/Julia MacDonnell of Keppoch, c.1665–c.1729) that we find a noblewoman who unashamedly uses her poetry to give a female perspective on the society in which she lives. Sìleas was a fiercely partisan Jacobite and MacDonald, a committed composer of Catholic hymns in a period of Presbyterian ascendancy, but she was also a proud and protective mother, who in her songs seems to consider herself a moral guardian of young women. There is evidence in her poetry that her warnings about the dangers of unchaperoned encounters with young men were borne of personal experience, 'Mo nianagan bòidheach/ nam b' eòlach sibh mar mise,/ Mun a bhrosgul bhréige/ seal mun éirich air a' chriosan' ('My lovely girls, if only you were knowledgeable, as I am, about the false flattery that precedes the rising of the girdle!').[16] Some accounts suggest that she was not exactly a paragon of virtue in her younger days,[17] and a strand of commentary and popular tradition has persistently shown disapproval of this aspect of her work, in spite of the conservative morality advocated in her songs, which suggests that her transgression lay in 'merely composing on the subject of sexuality'.[18] It is in her poems to her children that Sìleas stands apart from Màiri nighean Alasdair Ruaidh and Mairearad nighean Lachlainn. She shows her love for and pride in her children, as well as her grief over the death of one of her daughters. This indicates that she saw herself as an individual as well as a clanswoman: her concerns, though not necessarily those of the clan, were equally valid subjects for her poetry, and we should perhaps attribute this 'modern' stance – unseen hitherto in any of our sources – to her exposure to Scots and English literary traditions in the north-east where she settled.[19] Sìleas was a noblewoman, the daughter of Gilleasbuig (Archibald) Macdonnell of Keppoch, and this status is reflected in her poetry. Her outstanding lament for Alasdair Dubh of Glengarry[20] shows her blending classical panegyric with the personal, heartfelt lament to create a masterpiece of controlled, poetically expressed grief, while her equally polished lament for the harper Lachlan Dall[21] firmly places her in the upper echelons of Gaelic society: only noble houses would have been visited by travelling harpers, and it is clear that Lachlan was a frequent visitor to Sìleas' home.

Despite the glimpses of their world which we gain from the songs of the high-born women of Gaelic Scotland, it is not from them that we gain any insight into the way of life and expectations of the majority, but in the vernacular poetry of the 'ordinary' women, the lower classes, whose work-songs, love-songs and laments make up the main body of female Gaelic verse produced under the clan system. These are the poems of the nurses and foster-mothers of the leaders of their day, the secret or spurned lovers, the mothers of children, either in or out of wedlock, and the workers who composed songs to make the execution of their back-breaking chores a little easier to bear. As Alan Bruford notes, the work-songs 'were largely a women's preserve, with words reflecting a women's viewpoint'.[22] The work itself also seems to have been mainly a female preserve, as Dr Johnson notes the somewhat unequal division of labour during reaping in Skye in the late eighteenth century: 'The women reaped the corn, and the men bound up the sheaves. The strokes of the sickle were timed by the modulation of the harvest-song, in which all their voices were united'.[23] It is not too hard to imagine that, in a society where inter-clan as well as national warfare was a frequent occurrence, the women would have been relied on to tend the animals, see to the crops and look after the house and family, while their men were away fighting, and that this pattern continued even when the men were at home.[24]

The work-songs composed by women are in some ways the least exciting of their compositions in terms of content and imagery, but they are extremely interesting in social terms. The waulking songs in particular were often composite productions, with several women contributing sections of the song, which was held together by a refrain, usually consisting of meaningless vocables. This explains why so few waulking songs which were composed as such, rather than merely adapted for use, have an ascription, and also why their subject and tone change – sometimes radically – at one or more points during the song. It is easy to understand how this would happen as the main singer, and thus the focus of the song, would change during the waulking of the tweed – a process which took several hours – while the chorus acted as the glue which held the completed patchwork together.[25] Interestingly, very few of these songs actually mention the process of waulking the tweed – the important thing in these songs is maintaining the rhythm to which the work is done, rather than describing the work itself. Many of them were adapted from rowing songs, as the rhythm was similar. Waulking songs were also used as a form of verbal combat, a jousting weapon between singers of rival clans. The encounter between Nic Iain Fhinn, representing MacNeil of Barra, and Nic a' Mhanaich, representing Macdonald of Clanranald, which produced the song *Cha tèid Mòr a Bharraigh Bhrònaich* ('Mòr will not go to miserable Barra') reportedly ended with the Uist female bard falling dead at the waulking board, so thoroughly had she been insulted by her Barra counterpart.[26] Satire was considered a dangerous weapon, with supernatural powers, a superstition which probably goes back to the druidic roots shared, many believe, by the professional hereditary orders in Gaelic society, and a woman who could wield such a weapon effectively may have been regarded as a kind of witch. Indeed, Màiri nighean Alasdair Ruaidh and Mairghread nighean Lachlainn were both reportedly buried face-downwards, which was the Norse method for burying a witch.[27] We have no extant satires which are unequivocally the composition of either female bard, but whether or not they were indeed buried in this way in order to tame their supernatural powers, it has been suggested that such 'traditional memories' may be a revealing expression of a deep fear of women poets 'and their powers of transgression, whether potentially imagined or actually realised'[28] in Gaelic society.

Many, if not most, of the women of the period whose songs survive were fiercely partisan supporters of their own clan, and this was magnified if they had a place in the household of the chief. Among the most important positions of trust were those of nursemaid or wet-nurse to a chief's child. The importance placed on such an honour is best summed up by the lament composed by Màiri Nic Phàil[29] in which she grieves for her former nursling who has been drowned. It is only in the ninth and final stanza that she mentions that her own son was lost in the same incident. Nic Còiseam famously travelled from Eriskay to North Uist to tend to the wounds of her foster-son, Dòmhnall mac Iain mhic Sheumais, after a battle in 1601,[30] showing that the ties of fosterage or nursing did not end with the adulthood of the woman's noble charge. In fact, very few of the songs by women to their foster-children are to the child: most are addressed to the adult, and follow many of the standard conventions of panegyric praise. There seem to have been many female poets who used an accepted female verse form to produce poetry which was, to all intents and purposes, a variation on bardic praise poetry. Màiri nighean Alasdair Ruaidh famously rejected an accusation of just such a composition by declaring that her song was merely a croon, a 'crònan'[31] and thus permitted.

Cradle-songs form a substantial part of the store of women's songs from the days of the clan system, and they often serve a dual function, allowing women to compose panegyric poetry without obviously stepping on the toes of the trained bards.[32] As well as panegyric verse, cradle-songs gave women a voice on political matters and the social changes which ensued, changes which could adversely affect her charges. In B' fheàrr leam gun sgrìbhteadh dhuit fearann[33] ('I wish your land were set in writing'), a song composed to a child of Clan Cameron some time before 1540, the nursemaid shows her understanding of how the power of the pen and the charter was beginning to be of more importance than the power of the sword when it came to clans having a legal right over the territories they had in many cases held for generations. She lists all the lands which would be written in a charter as belonging to her charge, allowing us to identify him as '"Eobhan Beag Mac Dho'ill 'ic Eobhain" [. . .] the grandson of the famous chief Ewan Allanson'[34] and she is evidently worried that the lack of such a formal document might put the Cameron claim to those territories at risk. There is also a strong indication as to the position, if not the identity of the composer of the song: 'The lullaby must have been composed by the nurse, who was one [of] the clan. Had it been the mother that composed it, she would have made loving mention of the child's father, but the nurse would ignore him as he died without attaining to the honour of being chief, and she could only feel entitled to be proud of her nursling as the offspring of a line of chiefs'.[35] This is, of course, assuming that the child's mother had loving feelings for his father, which, in what was probably an arranged marriage, is not necessarily the case.

One of the more interesting aspects of the role of women in this period is the attitude towards extramarital relationships and illegitimacy. When it came to the upper echelons of Gaelic society, most marriages were little more than political alliances forged between clans, rather than any kind of love-match. There is plenty of evidence in Gaelic women's songs of the heartbreak which these arranged marriages caused, such as Turas mo chreiche 'thug mi 'Chola ('A ruinous journey I made to Coll'), in which (according to one attribution) the sister of the Campbell of Auchinbreck killed at Inverlochy in 1645 bewails her abuse at the hands of her husband, Maclean of Coll, and his household: 'Rinn iad mo leab' aig an doras/ Comaidh ri fearaibh is ri conaibh' ('They made my bed at the door, alongside the menservants and dogs')[36] or Ged is grianach an latha ('Sunny though the day may be')[37] where the daughter of Macleod of Dunvegan has to leave behind the man she loves and return to her husband. Emotions had no place in the realm of inter-clan relations, and women had little or no say in the major decisions which would affect their future happiness.

While it was deemed acceptable, and in fact seems to have been expected, for a man of noble birth to have illegitimate children by lower-class women, most of whom were acknowledged and brought up in their father's household,[38] it was a different story for a noblewoman who had a child by a lower-born man. *Biodh an deoch seo an làimh mo rùin* ('May this drink be in my love's hand')[39] in one of its incarnations is said to be the composition of a daughter of MacDonald of Clanranald who was exiled from her father's household and separated from her child as a punishment for her 'crime'. (It has to be admitted that a far worse fate befell the child's unfortunate father, who was torn apart between two horses.)[40] We have no songs of a wife forced to tolerate, if not raise, her husband's illegitimate children, but we do have a song from a low-born mother forced to hand her child over to his noble father. Beathag Mhòr's *An Cùl Bachalach*[41] ('The curly pow'), tells of how her child's father is preparing to marry, and Beathag gives him some advice on his choice of wife. This is not, however, based on how good a wife she will be to him, but how good a stepmother she will be to Beathag's child: 'Is ma bhuaileas i le fuath e/ guma luath 'n a chlachan i/ Ach ma bhuaileas i le gràdh e/ guma blàth fo t' achlais i' ('And if she hits him out of hatred, may she be soon for the churchyard, but if she hits him out of love, let her be warm in your arms').[42]

Other women's songs describe having an illicit relationship with a higher-born man, but there is at least one Gaelic song which takes the attitude, to a somewhat disturbing level, at least to modern-day sensibilities, that a relationship with a nobleman was something to aspire to at all costs. In *An cuala sibhs' a' mhoighdean cheutach* the singer dismisses the distress of a young woman who has evidently been raped, declaring that she would not have put up a fight if the young man in question had turned his attentions on her: 'An cuala sibhs' a' mhoighdean cheutach/ Air an tug Niall Bàn an èiginn [. . .]/ 'S truagh,a rìgh nach b'e mi fhéin i./ Cha sracainn broilleach do léineadh'.[43] ('Did you hear the handsome girl who was raped by fair-haired Neil [. . .] It is a pity, lord, that I was not her. I would not tear the front of your shirt.') Though one should be cautious in extrapolating from one lone example (whose survival at the waulking-board right into the twentieth century may always have owed more to its memorable frankness than to sympathy with the sentiments expressed), the song may nevertheless imply an underlying acceptance of the *droit de seigneur*, and that even the most ignoble of acts was acceptable from a man of noble birth. The woman had no right to refuse, no rights over her own body, and even if she complained, sympathy was not guaranteed. The treatment of women as pawns in games of power, or as goods and chattels of their fathers, husbands and brothers, was not confined to the upper classes of Gaelic society. In the late seventeenth century Martin Martin records the buying of a wife by a man from the island of Rona[44] and in another instance the practice of a widower being immediately provided with a replacement wife is noted.[45] Previously, the treatment of women as possessions apparently even extended to a 'sale or return' basis for marriage: according to an 'ancient custom [. . .] long ago brought into disuse' a couple were handfasted, usually for a period of a year and a day, and if the husband was displeased with the match after that time, the woman was returned to her father's home, while any children resulting from this trial marriage were brought up by their father.[46]

Although most women in Gaelic society had no formal education, this did not mean that they had none at all. Johnson records that the ten daughters of the laird of Raasay were educated by their mother.[47] However, Johnson does not specify the form of this education, which was unlikely to have been anything of an academic nature. Indeed, later on in his memoir he notes that the only boarding school for ladies in the Highlands is in Inverness, and adds that, because of this: 'I suppose their education is generally domestick.'[48] Martin Martin also tells us that: 'Women were anciently denied the use of writing in the islands to prevent love intrigues: their parents believed that nature was too skilful in that matter, and needed not the help of education; and therefore that writing would be of dangerous consequence to the weaker sex.'[49]

There is a small but interesting group of poems from this period by women which are addressed to other women. Most of them take the form of the clan flytings (verbal duels) already noted, but there are also examples of panegyric and lament. One of the most powerful of these is the plaintive lament of a foster-mother for her fosterling, Cairistìona.[50] In this we find a description of the lifestyle of a young noblewoman at the turn of the seventeenth century, with the author listing the places, such as the royal court, which she and Cairistìona visited together, their pastimes: sewing, presumably embroidering, linens and silks, and the future – including marriage to a high-born man – which had been expected for her. Cairistìona is praised in terms of the company she keeps, with dukes and earls said to seek her out, and she is also praised as a scholar, which is highly unusual in a poem to a woman of this period.

What do the songs of Gaelic women tell us about their role under the clan system? We find that describing their function as 'workers, weepers and witches'[51] is not too wide of the mark, although they did not always conform to the expectations of their society. We have the paradox of one of the fiercest supporters of the clan system, Màiri nighean Alasdair Ruaidh, also being one of the worst offenders when it came to composing poetry which was outside the remit of the female poet; we have the noble-born Sìleas na Ceapaich composing morality poems based, it seems, on her own lack of restraint during her younger days; and we have women who accepted their fate as pawns in male power-games, but did not do so silently. However, the public nature of their poems tends to throw the focus outward, onto events and actions, rather than inwards to thoughts, feelings and personal aspirations: even the laments are to a large extent for public consumption, following accepted patterns, rather than subjective expressions of grief. That they were mothers, wives, sisters and lovers is evident in their poetry, that they worked hard is also clear, but there is little or no evidence that they aspired to the same status as their male counterparts, or even thought such an outcome desirable.

2 Modern

Michel Byrne

Despite the fundamental socio-economic transformation of the Gaidhealtachd post-Culloden, the traits delineated above are not radically altered until the later twentieth century. Neither was the pattern of women's songmaking shadowing a dominant male tradition, although a greater subjectivity (already adumbrated in the songs of Sìleas Macdonald) can sometimes be more readily detected. Ironically, the 'subterranean' communal tradition of the waulking board is 'discovered' by collectors and publicised only from the late Victorian era on, in a cultural ambience least disposed to appreciate some of its most distinctive features or to seek to reinject them into contemporary literary practice. (Such a development would have to wait till the modernists of the 1930s.)

With the collapse of heroic clan society, the predominant mode of Highland secular song in the nineteenth century had become that of township verse sustained and propagated in local ceilidh houses, while a more nostalgic music-hall tradition would gain ground among *émigré* urban Gaels.[52] If there are just enough survivals in print and in oral-anecdotal memory to indicate a significant incidence of female bards in the Highlands in the modern period, the twentieth-century evidence also suggests the primacy given to male performance of male compositions in the ceilidh-house environment blocked, in some communities at least, the exposure of female compositions and the possibility of their transmission into the communal memory stream. Further, women's own acceptance of their secondary role as passive carriers of tradition (outwith female-only environments) probably in itself discouraged their creation of songs aimed at community consumption.[53]

Spiritual songs (inspired by succeeding evangelical revivals in the Protestant Gàidhealtachd) and laments are two genres cultivated by female poets which were allowed survival in the oral tradition and occasionally given greater permanence through the printed word. Interesting lines of continuity are sensed from the folksongs of clanship society to the mystical hymns of the modern period down to the twentieth century.[54] In the workplace environment, judging by the corpus recorded in print or by sound technology from the late nineteenth century on, the waulking song tradition seems to have congealed. This meant that beyond the simplest improvisational courtship songs its practitioners were content to transmit a (considerable) repertoire from the 'high age' of the genre.[55]

As literacy of some kind increased across the region in both English and Gaelic, the potential of print to bring ballast to oracy or to add cachet to an oral poet's work was exploited. The vagaries or the censorship of oral transmission, therefore, no longer obstruct our overview of literary activity. Thus there can be no doubt of the esteem accorded the lament attributed to Anna Campbell of Scalpay for Alan Morrison her fiancé (drowned in 1768). This survived orally to the present day in various guises although it was only recorded in print from the later nineteenth century.[56] The printed record also allows us to note the activity of two very different contemporaries, the 'nouveau-panegyrist' Mrs Cameron of Lochaber who twice published her small book of praise songs to the military gentry, and the Perthshire farmer's wife Margaret Gow née MacGregor (Mairearad Ghriogarach). The latter's substantial and unusually individuated corpus was anthologised by her step-grandson after her death.[57]

Prominent in her day was the well-travelled and prolific Mary Mackellar née Cameron (1834–90), who published poetry, songs and essays in Gaelic, Scots and English.[58] Although an intriguing, multi-faceted writer who one suspects might bear interesting comparison with her contemporary Lowland peers, the romantic, sentimental tone of much of her work (as well, perhaps, as its over-dependence on literacy) has almost written her out of both literary history (until recently) and the oral canon. (The low incidence of female subscribers to Gaelic books at least earlier in the century should be noted.)[59]

The only female voice of truly lasting, national impact – and indeed still the most acclaimed of all nineteenth-century Gaelic poets, male or female – is that of Mary MacPherson née MacDonald (Màiri nighean Iain Bhàin – Màiri Mhòr nan Òran or 'Great Mary of the Songs' – 1821–98, *fl.* 1875–). A nurse by profession and a widowed mother by the time her gift for songmaking emerged, nourished by a vast knowledge of Gaelic song, Màiri Mhòr's practice of composition was entirely grounded in orality. Some of her campaigning songs for the Highland Land League were, however, also diffused through newpapers, and her considerable output was collected into print in her lifetime.[60] Her identification with the political struggles of the

1870s and 1880s, her well-observed lyrical evocations of her native Skye and the expression of personal grievance that links her to the anonymous female song corpus of previous centuries underlie her appeal. Beyond these factors, however, Màiri's genius perhaps lies in her assured application of traditional modes of praise and dispraise to the modern political and social realities of her day.

That in itself may be enough to link Màiri Mhòr to the Modernist literary poetic developments of the 1930s, which kicked back so vehemently against the Celtic Twilight tendencies of some of her peers and certainly of the intervening decades. Equally, it is difficult to deny the poetic debt owed by Sorley Maclean (1911–96, fl. 1930s–1940s) to the predominantly female tradition of the 'old songs' (which Maclean also championed as a literary critic), whether as models of expressive intensity and subjective, indecorous frankness, or as a metrical inspiration for his own peculiar sprung rhythms. There is no reason to challenge the pre-eminence accorded the all-male 'Famous Five' – Sorley Maclean, George Campbell Hay, Derick Thomson, Iain Crichton Smith and Donald MacAulay – in the establishing of a Modernist written intellectual poetry in Gaelic, freed from the conventions of song and the traditional expectations of its public.[61] Nevertheless, the quiet modernism of schoolteacher Ciorstai NicLeòid's small volume of 1951 should not be ignored,[62] nor the ambition of Màiri NicGill-Eain (Mary M. Maclean, 1921–2004) of Grimsay, Uist – winner in 1957 of An Comunn Gaidhealach's then prestigious annual Bardic Crown (the second female recipient since 1923)[63] – and her insistence that 'although I have made songs, most of my work is written, literary poetry in the modern European tradition'.[64]

Women continued to contribute to the declining practice of community verse and spiritual verse into the second half of the twentieth century,[65] although no such creativity was seen in transposing traditional forms to new song-writing in the increasingly popular rock/country idioms. While musical modernisation became ever more frequent, women remained most prominent in their role as carriers of traditional songs rather than creators of new material. To this day only one (male) song-writing team, Calum and Rory MacDonald of Runrig, has exploited the rock potential of the waulking-song format,[66] while women have concentrated on re-creating the waulking environment for modern performance of the corpus.[67]

Where women did emerge as major creative practitioners in the closing decades of the twentieth century was in modern written poetry (although the prolific short-story writing of Eilidh Watt from the 1970s on should also be noted).[68] Freed from associations of antiquarianism and nostalgia, echoes of Gaelic song – whether in rhythm, tone or imagery – are frequent in the work of three of the four female poets featured in the second post-war anthology of modern Gaelic poetry,[69] Meg Bateman, Catrìona NicGumaraid (Catriona Montgomery) and Màiri NicGumaraid (Mary Montgomery). Beyond the conscious 'pastiching' of tradition, however – most skilfully exemplified in Bateman's love lyric *S e mo ghaol a' ghrian san adhar* (My love is the sun in the sky) or in Catriona Montgomery's satirical *Gu Dòmhnallaich Aimeireagaidh* (To the American Macdonalds),[70] lines of affiliation can be tricky to isolate. This is because these writers, all university educated (including, to various extents, in Gaelic literature), would be as aware of their Modernist male predecessors (and those poets' debt to older Gaelic tradition) as of the older traditions themselves. And, of course, they are in addition acquainted with English, Scots, American or European literatures. Bateman, the most productive in this florescence, has the richest weave of older Gaelic influences in her poetry, while the work of the youngest poet in the anthology, Anne Frater, still a student when the anthology appeared and the most overtly political of the four, sits more comfortably in the company of the modernist innovators, with no striving for older echoes. While their relationship to Gaelic culture or Gaelic communities is a theme all four explore (in common with every contemporary Gaelic poet), the diversity of their concern is notable. Perhaps of interest is the lack of attention to their gender (though not to personal relationships) in these poets' work: Bateman has remarked that 'for writers of a minority language, culture is of greater significance than gender'.[71] It may also be the case, however, that the prominence of women bards in the early modern Gaelic canon (such as Màiri nighean Alasdair Ruaidh and Sìleas na Ceapaich, discussed above), and, in the later twentieth century, both the prestige given to the anonymous female choral song tradition and the high profile of Màiri Mhòr MacPherson, made the Gaelic context an easier or, at least, less conflicted one for young emergent female voices.

Nevertheless, the transgressive nature of some of these poets' deeply introspective explorations should not be ignored – in spite of the taboos of previous ages, the public, communal voice which they almost all occasionally assume may be a less fraught choice than the cultivation of the individualistic poetic ego. In 1997, Bateman spoke of the 'charges of aggression and immodesty', both from their communities and from their inner voices, with which women writers must grapple,[72] but in the Gaelic context this may have been truer of poetry than of the relatively baggage-free, tradition-light writing of prose fiction. Certainly, the strongest voices since that surge of poetic activity in the 1980s and 1990s (which Bateman alone has taken into the twenty-first century, in terms of published poetry) have been heard in prose fiction rather than in poetry. It should be remembered that one of the four 'moderns' mentioned above, Màiri NicGumaraid, is also a gifted short-story writer, and in 1993 published a novel, *Clann Iseabail*. This is still unique in its bold attempt to convey through its heroine an outspoken, even brash, search for political identity alongside an incisive portrayal of family relationships.[73] It may be that prose fiction, which has seen a remarkable boom since 2003 under the Ur-sgeul initiative, is where Gaelic women writers' literary energies are more likely to be directed in the foreseeable future.

CHAPTER THREE

Orality and the Ballad Tradition

Suzanne Gilbert

Until recently, scholarly rhetoric concerning oral tradition has hinged on 'simplicity', 'nature', and 'artlessness', words prominent in essentialist criticism of women's writing. Like so-called 'peasant poets' such as Robert Burns, women have been perceived as reflecting an artlessness which is authentic, part of their nature.[1] Artlessness has been constructed as an admirable quality, attractive to Romantic conceits of original genius and spontaneous composition, most frequently associated with women, children, a supposedly naive, unsophisticated underclass, and with their characteristic types of expression. While in some societies oral tradition may function as cultural capital, it also imposes constraints, discernible in the cluster of meanings linking 'artlessness' to nature and the culturally feminine. A profound ambivalence, coexisting since the eighteenth century, is encoded in definitions of the word: 'artless' has been glossed as 'devoid of art or skill'; 'unpractised, inexperienced, unskilful'; 'unskilled, ignorant'; or 'uncultured' but also as meaning 'lacking artifice, natural, simple'; or, in yet another sense, 'sincere, guileless, ingenuous'.[2] It can be used to describe oral narratives, songs, and ballads as authentic and unaffected, but also limited in their intellectual range.

Conversely, literary history shows male writers praised as artless if the writer is able to affect simplicity and guilelessness, as in John Dryden's assertion, 'Such Artless beauty lies in *Shakespear's* wit'.[3] Concerning his substantial expansion of the ballad 'The Child of Elle'[4] (7F), eighteenth-century antiquarian Thomas Percy asks that the reader evaluate his additions on the basis of how difficult it is to imitate 'the affecting simplicity and artless beauties of the original'.[5] Artlessness is nevertheless acknowledged as a powerful and significant aesthetic force: in a lecture on the nature of poetry, Hugh Blair writes, 'It is no wonder [. . .] that in the rude and artless strain of the first poetry of all nations, we should often find somewhat that captivates and transports the mind.'[6] Women occupy a central position in this aesthetic: in 1893, *The Critic* quoted Edmund Gosse as saying, 'The border ballads have no art, and yet are exquisite; and the history of poetry is adorned by certain female names which will always preserve their freshness, and which yet were entirely innocent of art.'[7]

Presenting a vexing problem for female aspirations to authorship, women and orality have been so close aligned as to be nearly indistinguishable, configured in a context which emphasises the national dimension to their creativity. This chapter traces the ways in which Scottish women have been associated with orality, with particular emphasis on the ballad, where authorship, gender, and nation are closely joined.

'Custodians' of Tradition

Oral tradition is by no means exclusively female territory. The family of writer James Hogg boasts a lineage of male storytellers and singers; and among twentieth-century Scottish travellers there emerged a number of strong male tradition-bearers. It is clear, however, that historically women have figured prominently, as writing women themselves have observed. Prefacing *The Collected Poems Lyrical and Narrative* (1902), A. Mary F. Robinson justifies her use of ballad form:

> We women have a privilege in these matters. [. . .] We have always been the prime makers of ballads and love songs, of anonymous snatches and screeds of popular song. [. . .] [S]ome old wife or other, crooning over her fire of sticks, in Scotland or the Val d'Aosta, in Roumania or Gascony, is probably at the beginning of most romantic Ballads.[8]

In *A Room of One's Own*, Virginia Woolf quotes Dorothy Osborne, renowned seventeenth-century writer of letters: 'I walke out into a Common that lyes hard by the house where a great many young wenches keep Sheep and Cow's and sitt in the shades singing of Ballads'.[9] Woolf notes Edward Fitzgerald's suggestion that 'it was a woman [. . .] who made the ballads and the folk-songs, crooning them to her children, beguiling her spinning with them, or the length of the winter's night'.[10]

Catherine Kerrigan asserts that the ballad 'presents a vital and sustained women's tradition', and that 'women played such a significant role as tradition-bearers and transmitters that it can be claimed that the ballad tradition is one of the most readily identifiable areas of literary performance by women'.[11] Observing that the major collectors of the ballad (Burns, Scott, Hogg, Greig-Duncan) all refer to women 'as a prime source of their material', Kerrigan notes the 'legion of male writers who cite their mother, housekeeper or nurse (Robert Louis Stevenson's "Cummie" comes immediately to mind) as their first teachers of old songs and stories'.[12] For Alan Bold, women have functioned as 'custodians of the oral tradition'; 'the ballads became old wives' tales', a description he says is not pejorative: 'They were stories passed from mother to daughter, perpetuated by women'.[13] He gives examples from as early as John Barbour's fourteenth-century poem The Brus, in which 'Young women quhen thai will play,/ Syng it amang thaim ilka day'.[14] Charles Kirkpatrick Sharpe acknowledges women as his sources for the songs collected in A Ballad Book (1823):

> These have been mostly gathered from the mouths of the nurses, wet and dry, singing to their babes and sucklings, dairy-maids pursuing their vocation in the cow-house, and tenants' daughters, while giving the Lady [. . .] a spinning day.[15]

David Buchan describes eighteenth-century singers, including Mrs Harris, daughter of the minister of Blairgowrie, who learned her ballads before she was ten years of age from 'an old nurse Jannie Scott, whose store of ballad lore was inexhaustible'.[16] William Motherwell commenting on a version of 'Gil Morrice'(83) taken from the recitation of Margaret Paterson, a native of Banffshire who 'learned the ballad there in her infancy', notes that it is '70 years since she committed it to her memory'.[17] Searching for additional ballads for the English and Scottish Popular Ballads (1882–98), Francis J. Child acknowledges that women 'have been the chief preservers of ballad-poetry', and entreats 'the aid of gentlewomen in Scotland [. . .] who remember ballads that they have heard repeated by their grandmothers or nurses'.[18]

Women have also excelled at lyric song. Throughout the eighteenth century and beginning of the nineteenth, Scottish songs that had passed through oral tradition were appropriated and shaped by female authors. Jean Elliott (1727–1805) re-worked 'The Flowers of the Forest', an old song still sung today about the Battle of Flodden Field. Joanna Baillie (1762–1851) was celebrated as a dramatist but also known for popular songs based on legends and ballad narratives, such as 'Tom o' the Lin'. Isobel Pagan (1740–1821), an Ayrshire singer, included in her repertoire her own version of 'Ca' the Yowes to the Knowes', a song made famous by Burns. Drawing on traditional tunes, forms, and motifs, women also composed new songs. Anne Lindsay, Lady Barnard (1750–1825) authored the poignant 'Auld Robin Gray', known to have inspired poets such as Wordsworth. Carolina Oliphant, Lady Nairne (1766–1845) penned many songs anonymously as 'Mrs Bogan of Bogan', including the well-known 'The Laird o' Cockpen', as well as a number of popular Jacobite songs.[19]

Besides their roles as informants and composers, women also figure significantly in ballad content. According to Bold, the 'powerful and awesome' figure of the ballad matriarch may be attributed to women serving to perpetuate tradition.[20] In some narratives women enact heroic deeds, such as 'Tam Lin' (39) in which Janet rescues the father of her child from the evil Queen o'

Fairies (another powerful female figure), or in 'Geordie' (209), another rescue narrative in which the heroine travels great distances to plead for her lover's freedom. Many narratives deal bluntly with romantic love in terms of realistic concerns about women's economic survival as in the abandoned, pregnant woman's lament of 'The Lass of Roch Royal' (76), or the tragic triangle of 'Lord Thomas and Fair Annet' (73) in which the lovely Annet is passed over for a wealthier rival.[21] Women's predominant role in traditional expression may be related to the historical function of songs and stories in quotidian life, relationships, and community; but whatever their origins, ballads have been shaped and marked over time by women's concerns.

Post-Union Traditional Informants

At a crucial point in post-Union Scotland, women became informants for collectors and editors such as Walter Scott and Robert Jamieson, who were driven by culturally-nationalist agendas to preserve elements of Scottish culture deemed under threat of extinction. In their zeal to capture the old songs, the collectors managed to preserve volumes of material but in so doing overshadowed their sources. Thus, despite women's importance to balladry, the canonical history of ballads has been written by the men who raided the countryside for gems to grace their collections. These Enlightenment-influenced collectors and editors associated oral tradition with national antiquity and original expression, to Blair 'the rude and artless strain of the first poetry' of the nation.[22] For Scott, the ballad can transport the reader to an earlier stage in history; it exhibits 'the National Muse in her cradle'.[23] In this construction, the song itself is gendered female and infantile, but the provider of the song is less important than the 'ancient minstrel' imagined as its original author. Indeed, Scott disparages his sources, believing that '[t]he original ballad suffered irrevocably from passing through the mouths of many reciters', which produced the 'impertinent interpolations from the conceit of one rehearser, unintelligible blunders from the stupidity of another, and omissions equally to be regretted, from the want of memory in a third'.[24]

The title of Sigurd Hustvedt's *Ballad Books and Ballad Men: Raids and Rescues in Great Britain and Scandinavia since 1800* (1930) traces the culturally masculine narrative of collection that carried well into the twentieth century. This language, suited more to adventure story than scholarly tome, reflects the spirit with which ballad collectors such as Scott and his associates pursued their purpose. On returning from a collecting excursion, Scott wrote to a friend, '[I]n defiance of mountains, rivers, and bogs, damp and dry, we have penetrated the very recesses of Ettrick Forest' and have 'returned *loaded* with the treasures of oral tradition'.[25] The ideal object of their quest was the 'pure' traditional ballad, the product of a simple people whose artlessness and closeness to nature compensated for a lack of sophisticated style: in other words, a fiction, a 'scholarly mirage'.[26] Given the scarcity of ideal objects, the goal then was to train the ballad for polite society. J. W. Hales and F. J. Furnivall also describe Percy's approach to his manuscript in gendered terms, as to 'a young woman from the country with unkempt locks, whom he had to fit for fashionable society'.[27]

Buried in the grand narrative of antiquarian ballad collection, however, is evidence that the recovery of valuable ballads and songs depended on generations of women who remembered this material. A glimpse of this may be found in records that William Motherwell left of his collecting for *Minstrelsy: Ancient and Modern* (1827). As Mary Ellen Brown shows, Motherwell asserted 'the trustworthiness of oral tradition', of the importance of sources, and of women's role in transmission; his greatest success was in collecting ballads from a group of 'old singing women'.[28]

Some 'Singing Women'

Close scrutiny deflates the myth of a homogeneous tradition-bearer: singing women differed widely in education and station in life. We know little about them, and their own reluctance to be named further obscures the record. In an 1802 letter to Robert Jamieson, Anna Gordon Brown writes that Scott's publishing of her name in the *Minstrelsy* has 'vexed' her, and she asks that Jamieson refrain from using her name in his *Popular Ballads and Songs* (1806).[29] Margaret Laidlaw Hogg, mother of James Hogg, reportedly chastised Scott for publishing traditional ballads and had no interest in literary fame.

Anna Gordon Brown, commonly known as 'Mrs Brown of Falkland', has been hailed by ballad scholars as 'the greatest informant encountered by any collector of traditional ballads', and as 'the most important single contributor to the canon of English and Scottish popular ballads'.[30] Child included all thirty-three of her ballads in the *English and Scottish Popular Ballads*, twenty of them privileged as 'A' texts, noting: 'No Scottish ballads are superior in kind to those recited in the last century by Mrs Brown of Falkland'.[31] Among others, she contributed 'Thomas the Rhymer' (37A), 'The Twa Sisters', also known as 'Binnorie' (10B), 'Child Waters' (63B), 'Young Beichan' (53AC), 'Lamkin' (93A), 'Sir Hugh, or, The Jew's Daughter' (155A), 'Willie and Earl Richard's Daughter' (102A), 'The Gay Goshawk' (96A), 'The Lass of Roch Royal' (76DE), 'King Henry' (32), 'The Cruel Brother' (11A), and 'Clerk Colvill' (42A). Mrs Brown's contributions are preserved in three manuscripts used by Scott and Jamieson.[32]

Born in Aberdeen a year after the 1746 Scottish defeat at Culloden, Anna Gordon was the daughter of Thomas Gordon, professor of philosophy at

King's College, and Lillias Forbes, who came from 'a singing family of the
Scottish highlands'.[33] In 1788 she married the Reverend Andrew Brown
of Falkland. She had learned ballads as a young girl in Aberdeenshire from
her aunt, Anne Farquharson, whom Brown's father credits with 'a tena-
cious memory, which retained all the songs she had heard the nurses and
old women sing in that neighbourhood'.[34] Though Brown's ballads generally
have been printed without music, she provided both Scott and Jamieson
with words and music in the 'plaintive style' of old Scottish melodies. From
an educated and musically literate family, she was acquainted with Percy's
Reliques, but insisted on having learned the songs orally[35] as in an April 1800
letter to Fraser Tytler:

> I do not pretend to say that these ballads are correct in any way, as they are
> written down entirely from recollection, for I never saw one of them in print or
> manuscript; but I learned them all when a child, by hearing them sung by the
> lady you mentioned [Mrs Farquharson], by my own mother, and an old
> maid-servant that had been long in the family.[36]

David Buchan underscores this female lineage: 'As far as they can be traced
[. . .] Anna Gordon's ballads are stories of a woman's tradition; her three
immediate sources were women, and the most important of the three, Anne
Farquharson, derived hers from the nurses and old women of Allanaquoich'.[37]
Farquharson's 'songs and tales of chivalry and love' provided 'high entertainment' to the young imaginations of the Gordon children; according to
Thomas Gordon, his daughter Anna had 'a memory as good as her aunt's' and
'almost the whole store of her songs lodged in it'.[38] Attesting to the power of
her early impressions, Brown wrote to Fraser Tytler,

> You judge rightly in supposing that I should take pleasure in recalling those
> scenes of infancy & childhood which the recollection of these old songs brings
> back to mind, it is indeed what Ossian call[s] the joy of grief the memory of joys
> past pleasant, but mournful to the soul.[39]

Robert Anderson writes that Brown kept the ballads 'as a little hoard of
solitary entertainment' until finally persuaded to write them down.[40]

Another 'ballad woman' emerging from the eighteenth-century drive to
preserve tradition was Margaret Laidlaw Hogg (1730–1813). Some of the
eleven ballads for which she may be identified as informant include 'Clerk
Saunders' (69), 'Jamie Telfer' (190), 'Johny Armstrong's Last Goodnight'
(169), 'The Tale of Tomlin' (39), and, at least partially, 'Auld Maitland'.
The eldest daughter of a well-known storyteller, William Laidlaw of Phaup,
she was charged after her mother's death with the care of her siblings, which
resulted in her leaving school and painstakingly educating herself by reading

the Bible. At thirty she married Robert Hogg, a less than successful farmer. Gifted with a strong memory and active imagination, she soaked up the traditional songs and tales of the borders, as J. E. H. Thomson observed: 'As she had a vivid imagination and a retentive memory, she eagerly heard, and scrupulously retained, the legendary ballads that were floating about the Border district – many of these, it is to be feared, perished with her death.'[41] We know about Hogg only through anecdotes, especially those of her sons James and William. James describes his mother as 'a living miscellany of old songs'.[42] William's letters reveal a key function of traditional narrative in her day-to-day life: '[O]ur mother to keep us boys quiet would often tell us tales of kings, giants, knights, fairies, kelpies, brownies [. . .] These tales arrested our attention, and filled our minds with the most dreadful apprehensions'.[43] As Elaine Petrie observes, for Margaret Hogg the songs and stories served the purpose of amusement 'to keep the bairns out of mischief'.[44]

James Hogg records his mother's meeting with Walter Scott, who had approached her for a performance of 'Auld Maitland', a song with which 'he was highly delighted'.[45] Scott queried whether or not it had ever been in print – the ballad-collector's constant preoccupation – and she responded with her famous scolding:

> there war never ane o' my sangs prentit till ye prentit them yoursel', an' ye hae spoilt them awthegither. They were made for singing an' no for reading; but ye hae broken the charm now, an' they'll never be sung mair. An' the worst thing of a', they're nouther right spell'd nor right setten down.[46]

Here Hogg deploys his mother as representative of tradition in a pointed argument against antiquarianism, adding, 'My mother has been too true a prophetess, for from that day to this, these songs, which were the amusement of every winter evening, have never been sung more.[47]

In a different historical moment, similarly concerned with cultural and quasi-national identity, another group of women became recognised for their traditional skills. Many ballads, songs, and stories had been preserved among the travellers of northeast Scotland; these came to public attention during the Folk Revival that swept the country in the middle of the twentieth century. Arguably the central figure of the revival, Jeannie Robertson (1908–75) learned ballads from her mother and grew up travelling six months of the year with families for whom songs and stories were the chief entertainment. In 1953 she was 'discovered' by Hamish Henderson of Edinburgh's School of Scottish Studies, who first recorded her songs. In early life around the camp-fire, and as an adult living in Aberdeen, Robertson was acknowledged within her family circle as an outstanding singer. But as a mature woman immersed in the folk revival she became internationally renowned as a performer of traditional song. Through analysis of Robertson, James Porter and Herschel

Gower have documented the crucial relationship between singer and song, which has both aided the ballad's survival and illuminated another key to understanding women's connection to oral tradition.[48]

A significant finding in analysis of Revival singers is the songs' evolution over time in a repertoire, reflecting the individual ballad maker's input. Jeannie Robertson's involvement with a 'muckle' or big ballad exists on more than one level: her life experience is the unwritten part of the ballad text as she performs it. She responded in an intensely personal way, for example, to a variant of 'Edward' (13), 'My Son David', a ballad she learned very early from her mother and in adult life associated with the death of her own young son. According to Porter, ballad singing became for Robertson a 'transformative' act, 'a way of distilling the life-world and its experiences in a ritualizing gesture that compresses feeling, cognition and volition'.[49] Her approach to teaching ballads reveals the significance of transmitting this experience, passed on very deliberately to chosen family members. Nephew Stanley Robertson described the intensity of learning from his formidable aunt:

> If I was asking her for a ballad – asking her to teach me – she was very, very strict, very, very hard. 'All right, laddie, I'll learn this song, but I want you to sing it right, sing it proper, an' sing it real.' If I did not sing it *exactly* as she told me, I was in trouble.[50]

Jeannie Robertson's daughter Lizzie Higgins learned ballads from her mother and became a well-known performer in her own right. She too recounted the learning experience, but as relived in every performance: 'I dinna see my audience, I see her and me a wee kid lang afore the war. An as Am singing Am hearin' her singing.'[51] At the very moment of performing a ballad before an audience, Higgins re-enacted the moment of engagement with the source, her mother–teacher; the memory is tied to a point in childhood but carried into the present so that past and present coexist. She sang 'Lord Lovat' (75) only when 'in top form' because of its special significance as a lullaby her mother sang to her when she was very young.[52] She asserted, 'every one o' these songs, ballads and pipe tunes we sing, they mean something to us privately'.[53]

This sentiment is shared among singers performing today. Fife native Jean Redpath reports, 'I can never sing a ballad that I don't feel like singing. [. . .] I don't think they work unless they come out of your gut'.[54] Dundee-born Sheena Wellington had to change 'Sheath and Knife' (16) because otherwise singing it was too painful:

> I wasn't sure that I wanted to learn the song, and it took me quite some time to get it learned. And I realized afterwards, after someone pointed out to me that I had altered the tune, that a reason I found 'Sheath and Knife' so difficult is it's

a song that deals with a child's death, and I find them particularly difficult to sing. [. . .] I think we all tend to change the song in some way to suit our own interpretation of it [. . .].[55]

Shared by singers is the conception of 'muckle sangs' requiring a particularly intense involvement, a personal ownership that challenges the faceless anonymity that literary tradition has ascribed to ballad authorship.

Women's active, creative engagement with oral tradition has shaped both song and literature. A line may be followed from early singers to twentieth- and twenty-first-century practitioners of 'living tradition', exemplified by artists such as Jeannie Robertson, Sheila Stewart, Alison McMorland, Jean Redpath, and Sheena Wellington. Young contemporary singers of Scottish song incorporate traditional material into their repertoires. Singer-songwriter Karine Polwart professes a love of traditional ballads 'because of their ability to connect human experiences across the details of time and place, and to take on new resonances for new circumstances',[56] a sentiment expressed across generations of tradition-bearers. In another vein, writers such as Nan Shepherd, Violet Jacob, Jessie Kesson, Muriel Spark, and Liz Lochhead have been drawn to tradition, appropriating narratives, tropes, and cultural authority for their own, highly original, literary experimentation. Having memorised Border ballads through reading them 'repetitively and attentively', Spark recalled their significance to her: 'The steel and bite of the ballads, so remorseless and yet so lyrical, entered my literary bloodstream, never to depart.'[57]

CHAPTER FOUR

Enlightenment Culture

Pam Perkins

In the autumn of 1801, the Edinburgh editor and biographer Robert Anderson sought the opinion of his friend Eliza Fletcher (1770–1857) on the literary merits of a manuscript volume on female education. Fletcher had become a central figure in the overlapping circles of Edinburgh literary and legal society since settling there in 1791, but she had no publishing experience at that point, and in fact was to publish nothing in her lifetime, aside from a privately printed blank verse drama, *Edward and Elidure* (1825). She might have had that lack of professional experience in mind when she began her response to Anderson with polite self-deprecation, protesting that 'she has no pretensions to assume the offices of a Critic'. Nevertheless, she was willing to take on those 'offices': the bulk of the letter is a comprehensive attack on the volume, arguing that it fails on a number of levels, but perhaps most drastically in its disregard of what Fletcher presents as the one essential in female education, the cultivation of 'a sound and vigourous understanding'.[1]

The letter itself is a tacit demonstration of Fletcher's claims to such an 'understanding', but also exemplifies an aspect of women's literary history that has tended to be overlooked. If Fletcher is remembered at all today, it is mainly for her daughter's posthumous edition of a memoir and some of her correspondence but, as Anderson's request for her comments on the volume indicates, she had built a solid place for herself in the literary world of late Enlightenment Edinburgh. Fletcher was not unique in this respect: there were a number of Scottish women throughout the eighteenth century who, despite publishing little or nothing of their own, were considered 'literary ladies' by their contemporaries and were seen as contributors to the literary and intellectual life of the time. Looking back at Enlightenment Edinburgh – or Glasgow, or Aberdeen – it is easy to assume that these were entirely masculine worlds in which women hovered demurely in the background, relegated to needlework and gossip. Choosing not to publish was not, however, the same thing as choosing not to write or to cultivate literary interests. In recognising that point, one can start to reconsider the place of women in Scottish Enlightenment culture.

Looking back at the long eighteenth century, Scottish women of letters remain less visible than their English or French contemporaries. The most obvious reason for that comparative invisibility is that so few Scotswomen of this era chose to commit themselves to print, and those who did usually favoured briefer, more ephemeral literary modes, especially songs and occasional verse. As Roger Emerson has noted, there were no eighteenth-century Scottish women publishing 'on metaphysics, mathematics and natural philosophy, no interesting moralists or historians'.[2] Yet, as Emerson goes on to make very clear – by providing a historical survey of the period that draws on records of over a hundred Scotswomen who 'belong with the enlightened intelligentsia'– such negatives and absences provide, at best, only half the story.[3] This gap between the number of women who published and those with demonstrated intellectual tastes might not be that surprising; after all, the Republic of Letters, that Enlightenment ideal of free intellectual exchange, was a world that celebrated literary conversation and familiar correspondence. The French salons, and the women who led them, might be the most familiar example of women's contribution to the intellectual sociability of the Enlightenment, but it was a Scot – David Hume – who insisted on the absolute necessity of bringing together the 'learned' world of men and the 'conversable' domain of women in order to avoid one sinking into obscurity and barren isolation or the other drifting into empty frivolity.[4] Moreover, by the end of the eighteenth century, it had become something of a commonplace in British literature that Scottish women were unusually interested in intellectual pursuits. Edward Topham, an English soldier who visited Scotland in the 1770s, contrasted the tendency of his countrywomen to lose themselves in the 'Oeconomy of a Tambour-frame' with Scotswomen's taste for '*conversaziones*' at which they demonstrated both their 'fondness for repartee' and their skill as 'critics in the English tongue'.[5] Nearly half a century later, John Gibson Lockhart made a similar point in a more sardonic manner as, in the voice of a fictional Welsh traveller, he described Edinburgh women's topics for party conversation, which (according to him) ranged from such predictable subjects as the *Waverley* novels to the more esoteric pleasures of 'that delightful – that luminous article in the last number [of *The Edinburgh Review*] upon the Corn Laws'.[6]

This idea that, for good or bad, mixed intellectual sociability was a defining feature of actual Scottish society – and not just of the quasi-allegorical Republic of Letters envisioned by Hume – stretches back well before Lockhart or Topham. Around 1790, Elizabeth Mure of Caldwell, looking back from the slightly disenchanted perspective of old age, contrasted a contemporary, English-inspired fashion for an increasing social segregation of the sexes with the early- and mid-century Scottish practice of having both sexes pass their evenings together around the tea-table. In those gatherings, Mure writes, 'every thing was matter of conversation; Religion, Morals, Love, Friendship, Good manners, dress. This tended more to our refinement than any thing ellse [sic].'[7] Mure was not, admittedly, celebrating any sort of female scholarship; she endorses wholeheartedly the idea that women should learn from conversation with men rather than from reading and private study. Even so, the society that she nostalgically evokes is one in which women are expected to engage in an exchange of ideas, rather than simply to occupy themselves with gossip or cards.

In her treatment of women's intellectual tastes, Mure, like Topham, and Lockhart, focuses strictly on the ephemeral medium of conversation, but what is probably more interesting to twenty-first-century readers is the point at which this 'conversable' world slides into the more familiar one of literary work. The divide between the two worlds could be both flexible and porous, as can be seen in the Fair Intellectual Club, a group of women of literary tastes that apparently flourished towards the end of the second decade of the eighteenth century. According to the 1720 pamphlet that is almost the only record of the group's existence,[8] the Fair Intellectuals were a group of up to nine young, unmarried women (between the ages of 15 and 20) who chose to meet privately and in secret to enjoy 'rational and select Conversation' with other 'Persons who have the Talent of pleasing with Delicacy of Sentiments flowing from habitual Chastity of Thought'.[9] On the face of it, this group of Edinburgh women is a long way from the world of the Enlightenment salon: not only sexually segregated, its meetings were apparently built around a dauntingly sober-minded reading list dominated by sermons and conduct books. Yet the pamphlet itself – addressed in the first instance to the lover of one of the women and, more generally, to the all-male Athenian Society – forms half of a mixed literary 'conversation' and demonstrates a lightly witty side of the self-proclaimed Fair Intellectuals. The Athenians are being addressed by latter-day Edinburgh muses (the pamphlet underscores the playful allusion to the Muses in the number of members of the club), and the plans for recruitment in the event that 'Death, Marriage, or other important Occurrences' remove some of the members have a teasing air, given that the reason for going public is ostensibly a lover's indiscretion.[10]

This grammatical yoking of marriage with death also works as a delicately ironic counterpoint to the more conventional exaltation of a woman's domestic duties elsewhere in the pamphlet, while the detailed, quasi-parliamentary organisational structure set up by the Fair Intellectuals undercuts their predictable declaration that they refuse, with properly feminine modesty, to touch on political matters. (The tacit celebration of parliamentary authority and procedures would be a more or less overt declaration of political allegiances, perhaps especially in Scotland, in the early years of Hanoverian rule.) However restrictive the female intellectual pursuits explicitly recommended by this pamphlet, the anonymous author or authors demonstrate the ease with which sociable conversation can merge into sophisticated literary play.

Still, however skilled in the minor art of pamphleteering, the Fair Intellectuals remain minor and historically obscure figures – not even the individual names survive – and so they offer, at best, limited evidence of women's place in Scottish Enlightenment life. Later generations of Scottish women were a little less ostentatiously discreet in their pursuit of intellectual interests, perhaps in part because of the growing cultural opportunities that opened to women during the eighteenth century.[11] They might still have avoided print, but especially in the generations active from mid-century on, one finds a flexible network of familiar correspondence, in which women take on an active role, along with their more famous male contemporaries, in literary criticism, debate, and more or less playful manuscript exchanges. Recent criticism has begun to pay renewed attention to the place of such epistolary networks and communities in the English and French Enlightenment traditions; as Moyra Haslett notes in her survey of real and imagined eighteenth-century English literary societies, it was a commonplace at the time that 'the social exchange of learning and wit' was 'not only the most important use of talents but also the most virtuous'.[12] Social authorship – to borrow Margaret J. M. Ezell's terminology for the manuscript exchanges of the late seventeenth century – has been less visible in eighteenth-century literary histories than in studies of earlier periods, perhaps in part because of the growing importance of literary professionalism in the period, something inevitably connected with print. What Ezell, along with critics Haslett, Betty Schellenberg and Harriet Guest, has shown, however, is that shifting focus away from print and individual authorship and on to the more sociable coterie literature gives a much clearer sense of the cultural roles played by eighteenth-century women. It also reminds us of the literary sophistication of these ostensibly informal, sociable exchanges. As Benedetta Craveri has noted dryly of the honed and polished literary correspondence of Mme du Deffand, one would hardly expect that a major participant in 'an artificial society whose every action and every word is studied should suddenly become relaxed on paper', even if she was, at least ostensibly, writing for a single private reader rather than a wide public audience.[13] Indeed, as Ezell has suggested, attempting in a familiar letter or through informal, occasional verse to amuse, stimulate, or challenge a distinguished writer (and, quite possibly, his or her wider circle of friends) could well be a more demanding literary exercise than writing for a diffuse, anonymous public.

The literary networks and coteries of mid- and later eighteenth-century Scotland did not, admittedly, achieve the same place in history as Elizabeth Montagu's London blue-stocking circle or the Parisian salons of Mme du

Deffand or Julie de Lespinasse. While this may be, in part, because the
Scottish circles were both more informal and more diffuse, there has also been
a tendency in Scottish literary history to remember the female wits and letter
writers of this period for a single work or for their association with a particular
famous man, as opposed to being part of a wider sociable network. Frances
Dunlop (1730–1815) and Agnes Maclehose (1758–1841), for example, are
known almost entirely because of their friendships with Burns, while Alison
Cockburn (1713–94), Jean Elliot (1727–1805), and Lady Anne Lindsay
(1750–1825) have maintained a place in literary histories mainly because of
a single lyric each (the two versions of 'The Flowers of the Forest' and 'Auld
Robin Gray' respectively). Yet Dunlop was by no means exclusive in her literary friendships, while Cockburn was very far from being either isolated or all
but silent. Later editors of these women's correspondence tended to be deprecating about their achievements: William Wallace, who in 1898 printed two
volumes of Dunlop's correspondence with Burns, explained that he had done
so only because those letters are 'essential [. . .] to a right understanding' of
the final decade of Burns' life, noting that while he has carefully transcribed
Burns' letters exactly, he has fixed spelling and punctuation in Dunlop's as
well as omitting many of her own attempts at poetry.[14] Two years later, when
Thomas Craig-Brown brought out an edition of Alison Cockburn's letters,
he justified the project by citing Sir Walter Scott's comment that Cockburn's
correspondence, 'if it continues to exist, must contain many things highly
interesting and curious'.[15] 'No further warrant', Craig-Brown adds, 'is needed
for printing these letters', but just in case any doubts remain, he underscores
Cockburn's literary taste and judgement by pointing to her remarkably
prescient admiration of Scott. 'To that remotest day', Craig-Brown writes,
'when the world shall cease to interest itself in the author of *Waverley*, some
interest must always attach to the old lady whose bright perception noted in
the child of six the marks of genius'.[16] Far from presenting Cockburn as an
author of interest, minor or not, in her own right, or even as a participant in
and observer of a complicated and sophisticated literary society, Craig-Brown
implicitly turns her into a footnote to the *Waverley* novels.

Treating Cockburn as a backdrop to Scott's imaginative vision or as a
source of quaintly antiquarian anecdote does her a disservice; while her
surviving letters are not polished literary works, Cockburn was nonetheless
writing not just to amuse and entertain her individual correspondents, but
also, and self-consciously, as a member of a extended literary circle. Although
she expressed a conventionally feminine horror of publication – 'As for printing, never fear', she told her long-time friend Robert Douglas in 1775, 'I hate
print' – she made a point of adding that 'I have been sung at wells to the
flowers of the forest', implying a distinct pride in her cultural impact beneath
the more obvious self-deprecation.[17] Some seven years later, she was still

providing Douglas with lightly self-deprecating commentary on her work. After an amused account of the elderly Lord Kames's decision to pose for a statue, she concludes, 'We authors [. . .] carry vanity to the grave with us', adding in the same mock-serious tone, that in case Douglas is 'laughing now at me classing myself with the authors' she has in fact 'seen myself in print; and once in a paragraph from Newcastle did I read an address of my own in Shakspear's stile to the King for the Peace'.[18] Such jocular reminders of her credentials as 'author' are reinforced by the stylistic play throughout the letters, in which Cockburn shifts from household gossip or day-to-day practicalities to playful raillery (lightly reproving David Hume for his atheism, for example, or encouraging Douglas to look for a bad-tempered wife in order to strengthen his Christian virtues) or to serious reflections on moral and social concerns.

These stylistic games are perhaps the most engaging aspect of Cockburn's sociable correspondence, and it is fairly easy to demonstrate that she was not expecting this literary play to remain limited to a single reader, despite her choice of a 'private' medium. Cockburn makes very clear to her correspondents that she is sharing their letters and any poetic enclosures with friends, and it is no less clear that she expects them to be using her correspondence in the same way. In a letter that tacitly invites the recipient to share it, at least in excerpts, with its subject, she tells Hume what to say to lure Rousseau to Scotland; later, when she makes comments about Allan Ramsay's Edinburgh property development that she does not want to get back to Ramsay himself, she makes a point of stating explicitly that this is information that is not to be shared. On a more practical level, Cockburn also used her letters to circulate other literary work. Most famously, she helped to publicise Burns by sending manuscript copies of his early poems to Douglas; she also helped to enlist subscribers for a volume of work by John Hoy, a much less successful peasant poet.

Cockburn's most famous letters, besides those that mention Burns and Scott, are those to David Hume, but her cultural network extended much more widely than one might gather solely from the excerpts of her letters that appear in work on the more famous writers. That is also true of the correspondence of many of her contemporaries. Frances Dunlop was important to Burns in part because she had had so many connections in the literary world that he was trying to enter. She helped bring him to the attention of John Moore, then the more famous writer, and made some effort to engage Adam Smith to help Burns through a patronage appointment. Dunlop clearly liked seeing herself in the role of patron: in one early letter she rather coyly disclaimed any ambitions in this direction ('I am far too little conversant in the world to matron the Muses with due splendour and propriety'), yet only a few months later, she was envisioning herself as a Scottish Emilie Du

Châtelet. 'I have been told Voltaire read all his manuscripts to an old woman, and printed nothing but what she approved', she wrote to Burns, adding, in case he missed the point, 'I wish you would name me to her office.'[19] That said, Dunlop's relationship with Burns was not simply one in which she read, admired, and praised: she also, however deprecatingly, offered her own verse to him, and he in turn shared it with other literary friends, such as the novelist Henry Mackenzie.

The point made here is not that Dunlop is a lost or neglected poet in her own right, but rather that her letters to Burns, shifting as they do from poetry to prose, from playful praise and gossip to serious news, critiques and advice about his own work, exemplify a type of writing that flourished in the literary circles of later eighteenth-century Scotland and which women, in particular, employed. Looking back, from the perspective of the 1840s, on the Scotland of his youth, Hugh Miller reminisced about the 'type of literary lady now well nigh passed away', women who exemplified in their correspondence 'minds embued with literature though mayhap not ambitious of authorship'.[20] Focusing on his native northeast, Miller moves us away from Cockburn and Dunlop and turns instead to Elizabeth Rose of Kilravock (1747–1815), Anne Grant of Laggan (1755–1838) and Helen Dunbar of Boath (1775–1835). Miller praises these women by inviting the reader to imagine 'what delight they must have given to the circles in which they more immediately moved',[21] but it is easy to lose in such praise, which implicitly relegates the women to a closed, private world, how extensive those circles actually were. Elizabeth Rose, best known now for her correspondence with her cousin Henry Mackenzie, was also an acquaintance of Lord Kames – on sufficiently familiar terms to plead with him to be merciful in one of his court cases[22] – and of Robert Burns. By the end of the century, she was well enough known for Anne Grant, who had never met her, to take Helen Dunbar's report of Rose's praise of her manuscript verse as significant encouragement in her decision to move into print. (Grant jocularly described Rose's 'elegant criticisms' as 'an excellent cork jacket' to help keep her afloat as she ventured into the swampy world of publication.)[23] According to the rather deprecating account of a Victorian biographer, Rose developed a literary reputation mainly because her 'indiscriminate and voracious reading' marked her out 'in a country where there was little learning in either sex',[24] yet the exchange with Grant points to a network that extended well beyond her country neighbours. More significantly, it highlights a real interest among women writers in later eighteenth-century Scotland in building an audience of sympathetic and informed readers outside both the public world of print and the more confined world of face-to-face conversation.

This was also true of women who were not strictly 'literary' writers in the sense we tend to use the word today. Elizabeth Hamilton (c.1756–1816), remembered now mainly for three polemical novels (on topics ranging from Anglo-Indian relations to Scottish cottage life), was at least as interested in moral philosophy and theories of the mind as she was in writing fiction, and was able to cultivate those interests through both conversation and correspondence with some of the leading thinkers of her day. Notably, she saw her essays on moral education as being in conversation with those of Dugald Stewart, who also inspired her ambitious plan to write a series of historical biographies to illustrate his theories of moral philosophy. (Only one, a biography of Agrippina the Elder, was completed.) Her interests extended into science and travel: according to letters that the traveller and physician Henry Holland wrote to his father, Hamilton took an active role in helping him prepare his account of his 1810 travels in Iceland for the press. While Hamilton's name was not associated with the book in any published sources, Holland's correspondence makes very clear the ways in which his sociable exchanges with her shaded into professional literary advice.[25] Nor was Hamilton unique in this respect. More than a generation later, Eliza Maria Campbell, Lady Gordon Cumming (1798–1842) won the praise of both Louis Agassiz and Hugh Miller for her work on fossils, and while she did not publish anything significant of her own, there is no doubt that she saw herself as working in partnership with the scientists with whom she corresponded. 'I am breathless to be at work again', she wrote the geologist Roderick Murchison just before her death in childbirth, urging him to send an account of the Russian fossils he had been examining.[26]

The best-known science writer among the Scottish women of this generation was, however, Mary Somerville (1780–1872). While her career extended well into the Victorian era, Somerville's earlier life exemplified the fluidity of the social and intellectual worlds at the tail end of the Enlightenment, an environment that was not particularly friendly to intellectual young women. Late in life, looking back on her childhood, Somerville had no difficulty recalling the discouragement she had faced in the pursuit of her interests, from the aunt who was scandalised by her neglect of her needle to the sister-in-law who hoped marriage would turn her away from her books to more properly wifely pursuits.[27] Yet ridicule and hostility were at least somewhat balanced by her social interaction with some of the major players in the intellectual life of late Enlightenment Edinburgh, including Henry Brougham, John Playfair, and William Wallace, Professor of Mathematics at the University of Edinburgh. Playfair and Wallace advised her in her study of mathematics in general and of Laplace's *Celestial Mechanics* in particular, while Brougham launched her publishing career by soliciting a translation of *Celestial Mechanics* for his Society for the Diffusion of Useful Knowledge. Even as Somerville's autobiography offers a sharp retrospective glance at the hurdles that a woman had to overcome if, in the opening years of the nineteenth century, she chose to pursue an interest in science, it also demonstrates the ways in which she was able to use private sociability as a springboard into life as a public intellectual.

The problem in foregrounding social and epistolary networks in this way is that conversation and even correspondence are ephemeral media. Somerville might have left a large body of published work, but she is an exception in that respect as in so many others. The Victorian antiquarian Cosmo Innes commented in passing on the sheer 'mass of [Elizabeth Rose's] hand-writing' in the Rose archives,[28] but when, in the 1960s, Horst W. Drescher published Mackenzie's letters to Rose, he was unable to trace any of Rose's side of the correspondence and had to content himself with Mackenzie's letters alone. The result is a vivid illustration of Rose's wide-reaching intellectual curiosity, but one in which she inevitably remains a silent partner. Moreover, the notorious tendency of nineteenth-century editors to edit and 'improve' correspondence means the letters that survive only in posthumous print editions have to be treated with caution. Elizabeth Benger, whose biography is the only source for much of Elizabeth Hamilton's correspondence with contemporary literary figures, cut extensively and changed identifying details, as comparison with the few surviving manuscripts of Hamilton's letters indicates; likewise, Thomas Craig-Brown and John Peter Grant made significant cuts when they edited Alison Cockburn and Anne Grant. Even so, partial records are better than none, and however much caution is needed in reading and evaluating these sources, they still offer more than a mere footnote in the literary history of the Scottish Enlightenment. If one judges by the publishing records, Scottish women of the eighteenth century were indeed isolated and almost silent figures, but the taste for intellectual pursuits documented in surviving letters, and the often playfully sophisticated style in which they explore their ideas, suggests that those women who did publish were anomalous not in their literary interests but simply in their having moved from social to print media. In evoking the dazzling scope and range of literary activity in Enlightenment Scotland, it is important not to overlook the women who were inspired by and shared in the literary conversations of their era.

CHAPTER FIVE

Domestic Fiction

Ainsley McIntosh

Mary Brunton and Susan Ferrier played a key part in the development of Scottish domestic fiction during the early nineteenth century. More specifically, working within a historical and regional mode, they figured among 'the first female writers to describe Scottish manners and Scotland itself from a woman's point of view',[1] pioneering a feminine tradition of Scottish national domestic fiction.[2] Although their work today is relatively neglected, they were highly popular novelists in their own time; Brunton's *Self-Control* (1811) was 'one of the few unqualified successes to come from Scotland before *Waverley*',[3] while Ferrier is the only female author to be named as a member of the 'Blackwood group'.[4] This chapter focuses on Mary Brunton's *Discipline* (1814) and Susan Ferrier's *Destiny* (1831), arguing that these women writers transformed the novel of manners through formal innovation (blending romance, realism and social satire), through treatment of thematic concerns such as marriage and money, by presentation of female subjectivity, and in their engagement with the historico-political process. The paradoxical mix of conformity and resistance to literary and social convention displayed in their fiction reflects not only the complicated position of women writers of their generation but more generally the socio-political tensions of the era in which they lived and wrote.[5]

As the titles of her two completed novels suggest, Brunton's fiction is founded on deeply moralistic and didactic principles. Offering cautionary tales of virtue rewarded and excess avoided, her heroines eschew passion and 'excess of self' in favour of self-containment and self-denial.[6] Nonetheless, Brunton's work is not a bland hybrid of the conduct book and the novel of sentiment. In her hands, as Peter Garside notes, the moral-evangelical mode offers 'fresh possibilities for psychological analysis and moral discrimination'.[7]

Discipline presents an acute study in female subjectivity through its use of first-person narrative technique. Part *Bildungsroman*, the novel records the narrating heroine's process of moral and spiritual improvement. Ellen Percy is in many ways a modern creation, with her social status operating as one marker of her modernity. As a member of the rising commercial class it is her wealth rather than her pedigree that secures her access to aristocratic circles in London. However, following her father's bankruptcy and suicide, Ellen must negotiate a new life of austerity that is antithetical to her formerly self-indulgent lifestyle. Sarah Smith suggests that Brunton's originality resides partly 'in her almost uniquely unromantic attention to the subject of money',[8] and critics agree that her fiction is 'firmly focused on the social and economic aspects of existence'.[9] Economic metaphors abound in *Discipline*; for example, Ellen's father divides and quantifies humanity on economic principles 'into two classes, those who were to labour for riches, and those who were to enjoy them' (p. 38).[10] He equates money with abstract values, claiming liberality as a wealthy man's privilege and drawing a correlate 'between riches and munificence' (p. 70). Reflecting her father's outlook and language, Ellen speaks of marriage to Lord Frederick de Burgh in the terms of transaction, reasoning: 'He wants fortune, I want rank. The bargain would be very equitable' (p. 46). Meanwhile, Ellen's guardian, Miss Mortimer, cautions her against the fortune-hunting Lord Frederick, describing contemporary male lovers as 'insidious spoilers' who come in pursuit of a woman's wealth rather than her person (p. 46). Connecting marriage with commerce Brunton draws attention to the economic realities that frequently underpin matrimony. By embedding an articulation of the commercial imperatives of early nineteenth-century society within her heroine's speech and actions, she creates a modern novel.

Confronting unromantic truths about love, Brunton also undercuts romantic notions of poverty and working-class life abstracted from the reading of novels. Ellen remarks that: 'Heroines of romance often show a marvellous contempt for the common necessaries of life; from whence I am obliged to infer that their biographers never knew the real evils of penury' (p. 252). She observes that:

> although nothing be more sublime than a life of charity and self-denial in the abstract, nothing is less so in the detail. [. . .] Poverty I had known only as she is exhibited in the graceful draperies of tragedy and romance; therefore I met her real form in all its squalor and loathsomeness, with more, I fear of disgust than pity. My imaginary poor had all been innocent and grateful. Short experience in realities corrected this belief; and when I found among the real poor the vices common to mankind, added to those which peculiarly belong to a state of dependence, – when I found them selfish, proud, and sensual, as well as cunning and improvident, – I almost forgot that alms were never meant as a tribute to the virtues of man. (p. 185)

As her words indicate, despite her conversance with the language of the counting-house, Ellen has no real concept of either economic or moral worth until she encounters misfortune. She then learns not only the value of both but also the important lesson that labour is its own reward (p. 246). This process of re-education leads her to make the radical declaration that she 'would far rather earn my bread by labour than by marriage' (p. 355), and reject Mr Sidney's marriage proposal despite it presenting a 'tempting alternative to labour and dependency' (p. 193).

Ellen's refusal of Sidney's offer on the grounds that she is 'not in love' (p. 193) reveals her personal growth and independence of spirit. Far from suggesting that she harbours sentimental notions about love and marriage, it reflects her growing self-awareness that, were she ever to marry, she 'would have a husband whom I could respect' (p. 150). In creating a heroine who rejects the traditional route to security through marriage, Brunton disrupts literary and social convention. The agency given to Ellen, allowing her to act decisively and triumph over economic and social hardships, presents a key way in which Brunton moves domestic fiction on from the 'flat' heroines and static conventions of the eighteenth-century romance novel, anticipating Ferrier's treatment of matters such as matrimony and 'sexual self-determination'.[11]

The need for employment leads Ellen to Scotland where exposure to both Lowland and Highland society forces her once again to negotiate cultural discourses which are alien to her experience. While in Edinburgh, Ellen is wrongly incarcerated, for a brief spell, in a lunatic asylum – a situation that functions as a metaphor for the cultural dislocation she repeatedly experiences in 'that larger mad-house, the world' (p. 294). As a town Edinburgh may be 'romantic' (p. 224), yet the trials that Ellen endures there are anything but. Failing to find work as a governess – the only channel that the 'customs of society left open to the industry of a woman' (p. 211) – she struggles to survive 'for Edinburgh, at that time, contained no market for the fruits of feminine ingenuity' (p. 244). Significantly, she sets up a 'woman's business network' selling handicrafts to sustain herself.[12]

Although the novel's tone is unwaveringly moralistic, a shift occurs when Ellen enters Scotland and the focus of *Discipline* diverges from didacticism into national tale. This change of mode is signalled in part by the introduction of footnotes containing historical, topographical, cultural and linguistic information about the Scottish Highlands. They provide personal testimony from an authorial/editorial voice and textual corroboration from works including *Graham's Sketches of Perthshire*, *Mrs Grant's Essays on the Superstitions of the Highlanders*, and *Letters from a Gentleman in the North of Scotland to his Friend in London*, which support both Ellen's observations and Brunton's fictionalisation of the Highlands. They also offer a comment on the changes sweeping the region as a result of 'improvements' wrought by modernisation and tourism. For example, it is lamented that:

> The 'land of the mountain and the flood' has of late been the fashionable resort of the lovers of the picturesque, and of grouse-shooting; [. . .] The accommodations for travellers are of course improved. It were devoutly to be wished that this had been the only change effected by such visitants. (p. 342)

The implied threat to cultural integrity betokens suspicion of increased southern British and Scottish incursions into the Highlands.

As critics recognise, in Brunton's fiction 'happiness and moral worth are associated with Scotland, specifically the Highlands'.[13] In conventional manner, she presents fashionable life in London as full of danger and temptation, which reaches its apotheosis in the orgiastic sensuality of a masked ball. This may be read as a critique of southern, metropolitan or aristocratic excess. However, if this mines an established literary trope, Brunton's contrasting depiction of Lowland and Highland life is less familiar, highlighting cultural discontinuities within Scotland as well as within Britain, and suggesting the untenability, even undesirability, of configuring a homogenous national identity.

Significantly, it is the female characters in the novel who act as cultural mediators. Charlotte Graham speaks to Ellen of 'the peculiar manners of her countrymen, and on the contrast which they offered to those of the Lowland Scotch' (p. 331), and Cecil Graham provides her (and the reader) with much information about Highland culture, even teaching her Gaelic. It is from Cecil that Ellen learns:

> how much the innovations and oppressions of twenty years had defaced the bold peculiarities of Highland character; how, stripped of their national garb, deprived of the weapons which were at once their ornament, amusement, and defence, this hardy race had bent beneath their fate, seeking safety in evasion, and power in deceit. (p. 251)

Isabelle Bour argues that this kind of historical specificity undermines a simple nostalgic 'longing for a lost past. [. . .] the Highlands do not embody a timeless past, but are presented as post-feudal, and as having suffered from the Forty-Five'.[14] This is borne out by Ellen's observation that in Glen Eredine 'Feudal habits were extinct; and the days were long since gone, when bands of kinsmen, united in one great family, repaid hospitality and protection with more than filial veneration and love' (p. 352), and by reference to the ransacking of the Castle at the hands of the 'Hanoverians' (p. 356). However, nostalgia is not entirely lacking and, as Duncan recognises, such grounding in historicity is in its turn challenged by Ellen's contradictory representation of Glen Eredine, including her claim that its tenantry cheerfully cut the landlord's corn without payment (pp. 353–4).[15] Brunton's presentation of the Highlands is therefore ambivalent, suggesting a tension between Romantic and realist tendencies in her fiction. The sense of backward longing for the lost (and potentially fictional) past pulls against the depiction of her female protagonists moving towards modernity.

Nevertheless, Ellen's initial impression of the Highlands satirically under-cuts Charlotte Graham's sentimental and imaginative construction of them and she admits that on entering the region she 'was somewhat confused between my own perceptions and the enthusiasm of my companion' (p. 341). When they stop at an inn situated in an unspecified liminal space between Edinburgh and Glen Eredine, Ellen describes the children of the region as 'little barbarians' who display a 'savage nakedness of legs and feet' (p. 342). She is, like Scott's Edward Waverley, 'thoroughly disgusted' (p. 344) with the squalor of her surroundings and the crudity of the local manners that she observes. Ellen's preconceptions of the 'cavalcade' that arrives to escort them from here to Glen Eredine are deflated by the reality of it consisting only 'of three horses of very diminutive size' (p. 344) and she is further disappointed when her first view of Castle Eredine reveals a more modern and less warlike building than 'Cecil's romantic tales of its ancient possessors' have prepared her for (p. 348).

Once in Glen Eredine itself, Ellen persists at first in considering its inhabit-ants to be 'little better than savages' (p. 354) and, in a scene that resonates in Susan Ferrier's *The Inheritance*,[16] believes herself to be confirmed in this notion when she witnesses Charlotte and Cecil discuss his impending death in front of James Graham (p. 360). However, the salient point is that local codes and customs are incomprehensible to a person placed outside the prevailing cultural discourse. Ellen's progression from alienation to assimi-lation resolves this issue but raises new questions by highlighting that this Highland community is one both situated in reality (through the correlates of geographical and historical specificity) and one that transcends a realist framework.

Ellen's acquired appreciation for Glen Eredine suggests that an affec-tive response to the Highlands is generated by associative emotions; the Highlands are not an intrinsically romantic terrain. As Ellen learns to love the Highlands and Henry Graham she comes to view the locale as 'the land of imagination' (p. 355) rather than the realm of a barbarous reality. Geographical and historical specificity blur as Glen Eredine is recast in terms of a mythical hinterland and returned to an earlier stage of societal develop-ment. The calmness of the landscape is reflected in the silence and calmness of its inhabitants suggesting an organic unity between the community and its environment (pp. 347–8). Springtime in the glen is likened to 'the first spring [that] adorned Eden' (p. 372), thereby positing it as the setting of an idyllic prelapsarian community, and Gaelic is similarly exoticised through Ellen's observation that Cecil's dialect 'was foreign rather than provincial' (p. 246).

Ellen's cultural sublimation is completed through her marriage to Henry Graham. In this final dislocation of identity she exchanges her name for 'a noble name, – a name which has mingled with many a wild verse, and many a romantic tale – a name which the historian and the poet shall celebrate' (p. 371). She is herself thus incorporated into both history and romance. As Chief of Glen Eredine, Henry Graham practises benevolent, paternalistic rule: 'in exercising almost the control of an absolute prince, [he] was guided by the feelings of a father' (p. 338). Equivalently, Ellen's status shifts from 'stepmother' to the clan (p. 359) to biological bearer of their future Chief: 'every one of this faithful romantic race is united to me by the ties of rela-tionship. I am the mother of their future chieftain. Their interests, their joys, their sorrows, are become my own' (p. 375). She reconfigures her role in socially constructed terms to become carer to the community:

> Charlotte and I were at no loss to fill up the hours of their absence in the duties consequent upon being not only joint housewives in the Castle, but schoolmis-tresses, chamber-council, physicians, apothecaries, and listeners-general to all the female inhabitants of Glen Eredine. (p. 371)

This form of female community and utility contrasts sharply with the nega-tive construction of femininity and sensual indolence that characterised the time passed by Ellen in Lady St Edmunds' 'temple of effeminacy' in London (p. 145).

Brunton's 'domesticated Highlands' operate in an emotional and imagina-tive space that is constructed in feminine terms of familial bonds.[17] Just as her Highland characters are made up of 'a kind of romantic abstraction' (p. 246), so her Highland community is removed from reality. This facilitates Brunton's engagement with issues that traditionally lie outwith the limits of feminine discourse. Ellen's character is refined as the narrative progresses; the novel itself undertakes a similarly transformative trajectory towards a height-ened and variegated potentiality, reflecting her personal development in its increasing formal and thematic complexity. 'Improvement' is not confined to the protagonist, but extends to the novel's structural properties, its politicised thematic concerns and its generic identity. Increasingly, imitation gives way to innovation and convention to experimentation in subject matter and literary form.

In this experimentation Brunton's work prefigures that of Susan Ferrier. Ferrier produced three novels which were widely acclaimed during the nineteenth century: *Marriage* (1818), *The Inheritance* (1824) and *Destiny: or the Chief's Daughter* (1831). The titles of her novels reveal their thematic concerns with marriage, money, property and class, and have tended to be categorised as 'novels about courtship, marriage and female education in the line established by Richardson, Burney and Austen'.[18] However, it is Ferrier's progressive treatment of these motifs and her contrasting depiction of Scottish and English manners that is of interest. Her work demonstrates an inherent cultural ambivalence, registered in part through narrative technique.[19] In each of Ferrier's novels narrative authority resides in an omniscient narrative voice expressed in Standard English. However, it is her subaltern Scots voices and characters that are richer, more robust and often outrageously funny. The competition of cultural discourses is thus foregrounded in her novels.

From its opening paragraph, *Destiny* both invokes and satirically challenges stereotypical constructions of national identity. The comparison of Scottish and English manners offered in the novel suggests that parochialism abounds on either side of the border. It is epitomised at its worst in Lady Elizabeth Waldegrave and the Chieftain Glenroy who embody unenlightened insularity, national prejudice and stubborn inflexibility. Their unsuccessful Anglo-Celtic union, ending in separation, may be a warning against refusal to adapt to a post-1707 world. Interestingly, Glenroy's anti-English sentiments stem from moral turpitude rather than national pride. For example, his initial suspicions of the English tutor diminish when he is satisfied that Mr Ellis's ways do 'not interfere too much with his own' (1: 26).[20] This suggests that Ferrier's satirical shaft is aimed at moral rather than national character, and is borne out further by her representation of landscape.

As in Brunton's work, landscape is inscribed with meaning. Anne K. Mellor suggests that Ferrier constructs landscape in specifically feminine Romantic terms, 'offering an alternative definition of the sublime as an experience that produces intensified emotional and moral participation in a human community'.[21] Ferrier's feminised discourse also represents the natural world as the locus of the inner life, countering the Burkean configuration of the sublime as an expression of the divine. Scenes set in nature, such as that in which Edith, Reginald and Florinda undertake a ferry-crossing as they depart from Glenroy, uncover true character and feeling, as well as develop the plot. The violent storm that breaks during this journey imbuing the squalls with 'all the sublimity of power and danger' (2: 65), gives expression to Reginald's emotional state and catalyses the dramatic revelation of his 'apostasy' of affection (2: 87). Prior to this pivotal moment 'when even the master-passion of the soul is overcome by stormy and sudden emotion' (2: 87), emotional truth has been encoded in location: Reginald declares love for 'Italy' (Florinda) but merely respect for 'Scotland' (Edith).

Mellor argues that Ferrier develops the 'feminine sublime' further by specifically equating sublime nature with human morality[22] so that Scotland operates as a 'moral testing-ground' in her fiction.[23] Florinda Waldegrave interprets Scottish scenery through the lens of Romantic poetry, declaring the road to Glenroy to be '[q]uite charming' because '[i]t seemed as if Scott's

beautiful description of the Trossachs had started into life' (1: 348). Her
inability to appreciate the Highlands in terms other than Romantic and
poetic suggests the inadequacy of such a construction and the inferiority
of her character. On the walk to church Edith is 'surprised and mortified at
the indifference, and even inattention, with which Florinda regarded the
sublime scenery around them' (2: 12). While Florinda favours the moonlight
and flowers of Italy (1: 411), Edith defends her 'own native land', declaring
her love for the 'the clouds and the mountains, the firs and the heathers' of
Scotland (1: 412). The correlation between moral worth and receptivity to
the Scottish landscape is clear.

Glenroy and his clansman Benbowie similarly lack the capacity to respond
satisfactorily to the Scottish landscape. Their spiritual dislocation is evident
on their journey to Inch Orran Castle:

> Glenroy and Benbowie did not seem in character with the scenery as they were
> borne along on the bosom of the blue waters, which reflected, as in a mirror, the
> varied beauties that skirted their shores; the gray rocks, the graceful pendant
> birch, the grassy knolls, the gushing streamlet, the fern-clad glens, the lofty
> mountains glowing with heather. (1: 45)

The semantic field is sensualised and feminised, in accordance with Mellor's
domesticated sublime, but the men resist integration into this inviting scene,
remaining unresponsive to such beauty: 'To the eye of taste and the feeling
heart there would have been rapture in every beam of light and breath of
heaven on such a day and amid such scenes. But Glenroy and Benbowie
cared for none of these things' (1: 45). They see the land in terms of 'price
and promise' (1: 46), and their spectacular surroundings merely evoke
visions of the economic gain to be reaped from fishing, farming and defor-
estation (1: 46). Glenroy rambles on to the last about 'the worldly objects to
which his soul still cleaved – his estates, his rents, his woods, his cattle, his
improvements – everything in short which could still minister to his pride'
(1: 260–1). Even on Reginald's return all he can speak of is the fact that his
'tenants had got the principle premiums from the Highland Society this year'
and the 'draining of Dhu Moss' and 'the plantation on the Skirridale Hill' and
the 'thinning of the wood' and his plans for 'the thinning of the Glenhaussen
Wood' (1: 263, 267).

The minister Duncan M'Dow is similarly obsessed with his 'augmentations'
and projected improvements to the manse. Like Glenroy and Benbowie he
has a large appetite for acquisition and drive for consumption (be it land,
money or more corporeal fare). Through their collective failings, Ferrier
offers a critique of the failure of patriarchal structures and practices, including church-based patronage.[24] Inch Orran denounces the greedy debauchery
of Glenroy, his friends and his son Norman: 'my life, sir, has been a life of

labour, of frugality, of abstinence. *Your* life, sir, is one continued idle, extravagant, intemperate soss' (1: 94), and bequeaths his estate instead to the 'temperate' Ronald Malcolm. Ronald personifies the progressivist values of a new generation of landowners that must necessarily challenge and overturn the feudal-like oversight of degenerates such as Glenroy.

During Ronald's absence from Scotland the fabric of Highland society is further torn apart by the profligacy of landowners, such as Reginald who, abandoning himself to the distractions of life in London, accrues enormous debts and neglects Glenroy estate. The detrimental effect of bad 'husbanding' and absenteeism is made explicit when M'Dow informs Edith that 'if it had not been for your friend Captain Malcolm, who bought some of the finest wood at Glenroy, I believe there would not have been a stick standing' (2: 315). Edith's concern over what will become of the dependant lower classes on the estate reveals her strong social conscience and knowledge of economic realities (2: 315–16). She preaches social responsibility to Florinda and engages sympathetically with the plight of the poor (2: 291–2). Her personal 'destiny' is thus bound up with that of Glenroy and her informed understanding of its socio-economic system holds the promise that her marriage to Ronald heralds 'the renewal of the Highland estate'.[25]

Nevertheless, as in Brunton's work, the stance taken towards the Highlands is ambivalent since their future is uncertain. Old manners are being 'broken down by modern innovation' (1: 68), not least because modernisation brings with it greater regional and national integration, causing division of opinion in the community. For example, a steamboat comes by twice a week with supplies and M'Dow proudly reports that he 'can even get a loaf of bread from Glasgow, within four-and-twenty hours after it's out of the oven' (1: 114). Captain Malcolm, alternatively, figures such advances in morally and culturally erosive terms, fearing that:

> primitive manners [. . .] no longer exist, except in the poet's page, or your imagination. Steamboats and stage-coaches have now brought each village and hamlet in close contact with some great town, even with London itself; and the evils the poet so beautifully predicted are, I fear, coming on apace. (1: 146)

Captain Malcolm's words suggest that traditional Highland culture has been relegated to poetry and the past; that it endures only in a feminised reconstruction of historical reality; and that increased intra-national interactions necessarily result in cultural and moral dilution. However, when the plot relocates to London not only is national and moral integrity preserved intact but national manners are thrown into relief, creating an enhanced opportunity to explore the consequences of cultural exchange.

Landscape now operates as a marker of national difference. Mrs Macaulay judges the trees in the South to be 'stiff pookit things' (2: 184), and both the narrator and Edith comment on the contrast between the English countryside and the 'more picturesque beauties' of the Highlands (2: 205; 2: 270). Edith's joy at exchanging 'the crowded streets and stifling atmosphere of London for the silent glens and free mountain air of her dear Highland home' (2: 413) may denote political commentary or simply personal preference. Less equivocally, Edith's return 'home' signifies social and spiritual restoration. Similarly (and like Brunton's Henry Graham), Ronald must make a redemptive return to Scotland to recover his true identity, end his self-exile and claim Edith as his love. Accordingly, he instructs her to meet him at Inch Orran: 'There let me find you – there let me claim you' (2: 384).

Juliet Shields' suggestion that *Destiny* prescribes a model of 'national division of moral labor' is problematic.[26] The novel essays a more complex engagement with national identity than this segregation of Highland virtue from southern rapacity implies. The vital point (as Shields admits) must be that these characters return to Scotland with enlightened and broadened perspectives, having learnt the value of cultural relativism. When Penshurst expresses regret that Edith 'should have been made acquainted with so unfavourable a specimen of English taste and manners' as the Ribleys' set, Edith replies 'I am more in the way of losing prejudices than of acquiring them. I have already got rid of a few since I came to England.' He responds: 'So have I, since you came to England' (2: 214). Reiterating the point, Edith informs Admiral Conway that 'England has rid me of some of my Celtic prejudices' (2: 272). She has learnt that moral virtue is not embedded in nationality and money is a 'universal idol' (2: 213). Meanwhile, Ronald embraces his British national identity when he remarks: 'I was not aware it was more fortunate to have been born an English than a Scotchman, since both are alike Britons' (2: 284). *Destiny* concludes with Mrs Macaulay rendering an 'old Hieland distich' into English so that Admiral Croft may understand it (2: 423–4). The readiness demonstrated by both mediator and recipient to engage in this act of linguistic accommodation ends the novel on a positive note, promising greater British national harmony via mutually sympathetic cultural exchanges. Brunton's and Ferrier's novels invoke an ambivalent dialectic of tradition and experimentation; romance and realism; sentiment and satire; regionalism and nationalism; nationalism and Unionism. Exploring these dualistic impulses in their feminine domestic fiction enabled them to negotiate the public sphere and engage with key questions about personal and national identity in nineteenth-century Scotland and Britain. Such fracturing subverts reader expectations and demands renewed interest in their fiction from a modern readership.

CHAPTER SIX

Janet Hamilton: Working-class Memoirist and Commentator

Florence S. Boos

Drawing on information from census reports and marriage registers and a minimal definition of literacy as the ability to sign one's name, historians have estimated that roughly 25 per cent of Scottish working-class women were illiterate in 1855, seventeen years before the Scottish Education Act of 1872 permitted (but did not require) districts to arrange for primary education.[1] Against a background of baseline estimates such as these, it hardly seems surprising that penury, cultural bias, familial subordination, and exclusion from secular working-class organisations reinforced the 'absence among working-class women of the self-confidence required to undertake the unusual act of writing an autobiography' which David Vincent mentioned in *Bread, Knowledge and Freedom*.[2] It was a striking event, therefore, when Elizabeth Storie's *Autobiography of . . . A Native of Glasgow: Who Was Subjected to Much Injustice at the Hands of Some Members of the Medical, Legal and Clerical Professions* appeared in 1859.[3] And it was even more striking when a working-class Scottish woman's insights in Janet Hamilton's twenty-four essays, 'Sketches of Village Life and Character', and more than two hundred poems found an unexpectedly wide public audience, making her possibly Victorian Scotland's best known working-class author.[4] (Scottish working-class women poets who published volumes before 1870 included Jane Adams, Catherine Pringle Craig, Margaret Crawford, Sarah Parker, Susanna Hawkins, Elisa Leslie, Margaret Mackintosh, Emma Price, Mary Pyper, Janet Reid, Elizabeth Soutar, Jane Stevenson, and Isabella White. As might be expected, many of the poems in their volumes are conventional in sentiment and expression. The volumes of poetry published by Scottish working-class women after 1870 exhibit a marked rise in self-confidence and sophistication.)

   That Hamilton's prose as well as poetry attracted readers seems apparent from responses to her two volumes. Reviewers for the *Morning Journal* and *Liverpool Albion* of her 1863 *Poems and Essays*, remarked that 'the essays [. . .] are elegantly, nay, eloquently written' (1 June 1863); and 'The prose sketches at the end of the volume, are at least equal in merit to the poetry; if anything, we are inclined to think them superior, while so rich is the grace and purity of the English in which they are written, that even a professedly literary man might study them with advantage' (4 March 1863). A faint undertone of Samuel Johnson's 'surprise [. . .] to find [writing by a woman] done at all'[5] hovered in the *Morning Journal* review. But other 'professedly literary men'– the *Athenaeum* reviewer, for example – considered the 1863 volume 'one of the most remarkable that has fallen into our hands for a long time past. It is a book that ennobles life, and enriches our common humanity' (June 1863). The 1865 *Athenaeum* reviewer (perhaps the same man) singled out her prose 'Sketches' for particular praise: 'Still more animated and characteristic are her prose sketches [. . .] Occasionally an anecdote is told which owes its charm less to incident than the shrewd and kindly veracity of the narrator'.[6]

The breadth of Hamilton's audience suggests that her reminiscences and opinions particularly reflected the inherent aspirations and frustrations of her working-class culture, as well the uniquely Scottish history of 'The Killing Time' and her ambivalent, often sceptical view of Victorian 'progress'. This chapter explores the background to Hamilton and the particular dynamics of her role, as she moves beyond poet to cultural commentator.

Life

A girl without formal education, an ardent reader from childhood, a married woman at 13, a mother of ten children (seven of whom survived), a matron who taught herself to write in her 50s (she had committed her own verses to memory), Hamilton lost much of her sight when she was in her 60s and was fully blind at 70.[7] Born Janet Thomson on 14 October 1795 at Shotts in Lanarkshire, Hamilton was the only child of James Thomson, a shoemaker and sometime agricultural worker, and his wife Mary Brownlee Thomson, who moved together to the village of Langloan (now a subdivision of Coatbridge) when Janet was seven. Mary Thomson accompanied her husband during two years of field labour, then worked as a tambourer (embroidress), teaching her daughter the same occupation. Janet Thomson's mother was the great-granddaughter of John Whitelaw, executed for his Covenanter beliefs at the Old Tollbooth in 1683,[8] and deeply devout. James Thomson, described by Gilfillan as 'an ardent reformer' (*PES*, p. 13) was a man of parts, who subscribed to the new village library, which offered access to 'much good and solid reading',[9] and apparently had an interest in science which Janet Hamilton later memorialised with characteristic humour. Janet also remembered his anger and disgust when a neighbour, 'Auld Auntie Jamieson' punished little Janet severely for reciting a poem on the Sabbath, and his scorn and contempt when a local radical threatened him with violence if he failed to join a proposed 1819 uprising (*PES*, p. 422).

Her mother also reappeared frequently in Hamilton's recollections as an instructor in reading and religion:

> for as soon as I could read, she made me read a chapter from the Bible every morning, and this practice was never omitted for a single day, till I married and left the house; and [. . .] every night when I laid my head on the pillow, my mother's mouth was close at my ear, praying for me, and teaching me to pray for myself.[10]

She was less broadminded than her husband, however, and somewhat more austere:

> My mother, who was a very pious woman, did not at all approve of my ballad singing, poetry, and novel reading, and would often threaten to burn my precious store [of ballads], but a good fit of crying, on my part, always saved them. (ix)

Hamilton recorded one such encounter in 'Pictures of Memory'. When shown a volume of fairy tales and ballads by her eager daughter, Mary Hamilton responded that 'such reading may amuse,/ But will not make you good and wise'. Janet persisted, however:

> 'Oh, you shall hear,' the child replies:
>   Then warbled clear an old Scotch ditty.
> The mother's heart was moved; her eyes
>   Were brimming o'er with love and pity[,]

and Janet, 'like a dancing sunbeam, pass'ed/ Away into the summer air' (ll. 25–8; 31–2 *PES*, pp. 271–2). Hamilton seldom praised herself in print, but in this instance the power of the word evidently took precedence over the power of the Word. Hamilton told Gilfillan in later years that that she had nursed each current infant while reading, and had quickly hidden her copy of *Blackwood's* or Shakespeare in a carefully prepared niche in the wall when someone entered.

Many working-class autobiographers have expressed their yearning for education as a source of inner and outer fulfilment – life's great romance, as it were[11] – and Hamilton's longest prose account of her youth (three pages in all) consisted almost entirely of recollections of her early reading:

> I was never taught, never knew, do not know even now, any of the rules of grammar in composition [. . .]

> I do not remember when I became mistress of the alphabet, but I read Bible stories and children's half-penny books with eager delight before I was five years of age. When about eight, I found to my great joy, on the loom of an intellectual weaver, a copy of Milton's *Paradise Lost* and a volume of Allan Ramsay's *Poems*. [. . .] I soon became familiar with, and could appreciate the gorgeous sublimity of Milton's imagery. [. . .] With Ramsay I was at home at once, for I was beginning to get rich in the Ballad treasures of my country about that time; and a pathetic 'Aul Warl Ballant' would put the sweetie shop to a discount at any time when I was mistress of a bawbee.[12]

In old age she also recalled in conversation with Alexander Wallace that she 'could scarcely remember the time when her love of books was not her ruling passion', and that she had continued to read till two in the morning each day of her sighted life.

Adolescent conflicts between Janet and her mother may have been averted by her marriage in 1809 to her father's assistant John Hamilton, with whom she lived until her death in 1874. Wallace described him as a man who regarded his wife 'with singular devotion', (*PES*, p. 21), faithfully supporting her love of reading and bringing her armfuls of books from distant libraries (*PES*, pp. 16–17). Seven of their ten children survived to adulthood, five born before Janet reached the age of 20, and the last, a daughter, dying at five weeks when Janet was 30.

Implausible as it may seem, the unschooled ardent reader Janet Hamilton did not learn to write for many years: when she began to compose religious poems in her head at seventeen – and the mother of two – John transcribed about twenty of them. If these were the verses published as 'sacred poems' in the posthumous volume of her works, they are noticeably less sophisticated and more biblical in tone than later poems. After her third child was born she apparently left off composition for many years, but when she was about fifty taught herself to write a rough but firm 'printed' script (*PES*, p. 13).

Hamilton published four books in her lifetime, and her son James edited her posthumous *Poems, Essays and Sketches*. Age and complete loss of sight severely limited her production after 1870, but James's recollections provide a glimpse of her linguistic precision and independent character even when she could not see:

> Having been my mother's amanuensis, I may say that when I wrote a piece from her dictation, and afterwards read it over to her, she rarely made a correction on it. When her books were being printed, although unable from want of sight to read a line, she never would allow any one but herself to make any corrections on the proofs. I read them; she sat and listened, and an alteration of a word or a syllable from her own she would detect at once. She said if her writings

possessed any merit, it would be her own; and if there were blemishes in them, they, too, would be her own. (*PES*, p. vii)

Early Publications

Almost all working-class women poets whose work has survived benefited from the help of one or more reformist middle-class editors; Hamilton was no exception. Her first known appearances in print came at 55, in the publications of John Cassell, a publisher committed to the cause of popular education, the freehold land movement, and working-class political advancement. In 1850 he launched three self-help ventures specifically targeted at working-class audiences: the penny weekly *The Working Man's Friend and Family Instructor*; an essay competition for readers of *The Working Man's Friend*; and a companion volume, *The Literature of Working Men*, composed entirely of essays submitted for the competition.

Cassell's undertaking was extremely radical. The idea of a contest soliciting working-class writing which would then be published was literally 'empowering' to disenfranchised working-class readers: his call brought 800 submissions.[13] *The Literature of Working Men* was a unique instance of a nineteenth-century publication of works composed entirely by and for working-class writers, and its existence changed Janet Hamilton's life. In a period of tacit as well as explicit male discrimination, her submissions were accepted for publication in all three of Cassell's subsidised publications. Six essays were published in *The Literature of Working Men*, making her the most frequent contributor to the volume, and another submission on temperance appeared in *The Working Man's Friend*, in which Cassell included 'The Wayside Well', a poem praising his efforts on behalf of the working-class.[14] Cassell also published two of Hamilton's temperance essays, two essays on education and, in 1851 'To the Working Women of Britain', perhaps the most original of her early polemical essays. 'Sketch of a Scottish Roadside Village Fifty Years Since' (1851) later became the first of her 'Sketches of Village Life and Character'.[15] Cassell also sponsored a separate prize competition for 'social science essays' composed by members of the working class: Hamilton's remarks on 'Self-Education' brought her £2 for third place in 1859.[16]

No one had quite expected such accomplishments from an elderly working-class woman, and it was to the credit of Cassell's editorial staff as well as Cassell himself that they welcomed them. As Benjamin Parsons, an early feminist and one of *The Literature of Working Men*'s sub-editors, wrote in his introduction,

Only think that the spouse of a working man [Hamilton had described herself as a shoemaker's wife rather than as a tambourer] should write a discourse on

'The Uses and Pleasures of Poetry to the Working Classes,' and that the ease and elegance, and sentiments and composition, would be such as would do no dishonor to Mrs. Ellis or the Hon. Mrs. Norton.[17]

When Cassell's working-class competitions and compilations closed down a year later for lack of money, his project's circulation had both created a wider readership for Hamilton's work, making her, for example, 'an established favourite' with 'the readers of the [Airdre and Coatbridge] Advertiser'[18] and fostered her identification with the workers' movement. She dedicated her third volume in 1868 'loving and respectfully . [. . . t]o her Brothers/ THE MEN OF THE WORKING CLASSES' and followed it with a few lines of verse:

Ah, not low my aspirations,
High and strong my soul's desire,
To assist my toiling brothers
Upward, onward, to aspire.

In her final volume in 1870, she also expanded this dedication to 'her brothers and sisters of the working-classes'. Such gestures clearly expressed her gratitude for the encouragement and solidarity she found in the contemporary workers' movement.

Hamilton on Education and Alcoholism

The range of Hamilton's essays was determined to some extent by John Cassell's interests, but their topics – literacy, education and alcoholism – were natural for an autodidact who raised seven children and apparently endured the abuse of an alcoholic son. Her earliest essays were relatively formal and didactic, but the force of personal conviction and experience was apparent in their successors. In 'The Uses and Pleasures of Poetry for the Working-Classes' in The Literature of Working Men (1850) she expressed the hope that workers of sensibility, denied formal education and foreign travel, would seek comfort in 'that which remained behind' – imaginative literature as a source of inspiration, contemplation, social critique and consolation. Appropriately for her topic, she graced her plea with fourteen quotations from British poets from Milton onwards (whose works would have been available in cheap editions). An ardent supporter of independence movements, she also urged her readers to heed the words of Thomas Campbell's 'Pleasures of Hope' and support European democratic stirrings in general and the efforts of Hungarian revolutionaries in particular. Robert Burns was another of her heroes, along with the 'Corn Law Rhymer' Ebenezer Elliott.[19] The chief 'use' of poetry was ethical self-culture, however, and in her peroration, she concluded that 'amidst blasted hopes and wasted aspirations [the working man who loves poetry] may imbibe the very spirit of courage, patience, and resignation (p. 435).

Her political sympathies were more muted in 'Social Science Essay on Self-Education' (the essay which brought her the £2 prize), but her principal examples of 'self-made men' were a tailor and cooper who became ministers of the faith. She also addressed herself directly in this essay to those whose situations resembled her own, '[w]orking-women, daughters of working-mothers with families' who 'could not be spared for years to attend school' (p. 446):

> I venture to give my humble opinion that the proper study of womankind is woman; and I dare to say that the woman who takes up and thoroughly studies that interesting and sometimes intricate subject, will find ample scope for the exercise of her mind . . . and, above all, in the study and culture of her heart, affections, and feelings. (p. 447)

In a society in which a mandate for elementary education was a generation away, she accepted the inevitability of partial home-schooling, urging women entrusted with this to acquit themselves of it as well as they could, for the 'habits of religion, prudence, and industry' depended on their work. She also warned parents of the destructive effects of narcotics commonly given children, urged them to guide through affection rather than discipline, and asked them to educate themselves to read and discuss books with their children.

In 'To Working-Women' finally, she directly broached a painful topic, 'a sister addresses you, one of your class – the daughter, wife, and mother of working-men' (p. 456):

> Working-women, shall I here make the sad supposition that there are amongst us those who either cannot read at all, or do it so imperfectly that the sense is obscured or lost in the attempt? Alas for the woman who is thus engaged in the battle of life! She is indeed unarmed and undefended. (p. 458)

Even the relatively educated, however, have failed to fulfil their potential: 'we have [. . .] fallen immeasurably short of the standard attained by the females of the upper and middle classes, who [. . .] adorned the literature of their country' (p. 460). And for the first time she criticised her beloved 'Brothers [. . .] of the Working Classes' for their interest in matter not mind: 'is it not true that in early manhood the qualities you admire [. . .] consist chiefly in dress, complexion, and figure, with a piquant manner of uttering [. . .] silly repartees, and pretty nothings' (p. 461). Hamilton's essay is a rare instance of an address by a working-class woman to her fellow women. Her scorn for what would now be called 'women's socialisation' was not unique, but had the sting of personal experience and long observation, as did her confrontation of her 'toiling brothers' and the leaders of worker-education movements for their *de facto* devaluation of women. Perhaps alluding to the fact that adult education courses for workers were generally designed for men, she urged 'the necessity [. . .] of including the females of your class, and more particularly the young [. . .] in every movement for furthering the intellectual advancement of our order' (p. 462).[20]

Hamilton also devoted five of her early essays to denunciations of alcohol as an opiate of the working classes. The first European temperance movement arose in the west of Scotland, and its mutual aid societies and 'Band of Hope' activities for young people were as much parts of working-class life as were the densely packed pubs on its streets.[21] Hamilton contributed six poems to *The Adviser*, the Scottish Temperance League's illustrated magazine for children, in 1853–4, and dedicated her first volume to a local landowner who supported the cause.[22] In 'Counteracting Influences', her first temperance essay, Hamilton concluded with a poem in which a 'mourning mother' raged at the mysterious power of addiction:

> I have had, I have still, a stern warfare to wage
> With a monster so hideous, so hateful, and dire,
> It seems as I moved in a circle of fire. (*PES*, p. 484)

For all her fervour, however, Hamilton was a 'moral suasion' temperance advocate, not a 'Prohibitionist'. The Scottish temperance movement pre-ferred education and propaganda to prohibition in this period, and Hamilton was openly sceptical of the likelihood of governmental intervention through the force of law:

> It were useless in this matter to invoke the aid either of churchmen or states-men; for, generally speaking, the domestic usages of the one, and the rich results accruing to the revenue in the other, will always sufficiently account for the cold neutrality in the cause of temperance maintained by the first, and the nega-tive encouragement given by the last, to the unlimited manufacture, sale, and consumption of all kinds of excisable liquors. (*PES*, pp. 478–9)

Hamilton's predictions were more or less accurate: employers as well as the Church of Scotland opposed temperance initiatives. As Elspeth King observes, the Church had its own problems: 'The Reverend Mr. Houston of Gorbals Parish Church was one of the worst cases, having been charged nineteen times in five years with being "drunk on the streets, drunk in the house of God, drunk when performing the marriage ceremony and drunk in his own house".'[23]

Probably as a result of her defence of temperance and the importance of maternal teaching, Brian Maidment has characterised Hamilton's writings as a 'compendium of ferociously conservative attitudes'.[24] I see her as principally animated by basic ideals of autonomy and mutual aid. She did not, for example, believe that women should defer to men; that self-education should substitute for schools; that abstinence should be imposed by fiat rather than persuasion; or that statesmen have an *ipso facto* claim on respect. She believed in working-class solidarity, and drew on these ideals and her personal experience to suggest ways in which her brothers and sisters might find a better life.

'Sketches of Village Life and Character'

Hamilton published ten 'sketches' of the village life of her childhood, in which she recreated the customs and legends of her ancestors and gently rebuked or deconstructed some of their more manifest exaggerations.[25] As she put it in her preface to *Poems of Purpose and Sketches [. . .]. of Scottish Peasant Life and Character*, her motive was a 'desire to hold at times sweet (some will say uncouth) converse with dear old Mother Scotland, before her native Doric, her simple manners and habits, are swept away by the encroaching tides of change and centralization' (p. 5). In the opening 'Sketch' she appeals to her authority as participant:

> to give a true and graphic sketch or sketches of Scottish peasant life and character in 'days of langsyne', it is necessary that the writer should not draw his information from tradition and hearsay alone, but should, from childhood, have lived, moved, and shared, for a time at least, in the usages, customs, and opinions; in a word, in all the habits and actings both of the inner and outer life 'of that bold peasantry, their country's pride' – a class which is fast losing its identity. (*PES*, p. 351)

According to Hamilton, one pronounced characteristic of traditional Scottish 'peasant character' was a belief in revenge, ennobled as 'the actings of the retributive Providence'. Hamilton tried to mine such views for anagogic significance and to understand those who held them. She narrated a tale told by her maternal grandfather (1704–1801) about orphaned Mysie Fairlie, a servant who became pregnant by her employer's son, and was told by him that he would forfeit his right hand if he failed to marry her. After jilting her for a wealthier bride, he called Hamilton's grandfather on his deathbed to exhibit his putrid hand, blackened from gangrene, and to beg Mysie's forgiveness. Other examples of 'divine intervention' included a powerful dream which had allegedly appeared to Hamilton's great-grandfather, leading him on awakening to exchange his previous mode of life for sobriety and devotion. Hamilton does not 'suppose that this relation [. . .] will receive an unhesitating assent to the reality of the dream' (pp. 356–7), but duly offered for consideration the fact that he did alter the course of his life afterwards. On the other hand, she commended her grandfather for rejecting the narrow sectarianism of the period 'freely indulged in both by Seceders and Churchmen', as exhibited by publicly walking out of the kirk with his little son when a minister compared the Church of Scotland to the 'mother of harlots' (p. 365).

Other reminiscences record some of the many crises of remote rural life or describe her childhood awe of witches' charms and the country people's fear of '[ghostly] visitations [which] were sometimes fatal' (p. 378). As with the religious dream vision, she suspended judgement about 'the reality of [. . .] ghost[ly] intromissions'. In short, Hamilton respected her frugal ancestors' virtues, and drew on their 'auld warl' fables as sources for her 'sendings [. . .] set in my heart' ('Grannie's Tale', l. 8), but carefully distanced herself from their more extravagant details.

In 'Sketches of a Scottish Roadside Village Sixty Years Since' Hamilton expressed gratitude for the modest recompense of her work at the tambour frame, an obsolete profession which had once been 'amply remunerated': 'an industrious girl could not only earn a comfortable living for herself, but also assist her parents with the younger portion of the family' (p. 385). She recalled with respect the independent weavers of her region who 'by a moderate application to work for eight or nine hours a day, would earn a sufficient competence for all the purposes of life – his leisure hours being chiefly employed in the culture of flowers' (p. 385). She also described the traditional Scottish but and ben cottage in which she was reared, and averred that taken as a [vanished] class, [hand weavers] were the most intelligent, enlightened, and by far the most independent body of working men in the kingdom' (p. 386). In 'A Scottish Out-door Communion Sabbath in Times Gone By' Hamilton reproved some of the excesses she remembered from her ferociously conservative youth – the oppressive tedium of Sabbath observances '[. . .] leavened with something of Judaical strictness and austerity' (p. 396). She also deprecated the practice of outdoor preachments from ten in the morning to six in the evening, accompanied by a well-lubricated day-long feast and scenes in which drunken men fought near the church, 'surrounded by shrieking women, their Sunday clothes torn to tatters, blood streaming from their faces, and uttering the most horrid oaths' (p. 404).

By way of counterpoint, Hamilton also remembered people who lived marginal and unremarkable lives in quiet dignity, among them 'auld Robin', a lover of broadsides, and 'Auld Kirsty Dinsmore', an elderly spinster (in the literal sense of the word), who lived in a tiny round dwelling behind her family's cottage and taught her ballads:

How often when my peering, laughing face darkened the small panes, would that little, wrinkled round face, set in its rim of snow-white hair, turn round with a look of kindness in its pale blue eyes, and she would say – 'Come in, my bairn, an' I'se sing thee the sang thou likes sae weel.' (429)

Here and elsewhere, the elderly Hamilton remembered with particular affection the kind souls who had fostered her childhood gifts.

Aversion to armed conflict remained a deep and consistent feature of her thought. An ardent opponent of slavery, she recoiled from the carnage of the American Civil War, and wrote at least nine unreprinted anti-war poems for the 1863 and 1865 volumes, as well as a poetic meditation on 'The Horrors of War' (1870) in which she anticipated a bloody pan-European conflict. She also displays scepticism about the Napoleonic Wars of her youth. Citing lines on the devastation of war by the Scottish poet Hector MacNeill,[26] she sardonically recalled 'the days of Nelson and naval victory', when for 'too many of our village politicians it was sufficient atonement for the wasted blood and treasure of the nation that we could blow up the ships of the French at sea, or slaughter them by thousands on land (p. 386).

In 'Reminiscences of the Radical Time – 1819–20' Hamilton described an abortive uprising and neighbours who threatened to seize her home and tried to impress her father and brother into a doomed battle with troops encamped in nearby Airdrie. Even so, Hamilton sadly recalled 'the deep distress of the hand-loom weavers, occasioned by depression in trade, great reduction in prices, and scarcity of employment' (pp. 404–5), and the desperation of the insurgents as they marched through the village, 'with their lean, pale faces, unwashed, unshaved, and uncombed, thinly clad, and out at knees and elbows' (p. 405). Her final appeal was for peaceful reform, asking: 'who shall say that if our misguided brethren [. . .] had enjoyed the same privileges [as we], they would ever have, even in their trying circumstances, have supplied us with materials for writing Radical Reminiscences?' (p. 412).

In the end, Hamilton's 'people's history' left her with much to mourn, most conspicuously the ravages wrought by coal and iron smelting in her once-green and pleasant land. In 'Local Changes', the last essay in her last volume, she recalled a morning walk graced by bird songs on the banks of the Luggie in the spring of 1820, and observed that: 'the lover of nature has exchanged the whistle of the blackbird and the song of the thrush for the shrieking, hissing, and whistling of steam, and the once clear waters of the Luggie for a sink of stench and pollution' (Poems, p. 389).

A more personal burden in Hamilton's later years was her blindness. She sought to soothe her grief with appeals to redemptive memory. In 'A Ballad of Memorie' she wistfully recalled 'the [f]rien's o' my youth – a' gane, a' gane!/ An' I sit blinlins here ...' But even yet:

> the star o' memory lichts the past;
> But there's a licht abune

To cheer the darkness o' a life
That maun be endit sune.
(ll. 57–60)

In one of her last poems, 'The Skylark – Caged and Free', a woman who had enjoyed acute perception of visual detail recognises the bird's plight: 'the bard within thee burning,/ Heaven in thine eye, the dull earth spurning', as also her own: 'Thy prison song, O bird beloved,/ My heart hath strangely, deeply moved.'

Conclusion

There is a sense in which the trajectory of Hamilton's life was genuinely unique. Few literate working-class women had her literary gifts, strength of character and a measure of domestic encouragement for her efforts. Even fewer benefited from anything like the window of opportunity briefly opened by John Cassell. And fewer still had the grandmotherly authority to make impassioned appeals for women's education in Victorian Britain, or reflect on the mixed effects of 'progress', and have a chance that they might be heard.

A gifted woman raised in an essentially oral culture, Janet Hamilton survived long enough to become an astute mediator between shifting cultural views, and a cogent translator of her 'people's history' into written form. The topics she chose – education, temperance, regional history – were generally approved by the workers' movements of her time. But she infused them with more individual qualities: her wry sensibility; her temperamental pacifism; her faith in mutual aid and solidarity; her passionate advocacy of women's education; and her sage reveries of the 'auld mither Scotland' which lived on in her 'ballads of memorie'. Her assessments of the losses and gains of 'progress' expressed the ideals of her class, place and time, and her evocative essays remain among the best sources we have for an understanding of the lives and attitudes of the 'respectable' poor from within.

CHAPTER SEVEN

Private Writing

Aileen Christianson

This chapter considers the concept of 'private writing' in relation to letters, diaries and memoirs by nineteenth-century Scottish women. In most cases (although not all) they initially wrote for themselves, their family and other intended recipients, rather than for publication. Can their texts be read as 'private' or are they (however 'private') as much part of literary production as fiction or non-fiction intended for publication? One author discussed is Margaret Oliphant (1828–97), consummate professional published writer who began her autobiography as a private record but continued it as a piece of work to be published posthumously to provide financially for her niece.[1] Defining herself in relation to other more 'successful' writers and always driven by the need to make a living to support her family, she claimed a role more generally assigned to the male in the family in Victorian times. But other nineteenth-century women, without professional writing roles, produced private memoirs which gained posthumous life, for example, Elizabeth Grant's *Memoirs of a Highland Lady* (1897) and the scientist Mary Somerville's *Personal Recollections from Early Life to Old Age* (1873).[2] One text intended for publication from the outset is the 'Autobiography' of Ellen Johnston (1836?–74?), the 'Factory Girl', written and published as an intro-duction to her *Poems and Songs* (1867) to promote her hopes of an income from writing. The letters of novelist Susan Ferrier (published 1898) merit attention in their own right as well as illuminating her published writings.[3] The pre-eminent 'private writer' of the nineteenth century is Jane Welsh Carlyle (1801–66); with an entirely private function for her writing during her life, she became the most public of writers with the posthumous publica-tion of much of the extraordinary archive of her letters. Through these texts, this chapter explores the way in which 'private writing' claims a public life by the end of the nineteenth century, with accompanying expectations and ambivalences in reception.

The 'private' in 'private writing' is generally assumed to belong with the non-public nature of the material, that is letters, journals, memoranda books, written for private consumption. Karina Williamson's 'literature not primarily intended for print or wide public consumption'[4] gives an appropriately broad definition, which accommodates both letters and journals published posthumously and memoirs written for family consumption with later publication by family members (such as Grant (1797–1885) or Somerville (1780–1872)). Writing in 1845, Grant directly addresses her audience:

> Having got so far in these memorials of past life, the pleasure of the many half forgotten incidents now revived induces me to proceed in stringing together such recollections of our generation as can hardly fail, dear children, to be interesting to you. The feebleness of my health at present confines me so much to my room that I am neglecting nothing else while thus employing myself.[5]

The passage nicely encapsulates a defence against accusations of female time-wasting; confined to her room by 'feeble' health, she is not neglecting any of her proper female duties. Grant implies here and elsewhere that chapters were read aloud to her family,[6] reminding us that the idea of audience was implicit in private writing, either through reading aloud or by sending on. Williamson, primarily discussing late eighteenth-century examples (male and female), summarises:

> [U]npublished writings were virtually never 'private' in an absolute sense; that is, intended for closet reading by the author or recipient alone. It was common practice for personal letters, journals and memoirs to circulate within families, groups of friends or coteries of like-minded readers.[7]

Journals during the nineteenth century had a more completely private existence, self-penned, self-read, undistributed. Certainly Thomas Carlyle apparently did not know of those Welsh Carlyle kept for 1855–56. But letters could have a wide currency, at times written so that the direct recipient can make out one meaning while the audience's understanding is confined to the surface of the words, with the additional presumption that they might also be sent on to more distant relatives or friends. Welsh Carlyle acknowledges this directly when she writes to her sister-in-law: 'Please burn this letter – I mean dont [sic] hand it to the rest – there is a circulation of letters in families that frightens me from writing often – it is so difficult to write a circular to *one*.'[8] By drawing attention to the 'difficulties' of writing a 'circular to one', she foregrounds the idea of literary choices in relation to letter-writing.

The idea of private writing is extended to 'domestic writing' by Dorothy McMillan. She notes 'a great deal of work of primarily domestic origin like household books or letters and memoirs often privately circulated although not printed' and '[b]iographies of family and friends' belonging to a 'wider but still mainly private community', arguing:

> This kind of private writing which is designed for familial or coterie reading is, of course, difficult to discuss in aesthetic terms [. . .] the kind of shaping and polish that would be looked for in declared fiction might well be felt suspicious in the unvarnished 'truth' of letter and memoir.[9]

Williamson also finds the literary value of much private or domestic writing 'variable', although their value 'as historical sources and illustrations is unquestionable'.[10] Literary value and artistic choices are, however, found in all the examples discussed in this chapter, particularly in the case of Welsh Carlyle's private writings but also in Grant's *Memoir* and Oliphant's *Autobiography*. Johnston's text might be problematic in its style but, nonetheless, carries literary value in its tightly constructed appeal for an audience for her poems. Attention to literary and aesthetic value is deserved in all these texts, written as they are by women with an awareness of literary genre. They are as subject to 'revision' and choice as more conventional literary works, with their writing offering not McMillan's 'unvarnished "truth"' but a more skilled presentation of the truths of their material.

The opposition between 'public' and 'private' in relation to letters and memoirs is clearly expressed by the English writer Harriet Martineau (1802–76), a friend of Welsh Carlyle and an early nineteenth-century example of a professional writer, earning money by periodical writing as well as by her non-fiction and fiction works. She wanted all her letters destroyed; letters were so private that they should be allowed no posthumous existence. She believed that 'epistolary correspondence is written speech: the *onus* rests with those who publish it to show why the laws of honour which are uncontested in regard to conversation may be violated when the conversation is written instead of spoken'.[11] Welsh Carlyle was typically satirical about Martineau's request, seeing it as 'a diseased anxiety about her future biography', although she did comply: 'I have *done* the *practical* in the matter – keeping only an autograph for Helen – but for the rest, have told her that I must be allowed to retain my own *opinion*'.[12] Martineau's request illustrates views strongly held (but disregarded by many biographers) in the nineteenth century, with anxieties about control of private material combining with fears of betrayal of confidences. Welsh Carlyle is also aware of the ambiguities of connection between future biography and the 'privacy' of letters, although her response is couched as part of her ongoing satiric response to Thomas Carlyle; she rebukes him about the complexity of a piece of paper used for a letter: 'Such a mixed *m s*, with *flaps* too, may be a valuable literary curiosity "a hundred years hence"; but is a trial of patience to the Present Reader'.[13] In a letter to a nephew, with a (disregarded) request for burning, she directly references those biographers assumed to lie in wait for Carlyle:

Please to send what I am here writing *no further* – Indeed burn my letter – It is one of the disadvantages of being connected with a distinguished man, that ones own little obscure letters and speeches must be written and spoken always under a chilling sense of future Biographers! To say nothing of present Gossipers![14]

Her apparent expression of self-censorship is more honoured in omission as her reporting and discussion of Carlyle's daily life and events in her letters and journal is notably detailed and entertainingly opinionated, resulting in the revision of ideas about Carlyle later in the nineteenth century.

Beside her many letters, Welsh Carlyle also wrote other short pieces of private writing which were circulated to only a few chosen recipients. Her clearest piece of 'domestic writing' is 'BUDGET *of a Femme incomprise*', written in the form of a speech to the Houses of Parliament as reported in *Hansard*. Left for Thomas to find one morning when he came in from the garden, her current (1855) expenditure for the household is detailed, with an argument for an increased allowance:

I dont [sic] choose to *speak* again on the Money Question. The 'replies' from the Noble Lord are unfair, and unkind, and little to the purpose. When you tell me 'I pester your life out about money' – that 'your soul is sick with hearing about it' – that 'I had better make the money I *have* serve' [. . .] *all that* I call perfectly unfair.[15]

She then gives a long account of their household budget, throwing the metaphoric gauntlet to Thomas Carlyle: 'If I were a man, I might "fling the gauntlet to Society, join with a few brave fellows, and rob a Diligence". But my sex "kind of" debars me from that'.[16] Carlyle responded to the rebuke, writing on the document both his agreement and his admiration: 'The Inclosed was read with great laughter [. . .] The Piece is so clever, that I cannot, just yet, find in my heart to burn it, as perhaps I ought to do'.[17] It was not circulated further until after his death. Another short piece, 'Much ado about Nothing', a combined travel narrative and reminiscence about her return to Haddington in 1849 after many years, was sent to a new friend ('from all but the most sympathetic friend one would naturally withhold such outpourings of human egoism as is here written down') within a month of writing, but not seen by Thomas until after her death.[18] 'The simple Story of my own first Love', a humorous tale, was possibly sent to Kate Sterling, a young friend whose courtship by a Russian nobleman had recently been forbidden. It concludes:

[S]uch reflections did I let myself go to them, might lead me too far, – to the length namely, of my whole pamphlet [. . .] on *the Marriage-question*, which, I fear is too much in advance of the Century for being committed to writing; so long at least as the mania for *editing* and *publishing* everybody's *papers*, however come by, holds out.[19]

The fair copy, written in an exercise book, was seen by Thomas for the first time after Welsh Carlyle's death: 'Burn? No! 3 Augt 1866'.[20] Implicit questions of ownership are raised by the circulation of Welsh Carlyle's writing after her death rather than during her life, with subsequent awareness of her writing talent only possible because Thomas Carlyle gathered in her letters in the midst of his grief. His reading of her letters and other pieces led to the writing of these Reminiscences, a piece of domestic writing that Williamson sees as a continuation of an earlier tradition, while transforming it.[21] His decision that his Reminiscences and her writing should be published after his death contributes to controversy about the demands of privacy but also establishes Welsh Carlyle as a public writer.[22] After J. A. Froude's publication of Carlyle's Reminiscences, 1881 (barely a month after Thomas's death) and the three volumes of Letters and Memorials of Jane Welsh Carlyle in 1883 (including Thomas's editorial comments),[23] private truly becomes public.

Once the Pandora's box of 'private' writing was opened by the publication of the Carlyles' papers, that led the way for other privately intended writing to join the late nineteenth-century publishing phenomenon of relatives editing and presenting previously 'private' material in print form. Elizabeth Grant's Memoirs, written between 1845 and 1854, then edited by her niece Lady Strachey, were first privately published by subscription in 1897, then publicly by John Murray in 1898, with many editions following.[24] Susan Ferrier's Memoir and Correspondence, gathered and introduced by her great-nephew, and edited by John A. Doyle, was also first published in 1898.[25] Interest in Ferrier's letters undoubtedly lies in the light they throw on her writing of Marriage (1818) but they also have inherent value in the sharp, ironic analytic tones that Ferrier (1782–1854) uses, making it clear that the satirical Marriage is consistent with her talent and not an anomalous work. Binary oppositions between town and country are set up in her 1809 letter to Charlotte Clavering. Ferrier satirises the characteristics of the picturesque, opposing 'the enchanting season' in Edinburgh to 'vegetating at Inveraray', the seat of the Dukes of Argyll at the picturesque heart of the Highlands. Briskly characterising nature as 'decaying', with its 'dropping leaves, fading flowers, drooping trees' and 'the monotonous din of some tinkling rill or tumbling cascade',[26] she resists the romantic fervour of her time in her private writing as well as in her 'public' novels, 'her turn of mind' proving to be the 'very reverse of romantic', as a contemporary reviewer commented.[27] The publication of these letters (others having been destroyed at her request), described by her great-nephew as 'very lively and piquant in style', is justified as being of interest to those who enjoyed her 'clever and still popular novels' even though her life was 'so quiet and uneventful as to afford little scope for a memoir'.[28] The life is uneventful but the writing, private and public, is worthy of attention because of her literary skill, rather than the events of her life.

Peter Butter describes Grant as being 'Jane Austenish' with 'irony, wit, intelligence, firm moral judgements'.[29] But Grant is far closer to Ferrier in her wit, sharing ironic and satiric impulses, as well as her insistence on the importance of education for girls and young women. Grant's *Memoirs* are descriptive, casting back to a past world, with a more Edenic view of the Highlands of her childhood than Ferrier's:

> We grew strong and healthy, and we were very happy, revelling among the blackberries on the Doune till we were *tattooed*, frocks and all, like the American Indians; in the garden, stung into objects by the mosquitoes in the fruit bushes; in our dear broom island, or farther off sometimes in the forest, gathering cranberries and lying half asleep upon the fragrant heather.[30]

But there is much commentary interjected, often critical of the realities of the effects on children of various methods of upbringing:

> I had been so extremely good all this tour, well amused, made of, and not worried! that Miss Ramsay was extremely complimented on the improvement she had affected in my naturally bad disposition. As if there were any naturally bad dispositions. Don't we crook them, and stunt them, and force them, and break them, and varnish them, and do every thing in the world except let them alone to expand in pure air to the sun, and nourish them healthily?[31]

While her *Memoirs* are presented as a simple recollection of a past age and country, 'begun to please my children and my niece [. . .] May 1845',[32] they provide an opportunity for Grant to pass judgement on many of the people and habits she describes, criticising methods of child rearing, tartly pointing out the shortcomings of her parents and their generation. Written with mid-century attitudes, edited by her niece for late nineteenth-century sensibilities, even the shortened cheaper editions of 1911 and later carry enough references to illegitimate children, oddities of parental behaviour and criticism of educational habits to give a clear flavour of the original. Grant shapes the memoirs chronologically and, although they may lack the narrative discipline of fiction, the early and late nineteenth-century novels, Ferrier's *Marriage* and Oliphant's *Kirsteen* (1890), show similar aspects of early nineteenth-century Highland society. Both fiction and non-fiction provide a vivid sociological picture with strong criticisms of prospects for young women, and a foregrounding of Highlandism, gender and class.

Mary Somerville's recollections, covering some of the same period as Grant's, were equally begun mid-century and published in the late nineteenth century. Some of her purpose may have been similar to Grant's, but the opening is much more assertive and self-conscious:

My life has been domestic and quiet. I have no events to record that could interest the public. My only motive in writing, is to show my country women that self education is possible under the most unfavourable and even discouraging circumstances.[33]

Somerville's claim of her right to a scientific education and career alongside her domestic life is amply exemplified in *Recollections*; selected and published by her daughter the year after her death in 1872,[34] they take their place in the tradition of public Scottish women's life-writing. McMillan's edition, incorporating much from the manuscripts (including Somerville's opening statement above) that Martha Somerville edited out, provides 'a text that can be read simultaneously as the version of a Victorian daughter, Martha, and the production of her mother'.[35] Considered elsewhere in this volume, Somerville is included here as one of those women, born in the late eighteenth or early nineteenth century, who asserted their right to a life story, their private memoirs prepared by relatives for a public posthumous production. She narrates a vanished world in her reminiscences of her early childhood and education in Burntisland, before memorialising her personal and scientific life, ending in Sorrento with her ninety-second year and the words 'I am perfectly happy'.[36] Her memoir carries sociological and historical value; but there is also literary value, particularly in its observations of nature.

Ellen Johnston, with the shortest example of private writing discussed here, writes a tightly controlled 'Autobiography' (1867), using a conventional, even stereotypical, style.[37] The succinct presentation of her life contains oblique (but clear) reference to sexual abuse by her stepfather (her 'tormentor'), providing an early example that acknowledges of one of the most hidden aspects of a private life. She foregrounds the 'mystery of my life'[38] and her attempts to bear it. Of all my examples, except Martineau, Johnston is the only one writing directly for publication, but even here the publishing of her 'life' is part of a necessary advertisement for her poetry. McMillan considers that Johnston's 'appropriation of a second-hand literary discourse fights rather than aids the validation of her experience'[39] but Johnston still turns the form into a powerful example of the public presentation of self.

Of all the writers discussed in this chapter, Welsh Carlyle most clearly epitomises the overlap between the private (unpublished) and the public (published) visible in their work. With her prolific production of 'private' writing (at least two thousand surviving letters exist, as well the short pieces referred to above), she was defined as a writer by others after her death in 1866. There are many contemporary and subsequent descriptions of her storytelling abilities. Frequently and lazily claimed as a 'missing' novelist, her choice was to write privately; her reputation should rest firmly and justifiably on the skill and power of the life-writing that survives.[40] What can be seen in her letters, apart from her skills in irony and satire, is the power of narrative within an individual letter. These can be read as complete narratives; for example, writing to Thomas about an 1822 trip to Fort Augustus in the West Highlands she includes courtship, literary reference points and satire on the picturesque, within the frame of travel writing.[41] She self-references her skills as a storyteller by writing about her 'misadventures'; that could form a 'CHELSEAN *Nights Entertainments*' (invoking the greatest fictional storyteller, Scheherezade) but decides 'it would be better to keep my squalid difficulties to myself', till she could 'work them up [. . .] into a conversational "Work of Art"',[42] neatly encapsulating hints of pain, promises of dramatic events and awareness of artistic choices.

Oliphant, linked closely to Welsh Carlyle through friendship, had disapproving views of the posthumous publication of Welsh Carlyle's letters, at least in part because she felt that 'there is not the slightest evidence that she [Welsh Carlyle], at least, ever intended these narratives for the world',[43] introducing the concept of intention. Welsh Carlyle intended her letters to be read and shared by a small audience; the rhetorical flourishes of her style demand an audience, even if, as in her private journal, it is an audience of one. Given Welsh Carlyle and her audience/recipients' acceptance of the power and success of her letters, it seems unlikely that she was unaware of the publishable value of her own writing. Oliphant herself contributed to appreciation of Welsh Carlyle's literary skills, although she did so through her discussion of Welsh Carlyle's storytelling abilities rather than her writing skills.

Oliphant describes Carlyle's *Reminiscences* as 'like a missile, an angry meteor' in its presentation of Carlyle's views of his contemporaries, showing the 'inadequacy of personal impressions and highly wrought feeling to reach that truth of portraiture'.[44] Her misgivings about this publication of both Carlyles' feelings and opinions are expanded in 'Mrs Carlyle'. These two reviews constitute a kind of private writing, based as they are on her relationship to the Carlyles and her reaction to the publishing of private papers; they are as personal in content as what she wrote of them in her *Autobiography*. The fate of the Carlyles, all papers published, 'would be ruefully comic, if it were not tragical':

> An exposure almost unexampled in the range of literature, of everything about
> them – their most private thoughts and feelings, their quarrels, faults, compunctions, their uneasy tempers, and unsatisfied and unsatisfiable wishes – all
> set forth in a sort of pale electric light [. . . their] entire life [. . .] turned outside
> in for our edification.[45]

The publication of Oliphant's *Autobiography and Letters* in 1899[46] (two years after her death) in its turn contributes to the ambivalences surrounding private writing in the late nineteenth century.

Elisabeth Jay sees Oliphant's original 'fractured narrative' as having been organised by her editors into 'the cleaner lines of a conventional memoir', losing the 'narrative strategy of this experimental text'.[47] It was to this 'conventional memoir' that the contemporary reviews responded, developing the picture of her capacities that Oliphant had begun with her pronouncements on herself as 'very small, very obscure, beside them [George Eliot, George Sand], rather a failure all round'.[48] One wrote critically that 'Mrs. Oliphant, though one of the hardest working writers ever known, pursued her occupation largely as a trade [. . .] She was not in the great sense an artist' with her writing 'apt to be tedious and prolix'.[49] Oliphant anticipated these criticisms and to an extent caused them with her musings on her talent and her published works. In 1885, having just taken up again the first pages of the autobiography, she comments:

> I have written because it gave me pleasure, because it came natural to me, because it was like talking or breathing, besides the big fact that it was necessary for me to work for my children. That, however, was not the first motive, so that when I laugh inquiries off and say that it is my trade, I do it only by way of eluding the question which I have neither time nor wish to enter into.[50]

Smoothed and shortened, with complexities ironed out, the late nineteenth-century version of her autobiography contributed to the denigratory view of Oliphant as an overactive writer who failed to fulfil any artistic potential because of the demands she placed on herself to publish constantly as a support for her children and wider family.

What I have considered here is not McMillan's 'subterranean tradition' of unpublished non-fictional work,[51] but those writings, initially personal and private, to be shared with chosen recipients, which were 'public' works by the end of the nineteenth century. They provided at the time a visible stream of material which offered readers access to powerful narratives of life in nineteenth-century Britain. For us, in the twenty-first century, they not only raise important questions about the ambiguous boundaries between private and public, and the gender dynamics that underlie this form of literary production by women, but demonstrate the skill, techniques and choice of modes and genres exhibited by these writers.

CHAPTER EIGHT

Margaret Oliphant and the Periodical Press

Helen Sutherland

Margaret Oliphant's literary output was prodigious by any standards, including almost one hundred novels, fifty short stories, twenty-five non-fictional works and in the region of four hundred articles published in the periodical press.[1] These articles embrace a wide range of genres: Oliphant reviewed books and wrote historical and biographical articles, as well as literary criticism, guide books, translations and social comment. The range of periodicals publishing her work was similarly wide and included *Macmillan's Magazine*, *Fraser's Magazine*, *Contemporary Review*, the *Graphic*, *St James's Gazette*, the *Edinburgh Review*, *Good Words*, *The Spectator* and *New Quarterly Magazine* as well as *Blackwood's Edinburgh Magazine*, the journal with which she is most closely associated. This chapter explores the unique contribution of this prolific writer to that literary milieu but, through her, also assesses the place of women within the periodical press.

Oliphant's involvement with *Blackwood's* was more sustained than it was with other publishers, lasting for almost fifty years, from their 1852 publication of the novel *Katie Stewart*[2] in *Maga* (as *Blackwood's Edinburgh Magazine* was known) to her official history of the firm, *Annals of a Publishing House: William Blackwood and his Sons, Their Magazine and Friends* in 1897,[3] suggesting that it was a mutually advantageous partnership. It is, however, the nature of the advantages to Oliphant, rather than of those to Blackwood's publishing house, that is addressed in this chapter.

This was an important period for *Blackwood's*: although *Maga* sales began a downward trend from a peak of 7,537 copies per month in 1860, it still enjoyed considerable influence as a quality monthly journal for much of the period.[4] Women contributors were thus accorded an authority and a prestige which they would not enjoy in their own persons as women, and it this which accounts for the single-mindedness with which Oliphant sought entrée to the Blackwood circle. This was finally achieved in 1851 through the offices of David Moir, a family doctor, whose acquaintance Oliphant's mother had cultivated simply because he was a *Blackwood's* contributor (writing under the name 'Delta'), and through cousins whom her mother otherwise disdained but was willing to use to effect the introduction.

One of the attractions to Oliphant of publishing with *Blackwood's* was the opportunity to forge an identification as a *Maga* contributor. Laurel Brake argues that the practice (shared by *Maga*) of publishing contributions anonymously:

> supports the corporate identity of the journal as a journal and mitigates the differences of its individual contributors. In this respect such periodicals – despite their multi-authorship and distinct fragmentation into articles on different subjects – present themselves to the reader as a whole, as a book does.[5]

The obverse side of this is that the house style knits individual contributors together into a team with a corporate identity, despite differences in geography, gender or outlook. Oliphant was adept at using this disguise to enable her to explore some of the tensions she felt as a woman writer who was dependent on her pen to keep her family fed.

The Blackwoodian circle that Oliphant joined in 1852 had a clear corporate image within which she could mark out a place for herself. David Finkelstein takes this further, suggesting that the firm of Blackwood saw itself as a:

> creator of unique intellectual and social and work communities and spaces. The House functioned as a tightly run, male-dominated space, yet also suggested itself to prospective authors, both male and female, as an open, welcoming and inclusive club of sorts. It was run on paternalistic lines, with clearly defined roles, structures of command, and subdivisions of tasks and space one might consider typical of any proper nineteenth-century bourgeois household [. . .] It represented a specific social space, [. . .] an invisible arena that accommodated shifting bands of contributors and authors who were encouraged to meet and mingle, imbibe a common 'culture', and share common, unspoken assumptions about their identities within this large, all-embracing Blackwoodian ecumene.[6]

It was within this 'invisible arena', which was, nevertheless, mapped onto the familiar bourgeois household with its division of public and private spheres intact, that Oliphant created her own space from which to engage with the central concerns of life as a woman writer. Furthermore, this could be done from within her own family household so that she could continue the private matter of looking after her family while engaging in the public business of earning a living. In common with other women authors, Oliphant rarely had long stretches of undisturbed time for writing but worked within the midst of the household, fitting her writing around the claims of the family.[7]

If, as Julianne Smith suggests, writing is 'necessarily fragmented'[8] under such circumstances, it might matter less with periodical publication in which individual articles are themselves fragments of a whole, although it should be noted that the articles and reviews Oliphant wrote for *Blackwood's* were substantial.

Margaret Oliphant's writing represents concerns particular to women authors. The conflict inherent in a woman – and especially a mother – writing for publication at all, with its haunting fear that the writing itself had harmed those of her children who had died in infancy, is one.[9] The tension between the desire to undertake 'literary' writing and the necessity to engage in hack journalism, with the bitter awareness of the consequences of this to her reputation, is another.[10] Oliphant returns to struggle with these questions primarily in her *Autobiography* (published posthumously), while her contributions to *Maga* often featured the more public question of the rights and the role of women in the life of society. In discussing this, she used a range of rhetorical practices which make her stance difficult to pin down: there is no clear critical consensus on whether she was a proto-feminist or, as Valerie Sanders has it, one of 'Eve's renegades', an anti-feminist, albeit not an extreme one.[11]

In 'The Laws Concerning Women' Oliphant discusses the disadvantages suffered by women as outlined in the pamphlet, *A Brief Summary, in Plain Language, of the most important laws concerning Women, together with a Few Observations thereon* (London: Chapman, 1854) by Barbara Leigh Smith.[12] The voice she adopts is the male voice of *Maga*, appearing initially to accept that 'these laws which concern women do not seem at the first glance either just or complimentary'.[13] Having pointed out that the laws in question concern only married women, she proceeds to lay down the main planks of her argument. The first is that the 'laws which govern human intercourse are for the most part only fixed and arbitrary demonstrations of natural rights and necessities', and it follows therefore that the law cannot institute fundamental change.[14] Secondly she states the view (which for her was non-negotiable) that a man and wife are one flesh, and are so ordained by God and ordered by nature for the stability of society. This being so, it was the duty of law to defend them as one flesh, making it impossible for the law to intervene between husband and wife. Expanding on this Oliphant uses the children of a marriage as a test case to argue that if the law were to intervene, only injustice could result for, in the event of a breakdown in the marriage, to give children into the care of their mother is unjust to their father, while to give them to their father (the situation that actually existed) is to wrong their mother.[15] The only just course of action would be to take the children away from both parents and hand them over to the State – a course of action so unnatural and abhorrent that no one would ever choose it.

So far, so conservative, one might say. However, in the course of these arguments, Oliphant reveals an unusual and clear-sighted view of marriage which acknowledges that the law cannot create the 'union of souls and sympathies of which lovers dream; but has to do with the common security, the peace of families, the safe foundation of the social world'[16] without seeing it cynically as a matter of business to be arranged in the marriage market for the financial benefit of the parents involved. Her arguments also reveal a high view of the place and duties of women. In a marriage:

> [t]he man is the natural representative of his wife in one set of duties – the wife is the natural representative of the husband in another; and if anyone will tell us that the nursery is less important than the Exchange, or that it is a more dignified business to vote for a county member than to regulate a Christian household, we will grant that the woman has an inferior range of duty.[17]

Oliphant was not alone in holding a high view of the place of women in society, but hers is clearly marked out from the conventional perception implicit in the idea of the 'angel in the house' by its appeal to the responsibilities and commonplace, practical aspects inherent in the regulation of a Christian household, rather than a sentimental appeal to the idea of woman as morally superior, more refined and at the same time more delicate than man.

In the mid-1850s Blackwood's was more exercised by the conduct of the Crimean War (1853–6) and the subsequent state of the British army than interested in the rights of women, so Oliphant was alone in addressing the question in the pages of Maga. Later in the century the so-called 'woman question' appeared more frequently, with at least one writer using arguments very similar to Oliphant's in 'Laws Concerning Women'.[18]

Another aspect of the same question of a woman's role in society and her associated responsibilities and rights is found in 'The Great Unrepresented' but a different rhetorical approach is taken, for in this article on John Stuart Mill's support for the franchise for women, Oliphant adopts a female voice, beginning her argument with the statement: 'The present writer has the disadvantage of being a woman'.[19] Having touched on some of the advantages enjoyed by women, she then lists some of the wrongs they feel before acknowledging that the lack of a vote is a recently-felt wrong, rather than a popular grievance. She, nevertheless, hails Mill as champion, sans peur et sans reproche, of the cause of rights for women in the best traditions of knight errantry.

With characteristic ambivalence she then overturns the argument by pointing out that the women who signed the petition supporting the motion are exceptional women and not representative of women in general, for whom they cannot therefore fairly speak. It is a rhetorical manoeuvre which prompts the reader to question the basis on which one group of people can be said to represent another. If taken to its logical conclusion, this rhetorical strategy would question the entire political system, based as it is on the election of representatives, although it is unlikely that Oliphant herself would press the argument to that extremity. Furthermore, Oliphant argues that the women supporting the motion are not the same women who would be enfranchised should the cause succeed, for universal female suffrage is not the issue: it is widowed or single female householders alone who would be given the vote, and they were not asking for it. Oliphant then rehearses Mill's arguments that these women 'have nobody belonging to them [. . .] are their own protectors, and sometimes their own bread-winners but [. . .] pay their rents and parish-rates as punctually as their male neighbours' before offering a conclusion which is both an acceptance and a rejection: 'It is then, only justice that compensation be given us and we should be as other men.'[20]

Oliphant's rhetorical strategy of using the female voice here is more effective than the adoption of the male voice of *Maga* would have been, for it allies her as a woman writer with the women who are the subject of the article: as a woman writer she represents the 'Great Unrepresented' of the title. The strategy is not unproblematic, however, for Oliphant has already questioned the grounds on which one person or group of people can represent another. The reader barely notices this in her successful sleight of hand, however, and her ability to match rhetorical strategy to subject matter must be counted one of her strengths as a writer, and one source of her value to Blackwood's publishing house. The problem with Mill's argument is that in Oliphant's eyes it leads inevitably to women being treated as men, and for a woman to be treated as a man is for her to suffer loss, for she is 'under no very profound impression of the superiority of man! His shadow does not stand between her and the sun.'[21] Even a cursory reading of Oliphant's *oeuvre* reveals her view of men in general as inferior to women in general, but there is an irony here, for she has often had to assume the male voice of *Maga* to acquire an authority that as a woman she was denied in her own right. She goes on to explain:

> Our ambition is not of so small a character as to be satisfied with the privilege of voting for members of Parliament. Neither have we the slightest desire to be permitted to do as men do, and copy their occupations. We have our own, which are at least as important, and more in our way. When we happen to be compelled, by force of circumstances, to do things that are generally reserved for men, we have, in most cases, found that we were able to do them [. . .] If the poor souls were to try ours, the result might be different indeed. But [. . .] we are women, not 'lesser men' [. . .]. When our work slips out of our hands, and we

find our opportunities over, and that the world no longer stands in need of us, then it will be time to inquire whether we can find a different kind of situation, as it were, in the system of the universe.[22]

While the final sentence may hint at an openness to change as circumstances change, it could also suggest the author cannot envisage change of this sort in the order of the universe, which would argue an entrenched and conservative outlook, supporting Sanders' view of Oliphant as an anti-feminist. This, however, seems too settled an assessment: the suggestion here is that her views changed with changing times.

In both these articles Oliphant initially leads her readers to believe that the feminist point of view is being accepted, only to turn acceptance into a rejection which is the outcome of closely reasoned argument that accords women a high value, and sees their work within the home as being of at least equal worth to that of a man. Looked at in this way, these examples substantiate Elisabeth Jay's claim that Oliphant's 'anti-feminist conclusions were predicated upon a thoroughly feminist analysis'.[23]

In 'The Laws Concerning Women', Oliphant achieves her end using the male voice of *Maga* itself, encouraging the male section of the readership (and it was the most 'manly' of the periodicals as well as being a Tory one) to identify with the writer and accept the conclusions.[24] For 'The Great Unrepresented' she uses her own voice: this may be a reflection of an increased confidence, having established her credentials as a professional writer in the intervening decade, but was also an integral part of a strategy which enabled her to represent or speak for the vast majority of women whom she believed to be uninterested in voting. It is a more sophisticated argument, for in showing that the cause is an empty one, in that those for whom it is being fought see it as irrelevant, Oliphant turns John Stuart Mill from a knight in shining armour defending defenceless women into a Don Quixote figure tilting at windmills on a barren plain, and thus subverts the chivalric trope so popular in the nineteenth century.

By the 1880s Oliphant's stance on the woman question – though not her underlying principles – had changed. In August 1889 she published a number of book reviews in *Blackwood's* under the title of 'The Old Saloon'; a title which appropriates an exclusively male space.[25] The reviews open with an extended description of the writer sitting in Blackwood's library (another male space) during the month of August, thinking of friends and colleagues on their fishing and hunting holidays, thus establishing a masculine identity. One of the books under review has a special appeal to women, however: *Ideala: A Study from Life* by Sarah Grand, first published in 1888 but already in its fourth edition by 1889.[26] Oliphant describes this as ' one of the books which show the condition of the public mind, and what it is which secures the deepest attention at this particular moment among a large class at least of the more "thoughtful" readers' before arguing that:

> [i]t is the expression of a great many thoughts of the moment, and of a desire which is stronger than it ever has been before [. . .] for a new development in feminine life, for an emancipation which even those who wish for it most strongly could not define and scarcely understand.[27]

That it is not primarily political, nor about the enfranchisement of women is clear from the vagueness of the desire (it can be neither defined nor properly understood), but is a more general emancipation in which daughters will be as able to work for their living, and in consequence be as independent, as their brothers. Although Oliphant does not expressly endorse this desire for emancipation, she accepts it as a reality and neither condemns nor attempts to contain it.

In 'The Grievances of Women', which Oliphant was invited to write for *Fraser's Magazine*, her changed stance on the woman question is most clearly seen, for this covers the same ground as 'The Laws Concerning Women' and 'The Great Unrepresented'. In this case Oliphant speaks in a female voice and even in her own voice: as this was published in *Fraser's Magazine*, not *Blackwood's*, it carries her distinctive initials, M.O.W.O. The article begins with a refusal to join a political meeting, a confession that this is on the grounds of cowardice, and an acknowledgement of the debt to bolder women who were prepared to suffer the insults that their activism prompted. Oliphant's apology and explanation that 'the dash in our faces of such an epithet as the "shrieking sisterhood", for example, more effectual than any dead cat or rotten egg, would have driven us back, whatever our wrongs had been, into indignant and ashamed silence'[28] in effect aligns Oliphant and the other silent women of her generation with the shrieking sisterhood who are politically vocal and active.

It is a wide-ranging article which is concerned more with attitudes than actual wrongs, for according to Oliphant 'an actual injury is trifling in comparison with an injurious sentiment which pervades and runs through life'.[29] She touches on her sense of life being divinely ordered in her argument that 'when God put two creatures into the world [. . .] it was not that one should be the servant of the other, but because there was a certain evident and sufficient work to do' before reaching to the heart of the grievances felt by women:

> [T]he first, and largest, and most fundamental of all the grievances of women, is this: that they have never, since the world began, got the credit for that share of the work which has fallen naturally to them, and which they have, on the whole, faithfully performed through all vicissitudes [. . .] And I think that it is

one of the most astounding things in the world to see how entirely all the honour and credit of this, all the importance of it, all its real value, is taken from the doers of it.[30]

The high opinion of women that was revealed in 'The Laws Concerning Women' is here reinforced, leading to a brief discussion of the role of women in the professions, in which Oliphant states that the 'advantage to women of having a woman-doctor to refer to is incalculable'[31] and argues that this alone would justify the experiment of allowing women to qualify as doctors.

The remainder of the article is devoted to a discussion of the political enfranchisement of women, to which Oliphant was formerly opposed. Now, however, she writes:

I think it is highly absurd I should not have a vote if I want one – a point upon which I am much more uncertain. To live for half a century and not to have an opinion upon politics, as well as upon most other subjects, is an impossibility.[32]

So, why the change of mind? In part it may have been a response to the winds of change, the desire for a more general emancipation which Oliphant was to discuss in her review of *Ideala*. However, the main reason was that the law was about to change, making the payment of tax the *only* qualification for male voters; in this new situation Oliphant believes that it would be absurd to exclude women householders, although she argues strongly that the case is different for married women who have the vote through their husbands: their tax-paying household already has one vote and there is no justification for giving it another.

Oliphant ends the article with an even more strongly worded return to the chief grievance of women, which is that:

Whatever women do, in the general, is undervalued by men in the general, because it is done by women. How this impairs the comfort of women, how it shakes the authority of mothers, injures the self-respect of wives, and gives a general soreness of feeling everywhere, I will not attempt to tell.[33]

Oliphant's own sensitivity to these problems is everywhere in her *Autobiography*. Jay links her undermined authority as a mother to her feeling of being undervalued as a professional writer, particularly in her failure to secure an editorship, which would have eased her financial problems; a failure that she attributed directly to her status as a woman writer.[34] This demonstrates the porous boundary between personal life and professional work, which was a feature of the lives of women writers to a far greater extent than their male counterparts.

Although Oliphant was able to use the periodical press, and in particular *Blackwood's Edinburgh Magazine*, to explore her own responses to the woman question, either disguised as a male voice or more directly in a female voice, that voice required the endorsement of a male editor who could amend or limit her contribution to the debate. This is, of course, true of male contributors to the periodical press. As a woman writer, however, Oliphant faced other limitations, some of which were peculiar to *Blackwood's* and some endemic to the periodical press, which therefore affected all women contributors.

Maga had been established in 1817 as a Tory quality journal, and had jealously guarded that position. After 1860, however, sales began to dwindle, partly because of its refusal to use illustrations[35] but partly because the removal of stamp tax (1855) and paper tax (1861) led to the establishment of new journals which, drew sales (and contributors) from *Maga*.[36] Finkelstein argues that Blackwood's response was to focus on 'areas of known profitability'[37] and this led ultimately to a concentration on military affairs, the British Empire and geographical exploration[38] – areas from which Oliphant was excluded by virtue of being a woman.

More generally, the periodical press was becoming professionalised, a development that parallels the professionalisation of science during the late nineteenth century, for example. This meant that periodicals were increasingly seen to 'operate less as socio-cultural authorities in their own right than as forums for the exercise of a socio-cultural authority derived elsewhere – chiefly from the universities – that was vested in the university-trained individuals who exercised it as periodical editors and contributors'.[39] Oliphant and the other women who had been major, if anonymous, contributors to the periodical press for much of the nineteenth century were thereby marginalised, making it more difficult for them to place their work.

Oliphant's career, including her long association with Blackwood's publishing house, spans the period when the periodical press was at its most authoritative yet was also most accepting of women writers. *Maga* offered her opportunities for exploring in print her concerns as a woman and as a woman writer, with the most all-encompassing of these being the role of women in society, and the value of that role. What is striking about Oliphant is her belief that what women did was already supremely valuable, and did not require female suffrage or a political voice to make it so. Later in the century she came to accept that women ought to have the vote although she was far from sure she wanted it. This underlines the point that for her the value of women's work was inherent, and therefore independent of apparently irrelevant electoral representation.

Blackwood's Edinburgh Magazine provided Margaret Oliphant with the opportunity to discuss these concerns in public, but also gave her space to forge a number of rhetorical strategies to convey these concerns to the readership. Chief among these strategies was, of course, the assumption of the masculine voice of *Maga*, lending her an authority she would not have enjoyed in her own right as a woman. Oliphant was not unusual in facing these problems, for they were shared by most women who wrote professionally for the periodical press at this time, but as Elisabeth Jay notes, 'what was remarkable [. . .] was the degree, length and range of her success as a professional women writer'.[40]

CHAPTER NINE

Writing the Supernatural

Kirsty A. Macdonald

Creative interpretations and exploitations of the supernatural are characteristic of Scottish literature. Women writers in particular have negotiated
this fertile territory in myriad ways, from the traditional to the experimental.
What unites them all is an 'other' way of seeing. In Margaret Oliphant's 1880
novella *A Beleaguered City*, the women of the city of Semur readily identify
and acknowledge that the force overtaking their homes is the returning
spirits of the dead. The women welcome this as a positive visitation, allowing
them to make connections with those they have lost. The men, however,
refuse to recognise this irrational possibility, subscribing to fear of, and frustration at, that which they cannot understand. Time and again, Scottish
women writers have portrayed the supernatural as an ultimately positive,
ennobling force, causing or catalysing a welcome development. Encounters
with the supernatural are ultimately not sources of fear or malice, and tend to
leave protagonists transformed in some way.

This chapter focuses on texts in which such encounters occur in our recognisable world. These works can be defined as belonging to the genres of the
fantastic, magic realism, the ghost story and so on, rather than pure fantasy,
in which the action takes place in an alternative world. Exploring individual
works by specific writers from a range of periods, the chapter suggests a
paradigm of women's literary engagement with the supernatural that can be
extended to other texts. Margaret Oliphant (1828–97) is undoubtedly the
most significant nineteenth-century female writer of supernatural narratives,
and her story 'The Library Window' (1896) is often hailed as her most successful, and certainly most enduring. In poetry, Marion Angus (1865–1946)
uses the supernatural in both traditional and surprising ways, particularly in
the 1927 verse 'Waater O' Dye'. Similarly, Naomi Mitchison (1897–1999)
reworks traditions in her 1957 short story 'Five Men and a Swan', while
A. L. Kennedy (1965–) rewrites the conventional ghost story alongside an
enduring literary myth in her 1995 novel *So I Am Glad*. All engage with
long-established supernatural themes and motifs in unexpected and affirming
ways.

Philosopher Julia Kristeva's notion of the semiotic, as outlined in her post-structuralist study of signification *Revolution in Poetic Language*,[1] is especially helpful in thinking about supernatural literature, and writing by women in particular, in that it outlines an 'other' way of seeing and of writing that – via its connection to birth – may be particularly poignant for female artists. Kristeva formulates an unstable binary involving the two elements of meaning: the symbolic and the semiotic. The semiotic is comparable to Lacan's imaginary – associated with the mother (and prior to entry into the symbolic order). It is therefore an ambiguous location of both the production and annihilation of the subject, connoting the rhythms, drives and non-referential meaning of signification. The symbolic is the referential, the grammar and structure of signification, associated with social order. This binary thus parallels that of 'real' life and potential afterlife or otherworld in supernatural writing. Both elements are essential in the construction of textual meaning, allowing for a relationship between language and life. If the semiotic is that which precedes the formation of a coherent identity within society, or the symbolic order, then that which succeeds this – death, and the correlative dissolution of identity – can also be read as part of this semiotic force. Indeed, Kristeva describes the semiotic chora, the conceptual realm of these drives, as 'no more than the place where the subject is both generated and negated, the place where his unity succumbs before the process of charges and stases that produce him'.[2] It is a space where birth and death, renewal and annihilation, coexist.

Kristeva goes on to state that, 'in returning, through the event of death, towards that which produces its break; in exporting semiotic motility across the border on which the symbolic is established, the artist sketches out a kind of second birth'.[3] The writers discussed in this chapter employ a way of communicating and of expressing the human predicament that privileges the semiotic. What this leads to is indeed a kind of second birth, a renewal and development for protagonists, and subsequently for readers. This ultimately empowering form of the supernatural can be traced via key examples from the late nineteenth to the late twentieth century in Scottish writing.

Oliphant was able to conclude her short story 'The Open Door' (1882) with the realisation that 'things have effects so different on the minds of different men'. The psychological realism of this insight is in keeping with her other largely realist work, yet it occurs within a text that evinces the existence of something 'unseen', beyond death. This tension is played out more ambiguously in her other 'tales of the seen and the unseen', 'The Secret Chamber' (1876), 'Earthbound' (1880), 'The Land of Darkness' (1887), and most skilfully and significantly in 'The Library Window' (1896).[4] Oliphant's supernatural texts sit uneasily alongside her social realism, but at the same time they provide the more 'conventional', and often more renowned, texts

– such as the novels *Kirsteen* (1890) and *The Chronicles of Carlingford* series of the 1860s – with added resonance.

Oliphant had a strong and well-documented belief in a Christian God. Having moved away from the formal Presbyterianism of her early years, she developed her own theology, sympathising with Catholicism and its position on life after death, following the death of three of her children. Two further strands of influence on her supernatural fiction are the Gothic, which by Victorian times had established itself as a coherent literary genre with clearly identifiable machinery, and Scottish folk literature, in particular the ballads.[5] Equally, much of her fiction represents a continuation of the concerns surrounding Scottish identity articulated in her journalism.[6] Richard and Vineta Colby point out how 'the novels transfer to the realm of fiction a campaign she conducted intermittently through the pages of 'Maga' (*Blackwood's Edinburgh Magazine*)to break down what she regarded as naive stereotypes retained by English readers about Scotland and the Scottish people based on prejudice or on accounts by unreliable witnesses'.[7] Moreover, a concern with female identity and women's role in her society is also evident in her work. In her supernatural texts conventional national and gender identities are explored and often subverted through her treatment of established associations between the north and superstition, and women with madness and the irrational. Protagonists have both an individual and collective, although not necessarily traditionally recognisable, identity. She employs the conventions of folk literature, and of the contemporary Gothic to portray this dual identity. Yet as critic Margarete Rubik states, 'she is not concerned with the usual Gothic shock effects, but with psychological portraits of the "spirits" and with analysing the effects of the supernatural on the minds of the living'.[8] This mutually reliant dichotomy between the living and the dead, the seen and the unseen, is a shared motif in all of her supernatural texts.

What is glaringly unambiguous, however, is Oliphant's self-conscious construction, and subsequent subversion, of the hackneyed association between women, madness and the supernatural.[9] Madness, holiness and poetry are the three 'privileged moments' of particular semiotic insight that Kristeva pinpoints in *Revolution in Poetic Language*. However, Kristeva warns that a total retreat into the semiotic will result in death or madness: a problematic territory must be negotiated in order to harness the full creative energy of semiotic expression. Oliphant's characters walk this line. June Sturrock argues of Oliphant's supernatural fiction in general, that 'it is those characteristics culturally associated with the feminine that allow for such negotiations between the dead and the living. Qualities such as unquestioning love and openness to the irrational permit such liminal activity'.[10] Oliphant's critique of the enclosing female roles of her society reaches its height in the long short story 'The Library Window' (1896), one of her final, and finest, pieces of fiction.[11] The window of the title represents a portal into the world of the 'unseen'. Yet, significantly, even its existence – either as material or supernatural entity – is questioned. The young, bookish narrator believes she sees a window in the building opposite her aunt's house, while spending the summer there. Through this window, she intermittently witnesses the work of an indefatigable scholar, to whom she gradually develops an almost sexual attraction. However, the existence of the window is denied by her aunt's friends, and proves unlocatable when she herself visits the building, the College Library. The girl is eventually removed from her aunt's house as her interest in the phantom window and what lies beyond develops into obsession.

Penny Fielding has pointed out that some of Oliphant's texts 'are strikingly close to Freudian analyses of the operations of repression and its consequences'.[12] Indeed, a Freudian reading of the tale is possible in that the scholar appears in a study that almost precisely echoes the narrator's father's place of work. Moreover, the narrator herself admits that the scene is reminiscent of the legend of prolificacy surrounding Walter Scott: 'I trembled with impatience to see him turn the page, or perhaps throw down his finished sheet on the floor, as somebody looking into a window like me once saw Sir Walter do, sheet after sheet.'[13] In Lockhart's *Life*,[14] Scott is famously seen through a window, covering page after page with writing. In his famous essay Freud pinpoints a moment of uncanniness, as being when that which is assumed to be imaginary or fictional appears in reality. This legend is made uncannily tangible for the bookish protagonist, lending the narrative a metafictional dimension.

The girl's belief is put down to delusion by others, and to an ancestral curse by her aunt, whereby women of their family are at some point in their lives haunted by the apparition of a scholar murdered by their ancestor's brothers, after he rejected her because he 'liked his books more than any lady's love'.[15] Yet one incident towards the conclusion of the story maintains the ambiguity. Eventually, the figure behind the window stands up, opens the window and salutes the narrator. The open window is seen and remarked on as impossible by a local boy. This ambiguity can be read as representing Oliphant's views on the inaccessibility of artistic pursuit for women of her time. The narrator yearns for what the scholar has, believing – or at least hoping – it to be a tangible reality. Yet for this yearning she is judged unhinged by those around her, who assume this is a projection of her unconscious. The narrator is both the lady, saluted by the very man who has rejected all other women in favour of intellectual pursuits, and the scholar – the bookish teller of the tale, both participant in and creator of the parable. Ultimately, the narrator tells us, this supernatural encounter proves helpful in later life when, after becoming a mother herself, she sees the ghost as a welcoming presence: 'If it was he whom I have seen again, the anger is gone from him, and he means good and no longer harm to the house of the woman who loved him.'[16]

For Oliphant, then, those who attempt to access the semiotic, in Kristevan terms, as an alternative to the (patriarchal) symbolic as a means of signification and expression of identity, ultimately face madness or death. The narrator of 'The Library Window' is judged psychologically unstable for her particular insight and 'other' way of seeing. However, as Scottish psychiatrist R. D. Laing famously argued: 'Madness need not be all breakdown. It may also be break-through. It is potential liberation and renewal as well as enslavement and existential death.'[17] In Oliphant's work supernatural encounters are ultimately empowering and edifying.

Manifestations of the supernatural in women's writing are altered again during the primary translation of literary modernism into the Scottish tradition, the Scottish Renaissance. By now, the ideas of Freud and Jung on the imagination and the unconscious were passing into common currency, in part due to the influence of texts such as James Frazer's anthropological work *The Golden Bough* (1890–1915). These and other works lent academic credence to theories such as Diffusionism[18] and the survival of remnants of pre-Christian belief systems, or at least the possibility of their survival in however changed a form. Indeed, this period is characterised by the utilisation of myth and magic, engendering a connection with the ancient and ancestral through awareness and acknowledgement of current psychological research.

In terms of her supernatural writing, North-eastern poet Marion Angus acts as a conduit between traditional representations in the vein of the Scottish ballads and literary Modernist explorations. Angus's writing career spans the Scottish Literary Renaissance; she was publishing poetry throughout the 1920s and 1930s. Her 1927 poem 'Waater O' Dye' appears in her third collection *Sun and Candlelight* and presents a ghostly encounter with an ambiguous entity.[19] This entity suggests multiple interpretations: it can be read as an actual ghost in the form of 'some lang-deed wumman o' my kin' (l. 25), the projection of a troubled mind, or an aspect of the self that returns to haunt with desires and emotions usually repressed. The poem has most recently been interpreted as a groundbreaking expression of lesbian desire, owing to the ambiguity of the relationship between the female speaker and this 'lang-deid wumman'.[20] The relationship is intra-gender rather than inter-gender and the speaker focuses on the corporeality of the visitation: 'An' aye she hauds me for her ain,/ Flesh o' her flesh, bane o' her bane'. However, this female union provides supernatural knowledge of unexperienced (hetero-) sexual events, such as relationships with men and childbirth ('the feel o' babes, the luve o' men'), thus maintaining ambiguity throughout. In much of her verse, Angus shows a Modernist concern with fragmentation of the self that opens up the possibility of psychoanalytical readings. Here, however, the supernatural intrudes on a recognisable world, made clear through the use of actual place names: both the Water of Dye and the Hill of Wirran ('She gars me seek on Wirran's Hill' (l.9)) are landmarks in the Angus area of North-East Scotland, the poet's home territory. The inclusion of existing places gives the events in the poem a realist backdrop that heightens the ambiguity. Yet, regardless of the origins, the experience is clearly pleasurable. It is also enlightening in that the speaker is led to acknowledge her own mortality without fear. In the penultimate verse she looks 'bricht-e'ed' (bright-eyed) for 'wings o' Deith' above her head (l.21–2). This is a welcome epiphany, acting as an encouragement to truly live, experience and feel in the moment. The supernatural knowledge and edification obtained by the speaker is a common theme in Angus's poetry, and can be seen elsewhere, in 'At Candlemas', 'Hogmanay' and 'The Fox's Skin'.

Thanks to the re-energised employment of traditional supernatural elements by Oliphant and Angus, among others, the supernatural was available to later writers of the Renaissance and beyond. A writer who can fruitfully be placed within this context is Naomi Mitchison, whose life spanned most of the twentieth century, and who is renowned as a writer of science fiction, historical novels and fantasy as well as supernatural representations. She adopts traditional folk elements in a number of her stories, transforming and defamiliarising recognisable sources.

The proximity of the supernatural and the sexual, a subtle subtext in Oliphant's story and more overtly apparent in Angus's poem, is particularly striking in Mitchison's short story 'Five Men and a Swan' (written in 1940, but not published until 1957 as the title piece of a collection of short stories and verse),[21] a reworking of the classic Scottish supernatural short story. Like Angus's poem, the story has the feel and features of a ballad: the sparse but evocative language and presence of the supernatural. It relates the encounters between five fishermen who work on the same boat, the *Highland Mary*, and a being who can shape-shift between existing as a swan and a beautiful young girl. Mitchison uses this feminist revision of shape-shifter folk tales along the lines of the selkie legends in order to explore and critique the act of rape. The being in the tale is unambiguously supernatural, appearing only in human form 'once a month on the Saturday of full moon', and the story can be categorised as magic realism, since the characters unhesitatingly accept the girl's origins, and believe her to be a harbinger of bad luck. However, there is also a psychological aspect to her existence. The story opens onboard the boat, with a discussion about sex: 'all went on talking about women, though it was little enough they knew when it came to the bit, and less they had done'.[22] This suggests these lonely, unfulfilled men have somehow evoked her presence through their repressed desires. Rather than accept and enjoy what the girl offers, the men abuse her in turn, revealing a disturbing sexual aggression. We are told that her first suitor, the skipper of the boat, the widower Hat,

> had only meant to keep the Swan a short, short time to look fully at her and maybe to have her on his knee for a while, but not to be spoiling her. But when he had got her on his knee right, he needed to be holding her there, and one thing led to another and he went just a hairs-breadth too far with the Swan. And the third time he went too far with the Swan that night, he was that sleepy afterwards.[23]

In Kristevan terms, they have so fully subscribed to the symbolic (aligned with the masculine) that this encounter with a semiotic (aligned with the feminine) force shifts the balance in their lives. The only one of the five to treat the swan-woman with respect and to resist his lust for her is the engineer Alec. For this, he is rewarded with her care and protection, and is left at the conclusion of the story with an advanced understanding of the female position, and some hope for the future.[24] The range and diversity of Mitchison's creative output makes her difficult to label; what unites her work is an unfalteringly feminist perspective. As she said herself in her diary in 1942: 'My feminism is deeper in me than, say, nationalism or socialism, [. . .] it is more irrational, harder to argue about, nearer the hurting core.'[25] 'Five Men and a Swan' is a deeply political work, hinting at the covert patriarchy of many traditional tales, in which the symbolic order is only temporarily challenged before being restored fully.

More recently, A. L. Kennedy has also employed the supernatural in politically significant ways. Like Mitchison, Kennedy is concerned with rewriting and updating a myth in order to contemporise the traditional supernatural in her 1995 novel So I Am Glad. However, she reworks another myth entirely: central protagonist and narrator Jennifer meets and forms a romantic relationship with the ghost of Savinien de Cyrano de Bergerac, somehow translated from seventeenth-century Paris into late twentieth-century Glasgow. The novel succeeds in defamiliarising the conventional literary depiction of urban Scotland, via its refraction through a fantastic lens. Savinien, or Martin, as he comes to be known to Jennifer's housemates, is an alien, literally a 'man who fell to earth', who – or so he claims – finds himself dropped into Jennifer's middle-class home in the city to become the 'household's resident dead Frenchman'.[26] He can be interpreted either as an actual ghost or a projection of Jennifer's disturbed mind: the author is at pains to make explicit just how troubled Jennifer is throughout. The novel has been classified as magic realism, but given this central ambiguity, like 'The Library Window and 'Waater O' Dye', it can be much more fruitfully categorised as belonging to the genre of the fantastic;[27] we can never know the true nature of Savinien's presence. More important than Savinien's origins is the self-realisation and liberation from restrictive identities that his temporary presence provides. The ambiguous supernatural performs the translation from personal pain and suffering to political corruption and national malignancy, its radical departure from realism allowing it to metaphorise and embody the macrocosmic within the microcosmic. As Jennifer states, 'Apart from all the bad things in the world and all the bad things in my head, we were all right'.[28]

Jennifer is the archetypal, and self-conscious, unreliable narrator, taking her place in an identifiable Scottish tradition, perhaps most famously represented in James Hogg's *Private Memoirs and Confessions of a Justified Sinner* (1824). Not only does she relate the presence of an 'impossible'[29] ghost during a period of psychological instability after years of isolation, she is also – as she tells us herself – a professional liar. Through her job as a radio announcer, Jennifer is 'free to be a living bellows drawing and shaping air into fiction, to be a mouth without a brain'.[30] Moreover, the guilt she feels as a result of her job as 'media liar', relating disturbing news reports and advertising expensive and unnecessary products to an already anxious and saturated community, compacts her traumatised mental position further. Paradoxically, regardless of his origins, Savinien seems to be the only honest thing in Jennifer's life. He himself asserts, although this is reported by her, '"I was Savinien de Cyrano de Bergerac and I was true"'.[31] She ultimately loses Savinien after travelling with him back to Paris, as he either returns to an otherworld beyond life, or is resolved as a phantom of her own conception. Yet this loss paradoxically leads to the possibility of transformation, as she concludes, 'I will be glad'[32] and indeed proves to be, as the present tense of the novel's title suggests. The fantastic ambiguity surrounding Savinien's existence as supernatural or psychological is sustained to the end of the novel, so that the conception of any one singular interpretation or 'reality' is withheld. More significant than the resolution of his true nature is the defamiliarisation of Jennifer's predicament and her entire society that he temporarily provides, leading to a new self-awareness and healing. In Kristevan terms, Kennedy 'sketches out a kind of second birth' for Jennifer via her encounter with death and the semiotic.

In all these texts otherworldly beings appear within a secular context, a world recognisably our own. Encounters with what might conventionally be viewed as threatening or malevolent forces catalyse change and development, proving remedial rather than diabolic. Rather than being alarming and unsettling, these exchanges are at least enlightening, and even – in some cases – welcome and affirming. If the liminal terrain of the semiotic is successfully negotiated, it can lead to a positive transformation. Out of mystery, ambiguity and spectrality comes a deeper understanding of oneself and one's motivations and prejudices. The supernatural has maintained its presence in more recent Scottish women's writing, for example in the work of Margaret

Elphinstone, Alice Thompson and Ali Smith.[33] It continues to be employed in intricate and subtle representational modulations of reality, allowing modes conventionally perceived as escapist and popular to be renegotiated as politically relevant. Despite its well-documented and historically enduring presence as a motif in the Scottish literary tradition, Scottish authors will continue to write and rewrite the supernatural in productive, evocative and pertinent ways.

CHAPTER TEN

Interwar Literature

Margery Palmer McCulloch

From the vantage point of 1924, Virginia Woolf reflected that 'on or about December 1910 human character changed'.[1] Whatever specific events brought Woolf to view the century's first decade in that way, one ongoing happening was the increasingly vocal demand for new perceptions of women's place in society: in education, employment outside the home, female suffrage and, in particular, a rethinking of relationships between men and women. The writers in this chapter mostly have birth dates in the 1880s or 1890s, so their formative years as young women were in this challenging first decade. These young women, who were later to contribute so much to Scottish interwar culture, were already well on the road to becoming what Dora Marsden called 'Freewomen' (as opposed to 'Bondwomen') in the new *Freewoman* magazine she launched in November 1911.[2] Willa Muir and F. Marian ('Flos') McNeill both graduated from university in 1912 (Muir with a first-class honours degree in Classics) and took up appointments in London. Helen Cruickshank, whose family could not afford a university education, had already made her way to London in 1903 via Civil Service examinations. In 1908 Catherine Carswell won a ground-breaking legal case for the annulment of her first marriage when her mentally-ill husband attempted to kill her when she became pregnant, while in 1907 Lorna Moon eloped from her family home in Strichen, emigrated to Canada, and in the 1920s became one of the top three screenwriters in Hollywood.[3] In these interwar women writers, the independence of mind shown in their youth continued to influence the literary work they undertook in their later lives. Yet what is also demonstrated in their writings, explicitly or implicitly, is the insecurity which so often accompanied their bid for a more equal place in society.

Catherine Carswell, Willa Muir and Naomi Mitchison are three of the best-known female writers of the period, Carswell for her two novels of women's lives, her controversial novelistic biography of Robert Burns characterising Burns as a sexual being, and her memoir of D. H. Lawrence. Muir wrote two female-centred novels, together with the 1925 extended essay *Women: An Inquiry*, published by the Hogarth Press, and two satirical essays

in the 1930s on women in Scotland. She is also highly regarded as the translator, with her husband Edwin, of the novels of Franz Kafka, Hermann Broch
and other German-speaking writers. Carswell's two novels – *Open the Door!*
(1920) and *The Camomile* (1922) – and Muir's first novel *Imagined Corners*
(1931) are set in the period of their young adulthood in the early years of
the century; all three are strongly autobiographical works, more obviously
'life-writing' than the fiction of Mitchison where ancient world and other
non-contemporary settings work to conceal the subjectivity of her scenarios.

Carswell's *Open the Door!* might be interpreted as her interrogation of the
actual course her early life had taken, an attempt to understand this, while
The Camomile explores an alternative road, a narrative of what that life might
have been. As a single parent, Carswell supported her young daughter in
Glasgow and later London by literary journalism (thus unwittingly carrying
through Marsden's definition of the Freewoman as one who 'is to carve out
an independence for herself [. . .] produce within herself strength sufficient to
provide for herself and for those of whom Nature has made her the natural
guardian, her children').[4] It was through this occupation that she became
friendly with D. H. Lawrence. She had reviewed Lawrence's first novel
The White Peacock for the *Glasgow Herald* on its 1911 publication and been
'deeply impressed'[5] by it. She reviewed *Sons and Lovers* positively in 1913,
and met Lawrence himself in the summer of 1914 when he and Frieda visited
her in Hampstead. In late 1915 she was one of the few critics to review in an
objective way Lawrence's *The Rainbow*, the subject of much vituperation in
the press, and soon to be banned as an obscene book. Although Carswell was
not uncritical of Lawrence's fiction, it is clear in retrospect that both writers
were engaged in exploring, in a subjective and direct way, themes of human
sexuality and relationships between women and men in a changing modern
world. Lawrence wrote to Carswell about *Open the Door!* (several drafts of
which he read and commented on before its eventual publication in 1920):
'I believe that your book will be a real book and a woman's book: one of the
very few.'[6]

What is 'real', and new, about *Open the Door!*, especially in relation to
previous Scottish fiction, is its open exploration of human sexuality from
a female perspective. We first glimpse this in a cameo portrait of the young
Joanna at her family's summer holiday home in Perthshire, watching in innocent fascination as her adult male cousin's 'lean wrists and his long fingers'
skin a small bird: 'she felt herself a little fluttering bird in their cruel yet
skilful grasp'.[7] It is more conscious in the adolescent girl's wish for a relationship with a neighbouring young man in Glasgow, her disappointment at his
cautious responses to her own emotional excitement, her puzzlement with
regard to the power of feelings to disrupt the pattern of her normal daily life.
The satisfying of sexual desire, although not personal freedom, comes with

her hasty marriage to the strong-willed Italian scientist Mario. After his accidental death and her return to her Glasgow home, Joanna's search for understanding of her emotional life and the decisions it brings her to make, continues through a long-term sexual relationship with an artist who makes it clear that their affair cannot break up his marriage. While exploring female sexuality in new ways, *Open the Door!* is also a splendid Glasgow middle-class novel – again something of a rarity in Scottish fiction – and one that belies the comment of Duncan Thaw in Alasdair Gray's late twentieth-century *Lanark*, that the city has had no imaginative depiction in fiction. The book's lively dialogue and imagistic evocation of parks, streets, and social life draw the reader into the city's life in a way comparable to Clarissa Dalloway's evocation of Westminster in Woolf's 1925 novel.

Despite the prominence of its female characters and the modernity of its sexuality theme, *Open the Door!* is not an unequivocally 'feminist' novel. Joanna's search for emotional fulfilment is dependent not only on her own sexual desire, but on attracting and holding male desire; she is therefore hostage to an agenda set and controlled by the man in the relationships she enters into. The sections of the book which deal with her Glasgow youth and the release of her sexuality in marriage to Mario are convincingly realised (despite the deus ex machina element in his untimely death), but the later chapters of the book, which portray her unsatisfactory relationship in London with her artist lover, lack such conviction. The interactive social context, vitally present in its Glasgow chapters, is lacking in these later metropolitan scenes. Although she is supposed to be a successful artistic designer, we never see Joanna in her workplace, and the sense of freedom which the city affords the 'new woman' (a frequent topic in female modernist fiction) is not a motif in Carswell's metropolitan narrative.[8] Instead, this narrative becomes increasingly narrow and inward-looking, with the heroine alone in the aesthetically furnished little apartment she has established in an out-of-the-way mews corner of Mayfair, constantly waiting, like Tennyson's Mariana, for her lover to visit, and often equally disappointed: 'She only said, "My life is dreary,/He cometh not", she said.'[9] The denouement is similarly Victorian, when, their relationship having been finally ended by her artist lover, Joanna comes to a belated realisation of the worth of a long-term Glasgow friend and agrees to marry him: an outcome which follows closely the events of the author's own life.

Carswell herself emphasised the importance of objectivity in the work of art in 1926, when she criticised her friend Flos McNeill's attempts at autobiographical fiction, insisting that

> in an autobiographical novel of the kind you are trying to write nothing is any good until you get somehow a stage *removed* from the self of the story, outside of

that self, cool, critical, perhaps even hostile, having exchanged *human* sympathy for that very different commodity artistic or literary sympathy towards your characters.[10]

Carswell was a perceptive literary critic and reviewer, and although this advice is something she herself had been unable to carry through in the later chapters of *Open the Door!*, her second novel *The Camomile*, written in epistolary form, is a much more objective exploration of female emancipation. Its sexual theme argues out the need for a lack of hypocrisy, for openness with regard to sexual desire, and for a more equal partnership between men and women. In addition, the impersonality achieved by its author allows the narrative to address more widely the disabling factors in female lives. We see this in relation to prejudice against the heroine's wish to have a career as a writer (a familiar topic in women's writing of the period). 'Life', Ellen's doctor fiancé tells her,

is a bigger affair than books, and life is pre-eminently your affair. Wait till your hands are full of life, and I doubt if you will have the time or the wish to add to the mass of feminine writings already in the world.[11]

By 'life', her fiancé (in the euphemistic mode that is one of the book's targets) would appear to mean 'children'.

One intriguing feature in the majority of these interwar novels is that their female protagonists, even when married, do not have children. Similarly, mother figures rarely provide role models for their daughters, appearing either on the margins in disfunctional characterisations, or absent through death. This is the case with Julie, the mother in *Open the Door!*, dependent on her husband for order in her life, who, after his death, moves from church to church seeking unsuccessfully some kind of worship that can satisfy her unarticulated emotional longings. After her own death, she is characterised by her daughter as having 'failed'.[12] The mother is dead in *The Camomile*, apparently weakened by her obsession to be recognised as a writer; she abandons her daughter in Lorna Moon's *Dark Star* (as Moon abandoned her own children); and is both disorganised and insensitive to her daughter's intellectual ambitions in Nan Shepherd's *The Quarry Wood*.[13] She is largely absent from the plot of Nancy Brysson Morrison's *The Gowk Storm*, with her youngest daughter wondering 'what ships sailed into her harbour when she sat alone'.[14] In Willa Muir's *Imagined Corners* the mother of her young, university-educated heroine is unmentioned, and the place of her husband's mother taken by an unmarried indulgent aunt.

Other spinsters in Muir's narrative are characterised to some degree as eccentrics, as, for example, the woman who considers her personal identity to be that of 'a minister's sister'.[15] Such figures embody the 'surplus women' whose presence was increasingly causing concern after the First World War, but are far removed from the idealistic idea of the 'free woman' in Marsden's earlier journal for whom spinsterhood could be a fulfilling choice of lifestyle, as, exceptionally, we find in Nan Shepherd's *The Quarry Wood*.

With her university classical education and postgraduate study of educational psychology, Willa Muir is a more analytical and psychologically motivated fiction writer than Carswell. She brings an ironic narrative perspective to both her portrait of the young Elizabeth Shand and the east-coast community of Calderwick where Elizabeth comes to live after her marriage. *Imagined Corners* has been compared by some critics to *Middlemarch* as Elizabeth, like George Eliot's idealistic heroine Dorothea, finds her journey to self-discovery beginning after marriage. A significant difference, however, is signalled by the metaphors chosen to indicate that journey: while Eliot's structural metaphor is that of a web, suggesting entrapment, Muir's scientific metaphor of precipitation through a crystal dropped into solution is, philosophically, a metaphor of fluidity which can bring about change. Her novel, with its female-centred narrative, thus reflects and interrogates the changing contexts of a new century.

Muir succeeds in maintaining the kind of objectivity that escaped Carswell in her first book through her ironic, although sympathetic, narration, demonstrated in the hyperbole of clichéd imagery used to describe Elizabeth's state of mind when struggling to convey her passion for her husband to his unmarried aunt and substitute mother:

> She saw herself and Hector, living, growing, swimming, breasting the wind together. She thought of his strong neck, his swift and lovely feet [. . .] 'What have brains to do with it?' she asked looking up. 'It's a miracle, Aunt Janet; a miracle that sometimes takes my breath away.'[16]

Some time later, after one of the quarrels with Hector that are becoming a frequent occurrence in their life together, Elizabeth puzzles over the fact that once he is absent, her distress can so quickly lose itself in a return to her previous academic reading: 'She seemed to have become two separate persons [. . .] The whole of Elizabeth's world was in flux, although not exactly as Bergson had declared it to be.'[17] Muir's objectivity as author is assisted by her use of dream sequences and especially by the creation of two additional Elizabeth Shands in her narrative: Elise, older sister of her husband, who had abandoned Calderwick for the continent of Europe as a young woman and now returns as the elegant, sophisticated Frau Mütze, widow of a professor; and Lizzie, the rebellious young girl Elise once was, and with whom she hopes to make psychological peace in her return to her childhood home. Through these two actual characters, Elizabeth and Elise, and the Lizzie of

Elise's memories, Muir creates an interactive trio of subjectivities through which she can explore female experience. The ending of her novel is open and psychological, although in the context of the interwar national cultural revival it has sometimes been interpreted as anti-Scottish. Muir wrote to Flos McNeill in July 1931:

> You object to my letting Elise leave Scotland. Well, my dear, it was supposed to be 1913, when there was little Nationalism: also, I was thinking more of Elise, when I followed her, than of national sentiment: and Elise would not have stayed in Calderwick, however it might have benefited from her presence – which I don't deny. [. . .] I think I am right in conceiving that Elise & Hector were bound to leave it. Elizabeth was almost equally bound to come back: but all that I left to the imagination of the reader, being more concerned to present an illumination of life in Scotland than a reformation of it. [. . .] it is indirect, not direct propaganda that literature provides.[18]

Imagined Corners was begun in Menton in France in 1926 where the Muirs had gone with a commission to translate Lion Feuchtwanger's *Jüd Süss*. As a result of her becoming pregnant with her son Gavin, born in 1927, together with medical problems resulting from a difficult childbirth, and continuing pressures of translation work, the book was not completed and published until 1931. *Mrs Ritchie*, which followed in 1933, appears to show the negative effects of such pressure, while also offering a provocative link between her Hogarth essay of 1925, *Women: An Inquiry*, and her satirical *Mrs Grundy in Scotland* (1936). In contrast to the absent mother motif, and with a troubling relationship to the essentialist argument of *Women: An Inquiry* that a woman's physical and creative energy was entirely directed towards her given role as bearer of children, in *Mrs Ritchie* the mother figure is all too present, developing into a monster who destroys children and husband through her Calvinist obsession with Judgement Day and her own salvation. Muir said of her novel that she had 'lost control of it in the second half',[19] but it is, rather, the relentless control with which the author drives narrative and its main character to their apocalyptic end that makes this novel both terrifying and compelling. As earlier Scottish criticism read *Imagined Corners* in relation to George Eliot's writing, so some critics have situated *Mrs Ritchie* within a Scottish anti-Kailyard tradition which includes Brown's *The House with the Green Shutters* and Hay's *Gillespie*, or associated it with the religious duality theme of Hogg's *Confessions of a Justified Sinner* and Stevenson's *Dr Jekyll and Mr Hyde*. Such comparisons ignore the female ground bass of Muir's work as well as her modern study of psychology with its exploration of the relationship between conscious and unconscious being. For Muir, as for Wordsworth and Freud, the child conditions the adult it will become. The root of Annie Ritchie's terrible flowering lies in the uncaring denial of education to an obviously clever girl child; her suppression of violent feelings towards that denial eventually leads to the destructive control she exerts as adult over her own family.

Mrs Grundy in Scotland, often praised as a feminist work, could be read as suffering from the same 'direct propaganda' problem as *Mrs Ritchie*. Although the book was no doubt intended as a witty, ironical investigation of the situation of women in Scotland, Mrs Grundy bears too close a relationship to Mrs Ritchie for the reader to feel at ease in her company. In a lukewarm review, Catherine Carswell commented: 'Mrs Muir rumbles on';[20] and despite its angry hitting out in all directions, there is little in Muir's satirical account to yield either entertainment or productive insight. For all her intelligence and education, discursive or analytical essay-writing would not appear to have been one of Muir's strengths. The personal pressures she was under in the mid-1930s could only have further undermined her objectivity. In an uncanny sequel to her creation of the monstrous Annie Ritchie, the woman Muir employed to look after her young son during her translation work so terrified the boy with her stories of hellfire that he ran away from her into the path of a petrol tanker and was injured. Muir wrote years later in her memoir *Belonging*: 'I kept my sense of guilt under cover [. . .] and so began preparing an inward sump of self-accusation and grief.'[21]

Naomi Mitchison, born in 1897 and therefore one of the younger interwar writers, came from an upper-class family, but was denied the university education given to her brother since a daughter's destiny was thought to be the making of a good marriage. Initially educated at her brother's school for boys in Oxford, she was hurriedly removed when she reached puberty. She was subsequently educated by a governess, became a 'home student' at St Anne's College in Oxford, but did not take a degree. This discrimination probably influenced her future work as a writer where a keen exploration of the roles and capacities of women is present in both fiction and non-fiction. Unlike Carswell and Muir, however, her fiction, while woman-centred, is not set predominantly in the modern developed world, but ranges in setting from Scottish history to classical and primitive societies. It also includes fantasy and folk tale, science fiction and twentieth-century African settings. She differs also from her contemporaries by writing and publishing so prolifically – 'over eighty books [. . .], plays and poems, dozens of short stories, hundreds of reviews and articles and much unpublished work', according to biographer Jenni Calder.[22] Of particular significance in her historical writings is the narrative interaction of past and present, conditioned by Mitchison's personal experiences as a woman. As she commented: 'the life she was living and the books she was writing "tangled together"'.[23]

Among Mitchison's best-known novels are *The Corn King and the Spring Queen*, set on the shores of the Black Sea c.300 BC and drawing on the anthropological writings of James Frazer in *The Golden Bough*; and *The Bull Calves*, a product of her residence in Carradale on the Kintyre Peninsula in the 1930s and 1940s, but set in Gleneagles in 1747, shortly after the defeat of the Jacobites at Culloden. Both have women at the centre of their narratives. In *The Corn King*, as in her short story 'The Power of Light', the principal female character defies the elders of her tribe by rejecting the ritualistic role expected of her, escaping to lead a life of her own choosing. Historical events in *The Bull Calves* are told through the personal stories of Mitchison's own ancestral family, and especially through the experiences and perspectives of Kirstie Haldane. As the narrator comments when Kirstie's talk with her young niece is interrupted by the appearance of the men of the family: 'But the minds of the women were again on people and not on things.'[24] Through their effect on the lives of individual people we are brought to know and understand the public events of the period; the prospective resolution of conflicts – between men and women, higher and lower classes, Highlanders and Lowlanders – is played out through the coming together of individual characters.

Mitchison's feminism is part of her drive to change society as a whole, and towards the making of a more equal world. Such an ideal was not without its contradictions. In her 'Russian Diary', written during a visit where she hoped to study changes in male/female relationships resulting from the new Soviet political system, she speculates on her own responses to the 'she-sailors' she encounters on the boat journey:

> Would I want Lois [her daughter] to do that, be that, have that much praxis? Why should I want to insist that my children should have these other values, be in high-brow professions that make them feel as timid and valueless as I do? [. . .] I know I shouldn't like now to be a she-sailor myself.

She goes on to speculate whether 'having children is praxis' and whether this 'work of the body' is 'valueless [. . .] if one has them in comfort, with doctors and chloroform'.[25] Unlike most fiction by interwar women writers, the bearing of children is omnipresent in Mitchison's work; sexual desire is itself presented as part of this work of the body. In her short story, 'The Wife of Aglaos', set in revolutionary times in ancient Greece, a young ruling-class wife Kleta is sold as slave to a Macedonian commander. Escaping with her own child and the infant she has borne to the Macedonian, she finds herself the only woman among a group of insurgents who shelter her and her children. Rather than face the physical violation she had suffered from her previous captor, Kleta comes to an agreement with the insurgents that she will offer her body freely to each of them as part of her work in their small community: the men are all considered as father to the infants born as a result of their intercourse with her. In this viewing of childbearing as 'praxis', Mitchison comes close to Muir's theoretical arguments in *Women: An Inquiry* about woman's essential role being the bearing of children. Yet the overt physicality in Mitchison's descriptions – in relation to sexual desire, the awareness of changes to the body signalling the growth of new life, the satisfaction of breastfeeding – is very different from anything found in Muir, Carswell or other interwar writers. Most significant is the fact that neither in her fiction nor her actual life (Mitchison herself had seven children) did childbearing replace public work in the community, as suggested in Muir's prescriptive examination of female roles.

Virginia Woolf suggested women writing fiction could bring not only a different kind of sentence structure but also new material which reflected women's values.[26] This chapter has focused on female sexuality and the role of women in society, related themes dominant in women's writing in the interwar period, new in Scottish fiction, and bringing with them new stylistic approaches. Yet other preoccupations, often coexisting with female-led plots, contributed to the period's more general revival in Scottish writing. Nan Shepherd's *The Quarry Wood* tells the story of a young girl from a farming background and her struggle to go to Aberdeen University. Yet its most significant aspect is the revitalised use of the Scots language– not the modernist synthetic literary Scots of MacDiarmid's poetry, or the equally modernist refashioning of English in Scottish idiom of Gibbon's *A Scots Quair*, but the kind of vigorous everyday Scots speech that had been characteristic of Walter Scott's fiction. Lorna Moon's *Dark Star*, on the other hand, anticipates Gibbon in giving an impression of Scots speech, situating her English language narrative within the rich social and landscape markers of north-east Scottish life. Both books contribute to the language debates of the period, demonstrating that quality fiction can be written out of Scottish small town and country settings. Dot Allan took her preoccupation with women's lives into the lower social class of female city typists in *Makeshift* (1928) and in *Hunger March* (1934) focused (like Mitchison) on 'people' not 'things', describing disruptions to the lives of a group of city-dwellers accidentally caught up in the political events of Hunger March day.[27] Nancy Brysson Morrison's *The Gowk Storm* (1933), with its economic, ballad-like structure and tragic happenings, brought a new kind of poetic narrative into Scottish fiction.

Women worked within other genres too in the interwar period: Violet Jacob, Marion Angus and Helen Cruickshank participated in the Scots-language poetry revival; F. Marian McNeill is remembered for her work on the Scottish National Dictionary, for *The Scots Kitchen* and her four-volume study of Scottish folklore, *The Silver Bough*. Agnes Mure Mackenzie is important for her Scottish historical writing. Fiction writing was, however, the dominant genre, both in the number of women involved and in the innovatory nature of their work. Although forgotten for several decades, their books falling out of print and sidelined within the academic canon, these women were rediscovered during the 1980s and 1990s. Recognised by a new generation of women writers such as Liz Lochhead who wrote 'My country was woman',[28] their narratives of the attempt to be a 'free woman' in the modern world is an interactive and continuing one.

CHAPTER ELEVEN

Writing Spaces

Carol Anderson

In Margaret Oliphant's *Kirsteen* (1890), Kirsteen's brother Robbie and neighbour Ronald leave Highland Argyll, 'bound [. . .] in the Company's service for India', Robbie 'not sorry to escape' from dull Drumcarro 'to a larger life'.[1] Kirsteen tries to comfort their mother, who sniffs: 'You think going to India is just like going to the fair' (p. 31). But Kirsteen's love for Ronald enforces awareness of 'time and space' (p. 40) separating them. And when, to avoid an unwanted marriage, she travels alone to London, despite protests – 'you cannot travel the countryside like a servant lass' (p. 134) – Kirsteen's journey breaks spatial 'rules' relating to class and gender in the early nineteenth century.

In our age of global movement, interdisciplinary engagement with geography brings greater 'spatial awareness' to literary discussion. While Scots' reasons for moving around, within and beyond Scotland, have included emigration, Highland Clearance and Empire, women's experiences of spatial movement often differ from men's, differences shaping 'travel writing' in the broadest sense.[2] This chapter considers how female writers represent various kinds of space and 'real' or fictional movement of characters within them. It draws on the idea that space, whether in domestic interiors, city streets, region or nation, is not transparent but ideological, involving issues of power related to gender, class and other factors: 'space is never empty: it always embodies a meaning'.[3] As geographer Doreen Massey explains: 'the spatial is social relations "stretched out"', with interrelationships occurring 'at all spatial scales, from the most local level to the most global'.[4] From the early nineteenth, and into the twentieth, century, the dominant ideology was generalised as 'separate spheres': men having access to public space (work, culture, politics), women confined to private (domestic, familial) – an over-simplification of relationships to space.[5] Restrictions in mobility, influencing also inner or mental space, affect women from diverse social groups differently.

A key opposition examined by geographers is between 'a sense of movement, of history, of becoming' and 'a static sense of location, of being, or of dwelling'.[6] The writing considered here depicts, often unsettles, such oppositions through portrayals of women (like Kirsteen) leaving or returning home, travelling not necessarily abroad but across 'more everyday terrains'.[7] Dominant cultural associations exist between rootedness, 'the feminine' and 'home'. Yet notions of 'home', as domestic space, region or nation, are viewed by women themselves in complicated ways. Many value home, while others 'have had to *leave* home precisely in order to forge their own version of their identities',[8] women's mobility frequently linked to a quest for greater freedom and challenge to patriarchal structures.

There are dangers, though, of romanticising travel, especially for those (often the poor) forced from familiar surroundings. Victorian 'Factory Girl' Ellen Johnston, who worked in many places, remarks 'the unavoidable influence' on her life 'of the TIME and COUNTRY of my BIRTH', gender, industrialism, capitalism, class and empire also being factors. Comparing herself with the Wandering Jew, she notes: 'in all these wanderings I never enjoyed true happiness'.[9]

By contrast, Isabella Bird Bishop flourished through extensive, actively chosen solo travel, becoming in 1891 a Fellow of the Royal Scottish Geographical Society and in 1892 first female Fellow of the Royal Geographical Society. Listing these titles at the front of *Among the Tibetans* (1894) was an unusually assertive self-presentation.[10] Yet even Bird Bishop's physical movement was hampered; riding often side-saddle, as expected of a middle-class woman, may have caused her back problems. Her rhetoric, too, infused with colonial and class assumptions, illustrates the complexity of power structures shaping women's writing.

Much could be written about earlier 'travel writing'. But the early twentieth century, a period of great change – 'around 1910 a certain space was shattered'[11] – is particularly interesting in spatial terms. Growth of technology and 'the machine' brought new forms of transport, increasing physical mobility, altering experience of movement through space, and perceptions of relationships between space and time (also theorised by physicists and philosophers). Freud and others investigated inner space. Literary representations of space and mobility, evolving to meet the age's challenges, are frequently both literal and figurative, 'creating metaphorical spaces that try to make sense of the material spaces of modernity'.[12] Women's fight for political rights and mobility in other senses – considered 'dangerous' by opponents – contributed to shifts in gender relations and the emergence of modernism. Colonialism, too, is inextricably interwoven with modernity.

Yet while focus on 'placedness' brings growing recognition that modernist writing may emanate from locations other than the metropolis and western world,[13] Scottish women's writing of this period remains unevenly recognised. Attempting to add lines to literary maps, this chapter discusses three lesser-known fictions. With scale in mind (important to geographers), these are focused on locations of different sizes: small town, as explored by Violet

Jacob, the city, depicted by Catherine Carswell, and Highland farm by Nan Shepherd. Revisiting traditional male 'plots of wandering', such as romance or adventure, in which women are often excluded or serve as embodiment of home, these works probe tension 'between the thrilling possibilities of the unknown and the weight of the familiar, between a desire for escape and a sense that one can never be outside a binding cultural network'.[14]

In Joyce's 'The Dead' (1914), Gabriel Conroy, challenged to visit his 'own land' and people, retorts: 'I'm sick of my own country, sick of it!'[15] Jacob fictionally maps territory (region, nation) in *Tales of my Own Country* (1922) clearly not 'sick of it', but generally unsentimental, as in her 'Scottish' novels, notably *Flemington* (1911). Jacob's little-discussed novella *The Lum Hat* (written pre-1944), also undermines comfortable ideas of 'home'. Opening in small east-coast seaport Montrose, globally connected through trade, it focuses on young bourgeoise Christina Mills, whose limited horizons are partly due to personality. But through depictions of domestic, public and psychological spaces, the work explores power structures, portraying a class-stratified society that circumscribes middle-class women's mobility.

Remarking the difficulties of evoking Christina, the narrator describes a photograph 'taken in the very early days of the art'.[16] This self-conscious appeal to realism establishes temporal setting: mid-nineteenth century. Location, too, is insistently 'real' and specific. Christina lives 'in the Bow Butts, just where it joins Ferry Street on the way to the quays'; the house 'still stands', windjammers nearby, 'glittering water beyond' (p. 159). Social mores are detailed: cook Ann Wishart considers that 'the gentry should keep the pose thrust upon them by God' (p. 160); widowed bank-manager father likes Christina 'to preside at the eight o'clock tea tray, silent and well-attired' (p. 163); memories of Christina's mother 'sitting by a downstairs window' (p. 160) imply a female tradition of confinement to domestic space.

But the prose is metaphorical, too. Christina's nascent longings are figured in 'house' imagery: 'Yet there was something faintly curious in her mind, a semi-conscious fingering at the doorkey of life. But nothing that disturbed her' (p. 160). Vacillations – 'yet', 'but' – foreshadow tentative attempts at opening the door on a wider world through travel, linked to curiosity, imagination and power. Whereas Christina reads 'decorous' fiction literally, as if 'watching the life of a street through the cold window pane' (p. 167), the reader is challenged by spatial imagery and symbolism. The 'real' Montrose links, 'grassy spaces' between town and sea, become a liminal space where Christina's settled ways are unsettled by an ambiguous traveller-woman selling brightly coloured brooms from a caravan (simultaneously evoking domesticity, magic and freedom). Her account of London streets inspires 'the only progressive stir that had ever touched' Christina (p. 182), though the suggestion that Christina find a man to take her travelling implies prevailing attitudes.

Christina is dominated by symbolically suggested forces. She is known locally by her father 'Lummie' Mill's 'homely' nickname (p. 161), so-called after his unusually tall 'chimney-pot' hat, 'as much a part of the community as [. . .] the spire of the parish church' (p. 161). That hat moves through fictional space, connoting patriarchy and convention. In church – an important social space – Christina and father sit 'with the lum hat, like a third presence, occupying the end of the long red cushion' (p. 161), an 'unhomely' image.

When Christina encounters well-travelled, 'virile' Captain Baird outside church, we share her spatial perspective:

> She looked upwards at the great mass of stonework towering pointed above [. . .] and received from the moving clouds beyond [. . .] the sensation of being under something that was falling on her. Turning abruptly to earth, she met a direct look from Captain Baird who was replacing his hat.(p. 169)

Inner space is evoked, the Freudian unconscious implied, Christina obscurely connecting Baird and traveller-woman 'almost like forbidden things' (p. 170). There are hints again at phallic symbolism when Baird draws attention to his ship's male figurehead: 'the great torso that reared itself high above the horizontal line of the quay [. . .] awe-inspiring . . . because of a terrific solidity which held suggestion of latent violence [. . .] it made her shudder' (p. 175).[17] Embodying power, male characters are mobile, literally and metaphorically: her father 'glided along on a path of ledgers' (p. 163); significantly-named Aeneas, employed by a French manufacturer, travelling abroad (p. 162); Baird boasting of 'that rich merchant life' of the world's great seaports (p. 174), its financial, social and sexual opportunities. Ominously for Christina, he views 'the spectacle of the room of which she was the culminating point, with facile pleasure' (p. 171).

Christina's timid 'adventuresomeness' (p. 166) faintly echoes male adventure. Marriage to Baird brings travel; initially her 'wondering eyes roam' his ship's colourful interior, its 'red Utrecht velvet' and 'gold embroidered Indian shawl' (p. 175). But while her maid, Maggie, enjoys the voyage, middle-class Christina, terrified by a symbolically suggestive storm, abandons the 'thunderously male' ship (p. 200). She never reaches the intended Australian destination, but ashore, intimidated by Edinburgh's streets ('Barbados Place' heightening colonial connotations), glimpses a sweep, imagining, absurdly, she has achieved journey's end and 'landed among savages' (p. 196).

Christina, no inspiring, modern heroine, is a 'fearful self',[18] her 'adventure' abortive, her journey looping 'home'. But if the narrator remarks her limitations, many characters (notably Aeneas) are sympathetic, and when Christina's mobility is impeded by her 'voluminous skirt' (p. 195), readers may understand her in context. Baird's 'bad bargain', she is, like goods, 'shipped [. . .] back' (p. 204) to her father, her first journey alone.

The colonial adventurer sinks with his ship: punishment, perhaps. But how should we respond to the ending's rejection of romance convention? Although Christina does not desire remarriage (p. 214), we may recall Ann Wishart's disappointed singleness. Concluding images lend poignancy. As Christina's father advances across their town's 'spacious' thoroughfare, she sees 'the movement of his hat', and, 'just about to cross the threshold' of the post-office (p. 217), turns home to burn the letter accepting Aeneas. The reader is left to imagine her future, like her past, 'the chain of Sundays stretching back into vacancy on which she had sat in the pew' (p. 217). Like *Kirsteen*, *The Lum Hat* dramatises the past but this taut study of a restricted life is modern in its subtle use of images and symbols, its portrayal of social space and power structures shaping spaces of the mind.

By contrast, Carswell's fiction is notable for depicting modern urban life, as in her best-known novel, *Open the Door!* (1920). But her second, *The Camomile* (1922), equally deserves attention. It opens with a letter from Ellen Carstairs, giving a Glasgow address but no date, emphasising place. Real city locations occur throughout: street-names (Blythswood Square, Byres Road, Endrick Street); areas (Hillhead); names of shops (Dymocks) and coffee-shops (Brassey's). Ellen's narrative evokes the bustle of early twentieth-century Glasgow, its public spaces, churches and new Mitchell Library (opened in 1911).

Within the Glasgow-based letter, an older letter written in Germany introduces further spaces: Frankfurt and its cosmopolitan music school. The letter form implies a destination, London, making the metropolis a constant shadowy presence and reinforcing a sense of movement and provisionality. Ellen's family have recently moved (a 'flitting'), and itinerant characters like Miss McRaith and Don John suggest modern dislocation. Restless Ellen explores Glasgow on foot and by various modes of transport: tram-car, train, cab and motor car, with references to bicycles and 'the new aeroplanes'.[19] *The Camomile*'s fragmented form is influenced by, and embodies, urban 'flux' and movement.

The novel may be seen, too, in the light of female versions of (or responses to) the *flâneur*, a significant 'hero' of modernity,[20] free to travel the city, observing and being observed. Carswell seems concerned to 'validate a place for women in the masculine defined city',[21] showing Ellen as empowered in various ways. Finding independence though work, she rents a private 'Room', a space where she can make music and write, away from family and the dominance of religion at home.

Ellen is assertive in traversing urban space, though some (gender-inflected) experiences are challenging. Alighting from a tram, she calls at a flat where she glimpsed a young man playing the violin, imagining: 'Some foreigner, perhaps, struggling to make a living in the terribly uncongenial surroundings of Glasgow, after a distinguished studenthood, say, in Prague?' (p. 89). No: a silent, pink-eyed boy, playing 'The bonny, bonny banks o' Loch Lomond' badly, whose Glaswegian father leers at her. But Ellen enjoys tram-car travel, sitting 'opposite to a middle-aged man – not specially good-looking or smart – whose face I could have stared at for hours' (p. 96). The 'spatial conditions' of mass transportation forced passengers to acquire a new visual code: women learning to look, rather than being merely object of the male gaze.[22] Gazing into shop windows, Ellen is no mere spectator in the city, but a participant, buying herself clothes, consumerism here suggesting empowerment.[23]

Ellen is dissatisfied, however, with Glasgow, continually meeting acquaintances while longingly imagining London's anonymity (p. 11). Once resident in culturally complex Constantinople, she situates herself as a modern 'cosmopolitan', 'homesick – sick to get away from home [. . .] Everything that is foreign I greet with rapture like an exile returning home' (p. 7). Exile, of course, is a frequent condition of the modernist writer. Like many modernist characters, Ellen feels both inside and outside her 'home' culture.

Carswell's fiction also moves between urban and rural settings. In *The Camomile* Ellen makes many short journeys, including to Arrochar and Loch Lomond, seeming eventually to find in Highland landscapes a version of Hardy's 'primal things' (p. 60) against which to measure human life. Restlessly shifting between city and country, the novel implies a complex attitude to urban life, suggesting 'unfixed' notions of Scottishness and identity generally.

Ellen seeks the figurative 'road to one's own reality' (p. 30) as woman and writer, though actual travel brings anxiety. Struck by a Glasgow cab, Ellen recalls London traffic, envying the security of vehicular passengers, then musing metaphorically that remaining unmarried 'would be like coping on foot all your life with the world's traffic, not once getting a lift' (p. 179). Duncan drives her (by motor car) to Loch Lomond, but later Ellen journeys there alone, by train and on foot, finally recognising she can travel life alone, without marriage.

Like many female modernists, Ellen – and novel – are both anxious and rebellious. Tellingly, her friend Ruby is a caricaturist, and Ellen (like Jacob's narrator) uses wit defiantly (p. 172). The final section, 'Also, vorwärts', suggests onward movement (significantly in German). The British Empire remains unvisited; Ellen rejects travel to India with Duncan. But she will leave Glasgow to join her brother in New York, or share rooms in London with Jewish Ruby, a figure evoking outsider status and urban cosmopolitanism,[24] more positive than Ellen Johnston's wanderer and very different from Jacob's Victorian small-town Christina.

Nan Shepherd's works, especially *The Weatherhouse* (1930) and *The Living Mountain* (1977), attract growing attention following undeserved neglect. Her first novel, *The Quarry Wood* (1928), employing metaphors of adventure and discovery while critiquing colonialism, is also magnificent. Least discussed is *A Pass in the Grampians* (1933), fascinating as a modernist fiction located entirely in a remote place and actively *about* modernity. Novel and chapter titles ('A Kincardineshire Family') emphasise place. While clues about the identity of the 'Pass' are easily overlooked, references to mountain Clochnaben (p. 24) and historical beliefs (pp. 27–8) imply the Cairn o' Mounth. That the ancient sand and gravel road crossing the mountains here was tarmacadamised only 'shortly before the Second World War' [25] underlines wildness and isolation.

The word 'Pass', according to the *Concise Oxford Dictionary*, means: 'Passage through mountains; this as commanding access to a country'. It is also a noun suggesting change (as in 'things have come to a strange pass'), and verb, 'be transported from place to place; change (into something, from one state to another); die'. Such meanings hover in a novel exploring movement and change one summer when Bella Cassie – now singer 'Dorabel Cassiday' – returns to Boggiewalls where she grew up. Various characters' responses, to Bella and 'home' spaces, are charted. Chapter headings range around names; no single character is central, all exist as part of a community, interrelationships vital. Narrative structure is closely woven with content.

The novel opens with an old shepherd, Durno, sometime teller of tales and singer of songs,[26] recounting his encounter with Bella on the Pass – he driving sheep, she a motor car. In an apparent confrontation of cultures, traditional (or 'rooted') and modern, Bella in her car signifies the new machine age. Thus the novel begins as a drama about modernity, figured as a woman bringing change and mobility to a remote rural location, importing creations – motor car, gramophone, wireless – that alter perceptions of space and time. It ends with young Jenny, representing the future. But the novel's vision is far more subtle and complex than such a summary suggests.

Some characters, notably laird Andrew Kilgour, dislike change and movement. Aware he could not have left Boggiewalls, like his brothers, on colonial travels (p. 25), Andrew also fears Bella's 'terrible vitality', the 'demons of speed and din' coming with her: 'the dreadful tides of a new and incomprehensible life, that had already, he knew, submerged the cities, would rise pounding against the hills' (p. 28). Other farmers drive cars, but Andrew, in 'the old self-contained way [. . .] mended his own cart-wheels' (p. 58), whereas Bella's brightly-coloured car is 'like an advertisement hoarding' in the farmyard (p. 32). Although like Bella, Mary now works in London, she, too, resents Bella's return. Escape, then, can be in two directions. Having fled the restrictions – especially for women – of life in rural Highland Scotland, Mary wants Boggiewalls to remain unchanged, and to escape back to it when convenient.

The variety of women characters prevents simple notions of femininity.

Old Alison describes being beaten by her mother for wearing a lace collar to Kirk: "'I'll have no daughter of mine stravaigin' the roads like a Jezebel'" (p. 88). By contrast, 'consuming' Bella, one-time shop-girl and gargantuan eater, might be seen in relation to Rebecca West's rebellious female body 'characterized by riotous appetite, rebellious ornamentation, and aggressive desire'.[27] At the wheel of her car, in control of her movements, Bella shows new feminine roles evolving.

Jenny secretly learns to drive with Bella's young artist friend Barney (p. 57). As they motor by night, she savours sensations wrought by this new rapid mode of transport: 'Their movement was the one reality. The black shapes of hills, the rutted road, changing subtly under their lights [. . .] were no more than the framework that held this exhilaration, gave it position in time and space' (p. 62). Robert Macfarlane remarks that Shepherd's vision elsewhere anticipates French philosopher Merleau-Ponty's 'bodily thinking'.[28] Physical sensation is explored here through transport and dance. Bella sets up her gramophone 'outside the Inn where they had lunched, or on an open space beside the war memorial' (p. 73), and dances. Bella's effect on Jenny, 'tumbling her world into space (p. 75), suggests Bergson's *élan vital*; 'vital energy' is later mentioned (p. 86).

Infused with ideas of the time, the novel also self-consciously refers to contemporary arts. Jenny describes Barney's paintings as 'the kind of picture that you don't know what it is [. . .] all right in Paris and places like that, but rather odd when you know it's the Grassie Burn and Craig Clach' (pp. 29–30). Barney struggles to depict Bella's living motion, including her leg moving 'of its own volition' (p. 72). Bella mentions Cubism – 'your planes and cubes and all that rot' (p. 71). The novel itself, many-faceted, invites us to view characters and places from different angles.

Mixing styles, forms and voices, it melds ancient tradition and modern innovation. Sometimes the narrative voice seems biblical, or echoes folk-tale (p. 25). Plot elements (including Peggy's violent death), and the detachment implied by shifting point of view, echo balladry.[29] Characters and places are symbolic, yet 'Dorabel and Barney are persons [. . .] not codes' (p. 111). Joycean word-play occurs, with chapter headings like 'Bella Horrida Bella', the novel's modernist collage-like formal mix embodying movement and change.

While temporary visitor Bella builds a pink bungalow, Andrew's relationship to place is one of rootedness. He is not presented as backward or static, his memories evoking a dynamic vision (p. 24). However, his assertion that 'we couldn't do with many more folk hereabouts' is challenged by granddaughter, Jenny: 'The place is big enough' (p. 23), a response pertinent today. Binary oppositions are undermined. Past and present are not opposed; Bella may reject the 'family tree' (p. 38), but cannot escape her father, Durno, whose music has transmuted into hers. Movement can be both destructive (a woman's fatal fall) and creative, and interconnected with stillness: Jenny like a pool containing 'energy suppressed' (p. 23), Alison's stillness 'like the terrific immobility of a whirlpool' (p. 89). The name Boggiewalls suggests paradox. Even gender oppositions are subverted. Male and female roles are highlighted, and modernist representations of women satirically addressed through Barney. But Andrew and Durno are also 'ribs of the earth. The land made men like these because she needed them'; while the earth's qualities are 'embodied' in Andrew (p. 74).

All Shepherd's work offers an inclusive, holistic vision. Mary's return home is a 'journey' (p. 95) both physical and internal. This intricate novel, with its strongly metaphysical aspect, portrays movements physical, social and cultural, but also of spirit, mind and emotions, spaces 'below consciousness, where the dark tides run' (p. 37).

Jacob, Carswell and Shepherd, like other women writers of their time, 'were participating in a dialogue about the nature of modernity through their narrative depictions of women's changing locations'[30] – a dialogue with many voices. Other works interesting from spatial perspectives include Willa Muir's *Imagined Corners* (1935) and Naomi Mitchison's long story, *Beyond These Limits* (1935), set in the Paris Underground, its textual space including illustrations by Wyndham Lewis.

'Home', leaving, returning, and travel generally, are still potent subjects. Margaret Elphinstone's novels feature many travellers; in the inventive *Hy Brasil* (2002), Sidony Redruth visits an island composed from many fictional and real islands, ever-changing, suggesting the subjective nature of travel. Kathleen Jamie's beautiful volume about travels in Northern Pakistan, *The Golden Peak* (1992) was revisited and expanded, new title *Among Muslims* (2002) shifting emphasis from physical place to people. Leila Aboulela's poised novel, *The Translator* (1999) portrays a young Sudanese woman's journey and perceptions of space around and within her, in Aberdeen and Khartoum. In her moving *Red Dust Road* (2010), subtitled 'An Autobiographical Journey', Jackie Kay, adopted as a baby, traces her birth parents, white Highland mother and black Nigerian father. The topographical title suggests a road both real – to an ancestral African village – and metaphorical, the book's structure, aptly for the complex journey, looping back and forth in place and time.

Women's 'travel writing' follows such a journey, never simple, always interesting.

CHAPTER TWELVE

Experiment and Nation in the 1960s

Eleanor Bell

The early 1960s in Scottish literature are often readily associated with the sensational arguments of the 1962 International Writers' Conference and the infamous 'happening' of the 1963 International Drama Conference, where a nude model was wheeled across the balcony of McEwan Hall, much to the Edinburgh establishment's horror. The 1962 event was organised by John Calder, Jim Haynes and Sonia Orwell and lasted for five days, covering as many topics ('Difference of Approach', 'Scottish Writing Today', 'Commitment', 'Censorship' and 'The Future of the Novel'). Each day, tickets for the 2300-capacity McEwan Hall were sold out; there was a definite excitement in the air. The Scottish event was chaired by David Daiches and comprised Douglas Young, Robin Jenkins, Hugh MacDiarmid, Alexander Reid, Alexander Trocchi, Walter Keir, Sidney Goodsir Smith, Edwin Morgan and, the only female panellist, Naomi Mitchison. While it is the heated exchanges between Hugh MacDiarmid and Alexander Trocchi concerning the role of nationalism in Scottish literary studies that are often best remembered and most documented, this chapter reflects on the experimental work of Scottish women writers during the 1960s and the extent to which they engaged with prominent national debates at the time. Taking the 1962 Conference and Naomi Mitchison's contribution to these debates as its starting point, before going on to consider the work of Elspeth Davie, Margaret Tait and Helen Adam, it explores the ways in which, and perhaps some of the reasons why, the artistic objectives of women writers of the period were often quite different from that of their male counterparts.

Born in 1897, Naomi Mitchison was already in her mid-sixties by the time of the 1962 Writers' Conference. Known mainly for her historical fiction prior to the 1960s, Mitchison's prolific fiction and non-fiction writings had also veered towards controversial issues: sexuality, for example, in *The Corn King and the Spring Queen* (1931) and *We Have Been Warned* (1935).[1] An ardent and vocal campaigner for women's rights, Mitchison served on the committee and acted as a volunteer in the first birth control clinics in London set up by Marie Stopes; it is no coincidence that her writing is associated with a particularly feminist stance.[2] Despite such prominent, pioneering work, it is clear that Mitchison, at times, felt marginalised from Scottish literary culture, perhaps as a consequence of both her geographical location (being based in Carradale, Argyll) and her gender (readily aware of the particularly masculine literary culture around her). With many connections to writers of the interwar Scottish Renaissance, she felt the need to distance herself from what she referred to as 'the MacDiarmid-Poetry-Scotland crowd'.[3] In her self-portrait for the Saltire Society she comments, 'Although Hugh MacDiarmid was always very friendly, I was definitely not one of the bright and coming-up people.'[4] Despite her privileged background and aristocratic connections with the Haldane family, it would seem that some doors remained closed to Mitchison. One of the primary purposes of this chapter is to examine the extent to which some of Mitchison's female contemporaries similarly felt this outsider status, apart from Scottish literary culture while paradoxically active within it. It questions whether Mitchison, Davie, Tait and Adam self-consciously distanced themselves from debates surrounding nationalism and identity politics in favour of focusing on their respective experimentations with literary form, or whether their own reticent approach to such debates was more inherently linked to feeling silenced to speak on such matters because of their gender.

While Mitchison was an advocate for Scottish nationalism, her sense of detachment from certain aspects of Scottish literary culture is ironically evident when looking at the transcripts from, and her personal responses to, the 1962 Writers' Conference. The panellists at the Scottish event were invited to comment on issues such as the strengths of Scottish literature, the relevance of Scottish literary tradition and the extent to which Scottish writers were expected to deal with national matters in their own work. While discussions were largely dominated by debates surrounding nationalism and whether Scots or English was the most appropriate medium for writing Scottish literature, Mitchison's contributions appeared vague, disconnected from other panellists. Perhaps reflecting her then current interest in science fiction and rising concerns surrounding the nuclear threat, Mitchison made the rather cryptic comment that some of the most important writing of the time was emerging from university science departments.[5] While her statements, at times abrupt, make it difficult to pin down her intentions, she was clearly resisting the main topics and questions presented to the panel, working tangentially against them. In 1962 Mitchison also edited a large, 400-page collection of articles on politics, science, psychology and contemporary forms of communication entitled *What the Human Race is Up To* (Victor Gollancz: London 1962), a collection well received by leading scientific journals and praised for capturing, in brief, some of the most important scientific developments and their impact on human consciousness at that time.[6] Mitchison may have found the disputes of the Scottish Day of the Conference petty and somewhat inconsequential when considered alongside the larger concerns of the age that were consuming her thoughts at that time. In 1963 she sent a letter to *The Scotsman* making her thoughts on the event clear:

> Some of those who attended last year's Scottish Day at the Writers' Conference may remember that I seized the mike at the end and started apologising to the audience for the exhibition they had seen and heard, all the worse because, at the preliminary meeting, we writers had agreed on the heads of a technical discussion which might have interested an intelligent Scottish audience. The mike was cut out before the end of my first sentence. I still feel ashamed of that afternoon. On the other hand, it gave the Festival a boost in certain circles, which it might otherwise have missed. We who were the victims must console ourselves with the thought that we had been used in the good cause, one hopes, of increasing Festival publicity and the rolling in of the bawbees.[7]

The only woman on the panel, Mitchison was embarrassingly silenced at the end, prevented from making what could have been her central contribution of the day, an issue which has subsequently been glossed over in the available transcripts and recorded histories of the event.

In 'The Young Writer in Scotland', his article in the 1962 Writers' Conference Programme, Edwin Morgan called for the need to challenge the provincialism of Scottish literature in the early 1960s, commenting that 'there is no doubt that our literature as a whole . . . is like nothing so much as an anxious pedestrian swithering at the end of a zebra crossing: he cannot cross, he cannot cross! – he is afraid he will be swept away by wicked French anti-novelists, run down by noisy beats, sprung at by Red Cats'. For Morgan, Scottish literary culture had become 'dangerously conservative and tradition-minded'.[8] While Morgan, Ian Hamilton Finlay and Alexander Trocchi were all clearly working in an anti-traditionalist vein, the diversity and range of Mitchison's work has still to be fully interpreted along such lines.

Seldom categorised as an experimental writer, in the 1960s Mitchison was in many ways achieving the objectives called for by Morgan. While parallels with Alexander Trocchi's 'cosmonaut of inner space' may be somewhat out of place for this esteemed lady of Scottish letters, it is important to recognise that 1962 is also the year in which she published *Memoirs of a Spacewoman*, the first of her science-fictional writings in which she experiments boldly with gender and sexuality. The novel has subsequently been praised by critics as an important precursor to later writers of feminist science fiction such as Ursula Le Guin, Doris Lessing and Margaret Atwood, setting the agenda for future feminist forms of the genre.

Around the time of the Writers' Conference, through her long-standing friendship with Aldous Huxley, Mitchison was also drawn to experiment with the drug mescalin (this despite her husband, Dick, being a well-respected Member of Parliament). In personal notes held at the National Library of Scotland, Mitchison describes the carefully controlled circumstances in which one particular experiment took place, at home in London, in the presence of two scientific researchers (one a medical doctor) who were avidly observing and taking notes on her experiences:

> In England there was great interest in the less harmless drugs [. . .] Aldous Huxley, my old and dear friend, had written about them and how good they were. A doctor was trying to find volunteers. I was interested and agreed. The experiment was set up to be held in our flat in London one evening. Dick, at this time, spent most of the day in the House of Commons and this, one supposed, would only take a few hours. I was in good health.[9]

Mitchison, then in her sixties, remained open to the unconventional, even asking one of her daughters to be present during parts of this experiment to provide her with moral support. Highly unpredictable in her interests, it is also around this time that Mitchison left Scotland in order to take up the unlikely role as an adviser to, or, as she became known, 'tribal mother' to the Bakgatla tribe in Botswana.[10] While Mitchison resisted active involvement at the 1962 Writers' Conference, she was clearly challenging any lingering parochialism within Scottish culture in many ways, and on her own terms.

A contemporary of Mitchison's, the Edinburgh writer Elspeth Davie (1919–95) published four novels and five collections of short stories between 1965 and 1992, yet remains a marginal figure in Scottish literature. Part of the reason for this neglect is that Davie's writing is often abstract and difficult to categorise. Like Muriel Spark, her writing is pared down in ways that often lead to unsettling and defamiliarising reading experiences. Similarly, Davie appears unconcerned with the literary expectations of her peers, or the need to conform to any specific 'Scottish' agenda in her writing. Edinburgh in particular often features, yet for the most part only as a backdrop; her characters rarely have a strong connection with place. Rather, her characters exist as props for the investigation of ideas; by extension, the same could be said about the representation of place in her work.[11] Comparisons could be made with other avant-garde Scottish writers of the period such as Ian Hamilton Finlay and Alexander Trocchi, yet the complexities of her work suggest connections with French writing and the nouveau roman, or anti-novel, in particular.

Davie trained as a painter and for many years taught at Edinburgh College of Art. This interest in painting, colour and abstraction feeds directly into her writing and concerns with symbolism permeate several of her novels. In *Providings* (1965) and *Coming to Light* (1989), for example, ideas are more important than plot. Sometimes it is a focus on colour and its possible interpretation at philosophical levels, sometimes it is external objects and the ways in which we project feelings of interiority onto them, altering their meaning as a consequence, that emerge as themes. Yet both texts present an uncomfortable experience for the reader who is left to puzzle over the interpretation of such symbolism, when at a surface level it is more concerned with absences and abstraction. This sense of absence, of detachment and overall frustration with the reading experience can be directly linked to the aims of the anti-novel. Whereas conventionally the novel has been driven towards ending, a natural conclusion of the plot, anti-novel writers were more concerned with 'narrative as laboratory', where texts are viewed as artificial constructions rather than mirrors of the world, and the novel 'revels in the consciousness of plot as unnatural'.[12]

Davie's works are noticeably full of gaps and silences, of voids and things not explained, with little drive for a neat conclusion. Davie's novel, *Providings* (1965), for example, is more concerned with the estranging power of objects than the need to deliver a chronological narrative. The central character, Peter Beck, has recently left home and moved to another city one hundred miles away. The name of this city is not revealed; such detail is often regarded as superfluous in Davie's fiction, where the focus is directed towards more metaphysical examinations of belonging. Clearly playing off 'Beck' and Beckett, the novel examines the lonely existence of a character who seems trapped and controlled by material possessions, in particular by the large boxes of preserves that arrive in weekly parcels from his mother, the 'providings' of the title. These boxes arrive at Beck's lodging house with an alarming resonance, a heavy thud: the novel traces his inability to escape their haunting presence. Despite his disregard for them, the boxes arrive, regardless, so that Beck comes to feel suffocated by this struggle between familial and individual will. Beck leaves home and sets out to find his own form of freedom, yet the novel examines the powerful controlling forces of home and the difficulties involved in this process. The parcels from home, which clearly become a burden to him, are not something that can be easily or thoughtlessly discarded. He is in some way part of them and they become objects to be treasured as well as abhorred.[13]

Davie was married to the prominent Scottish philosopher George Elder Davie, yet, as in the case of other famous literary pairings (such as that of Edwin and Willa Muir, for example), her own work has always remained in the shadows. Similarly, Davie's characters are often those who avoid limelight. They are frequently figures who have lived too long in isolation, seeing the world as detached observers rather than as active participants. Yet the narratives refrain from being pessimistic and often focus on the need to 'get back to light', for characters to find a consequent sense of belonging. Throughout her fiction Davie takes her reader into uncomfortable spaces that do not so much raise questions about characters but rather the scope of fiction and the spaces it can reach. Her work thus connects with the writers of the nouveau roman who repeatedly presented the same kinds of questions to their readers, the uncertainties of the text drawing attention to the uncertainties of world outside and the inability to accurately capture lived experience. The often absurd world in Davie's fiction is part of this process of reflecting on the boundaries between fiction and reality and the extent to which this boundary is comprehensible. In Davie's fiction the major concerns surround interiority and journeys into the self: all other concerns, including those of the national, are pushed into the background.

It is perhaps unsurprising that Davie was published by John Calder. At this time, Calder was at the heart of experimental publishing, responsible not only for writers including Beckett, Alain Robbe-Grillet, Marguerite Duras and Nathalie Sarraute, but for bringing awareness of their work to public consciousness. In his memoirs, *Pursuit*, Calder commented:

> Elspeth Davie was a beautiful writer, with a fine style, but imprisoned in a kind of ivory tower from which she contemplated people and the things that make them tick with a gentle humour that showed her very accurate powers of observation. She was married to George Davie [. . .] and they both appeared on the surface to be shy and retiring, but this was, I think, a good example of still waters going deep.[14]

Consequently, it is the difficulty of Davie's work that has prevented her from being pigeonholed in any convenient way, the experimental nature of her fiction working against this at every turn.

Two other important figures of this period raise further questions about situating the work of experimental women. Margaret Tait (1918–99), was a film-maker, painter and writer, who over forty-six years produced over 30 films, 3 books of poetry and 2 volumes of short stories. During the early 1960s, Tait was living between Edinburgh and Orkney. Sharing some similarities with Davie's minimalist style, Tait's experimental films are anti-narrative for the most part, often focusing on images in quite meditative ways, and once again it is the unconventionality of her work which could begin to account for her critical neglect. Ali Smith, however, has claimed Tait as central to the recent regeneration of Scottish writing, commenting:

> Tait was a remarkable critical forerunner in her poetry of what's now a recognisable Scottish literary voice, one that took ten or twenty years after her own publications to come to the fore in newer voices credited with kick-starting the late twentieth-century renaissance in Scottish writing. She's a writer whose openness of mind, voice, structure, all come from the Beats and Whitman, crossed with MacDiarmid, but then cut their own original (and crucially female) path.[15]

Despite being a tenant in Rose Street, Edinburgh, from 1954 to 1973, Tait was never part of the Rose Street group of poets now made infamous by the Sandy Moffat painting 'Poets Pub'. In 1964, however, Tait did make a short film about Hugh MacDiarmid, then seventy-one. The film shows MacDiarmid at home, reading poems, and also outside, walking playfully along kerbstones, trying to retain his balance (Tait has described these scenes as if MacDiarmid were balancing on a high wire, somehow steadying the world beneath his feet).[16] While there was some correspondence between the two writers, they were never closely associated. MacDiarmid published some of her poems in his *Voice of Scotland* magazine in the 1950s, and also mentioned her work in his 1960 article 'Intimate Filmmaking in Scotland', yet Tait evidently did not feel inclined to make strong connections with her fellow, mostly male, contemporaries. Her poem 'Face-Kicking' from 1961, illuminates the extremes of all that she perceived to be wrong with Scottish literary culture at this time: 'The boors/ Are everywhere./ They kick you in the face./ Only in Scotland/ Do those who love you kick you in the face.'[17]

This troubled distance from Scottish literary circles is perhaps most obvious in the case of Helen Adam. Although born in Scotland in 1909, Adam moved to New York in 1939, then to San Francisco where she befriended Robert Duncan and became associated with many writers of the Beat movement, later moving back to New York where she died in 1993. While sometimes referred to as the 'Den mother of the Beats', and a central figure of the San Francisco Renaissance movement (especially for her musical *San Francisco's Burning*), Adam mainly chose to write in traditional ballad form – often drawing on her Scottish background and her interest in supernatural ballads, such as 'Tam Lin'. While this focus on the ballad form baffled many of her Beat peers, it fascinated others such as Duncan and Allen Ginsberg. Adam's eclectic style moved seamlessly between her interests in religion, myth, magic and the excesses of the bohemian culture around her, such as in 'Jericho Bar' ('Oh! Never hope to lure me home/ Before the break of day, For this is where the action is, And this is where I'll stay;/ With Uppers and with Downers, with L.S.D and Pot./ Till all the rats of Jericho/ Stampede to Camelot./ Don't grudge me dreams, Mother./ Dreams are all I've got/ Swinging Single at the Jericho Bar.')[18] While often cited briefly in Beat histories, Adam remains an outsider in both American and Scottish literary circles – perhaps owing to her eccentric ways as much as her gender. In his Post Office Lecture at the Edinburgh Festival in 2000, Edwin Morgan commented: 'Helen Adam is possibly unique in the sense that she would never have made anything of her poetry, even though she wrote a lot of it, if she remained in her native place. She was a latent poet who needed the jolt of an entirely different environment to bring to the surface what was subterraneanly there.'[19]

In terms of Morgan's call for young Scottish writers' literature to 'have the self-confidence to measure its creative life against the best and vividest examples from outside', the four writers discussed here were already deeply engaged in such pursuits in the early to mid-1960s. Each, though, either chose to remain consciously apart from Scottish literary culture of the time or, if they were directly involved (for example, in the case of Mitchison), often found such experiences frustrating, unsatisfactory and at times alienating. While Morgan has been one of the few critics to illuminate the importance of both Tait and Adam's emerging work, all four women have yet to be written into the history of the Scottish 1960s in sufficient detail. Each may have consciously resisted prominent debates concerning the national literary culture, or simply ignored them while following their own creative paths: for whatever reason their experiments reach far beyond the limitations of the provincial.

CHAPTER THIRTEEN

Genre Fiction

Glenda Norquay

The twentieth century witnessed an increasing momentum, in both critical output and the institutionalisation of teaching, towards establishing a canon of Scottish literature. That canon, as represented by school and university syllabuses and by the works that receive most critical attention and are the focus of theoretical contextualisation, has been predominantly shaped by an emphasis on the contribution of texts to our understanding of national identity. Subsidiary concerns, in thinking about writing by women, have been their advancement of the dynamics between national and gendered identities, their understanding of social inclusion and exclusion, and the concomitant literary experimentation as women develop their own voices. Much of the writing in this volume demonstrates such engagement with texts which foreground the relationship between literary form, Scotland's cultural autonomy, and the representation of a range of national, sexual and gendered identities: literature, in other words, which could take its place on a 'national' curriculum.[1] There is, however, another body of writing by women – and perhaps written predominantly for women – which, because of its apparently formulaic nature and commercial success, has received less critical attention and might appear to sit less comfortably on a school or university syllabus. This chapter focuses on two genres, detective and historical fiction, within that body of writing which also includes 'chicklit' and science fiction,[2] asking what 'genre fiction' might offer writers and readers, exploring its engagement with wider political issues more overtly addressed in 'higher' or more experimental literary forms and arguing that, with the writers discussed, it is their deployment of genre fiction's serial nature that gives the work its force.

Since second-wave feminism and its emphasis on fiction that addressed either significant social concerns or represented a literary experimentalism, there has been a growing recognition that formulaic fictional forms offer an ideal space in which to engage a large number of readers but also to subvert expectations. The explosion of American women's detective fiction, with a specifically regional emphasis[3] and a challenge to the conventions of form which at times threatens to break it completely,[4] shows how powerful this move into the sphere of popular writing can be both in challenging gender boundaries and in finely exploring geographical delineations of existence. In Scotland the pattern of using popular literary forms and tightly defined genres to articulate serious concerns is long-standing and well established. George MacDonald showed what could be achieved through fantasy and fairy tale; Neil Gunn and, more recently Iain (M.) Banks chose to work in dystopia and science fiction; and William McIlvanney's deliberate move into detective fiction with his 'Laidlaw' novels clearly paved the way for the commercial success and political reach of Ian Rankin's work.

The dynamics of the popular in terms of women's literary production has, however, been rather different. Since the nineteenth century women's relationship to the consumption of popular literary forms has been given a particular definition, with women being seen both as less discriminating readers and as more 'demanding' in their appetites for fictional fodder.[5] This perception was fuelled particularly in the twentieth century with the success of Harlequin and Mills and Boon romances, and later in the 1980s sex and shopping sagas or Aga sagas.[6] This gendered perception provoked and gave force to feminist appropriation of generic forms by some, in areas such as science fiction or detective fiction, while simultaneously allowing significant numbers of women writers to achieve commercial success in the fields of historical romance, romance, chick lit, and detective fiction without necessarily challenging their readers or engaging with specific feminist or political agendas. This chapter explores the work of writers who have clearly addressed the commercial market but who produce fiction that disrupts perceptions, offers fulfilment of various kinds and makes its own contribution to our understanding of culture and identity formations. Because it is the structural constraints and expectations of genre fiction – most notably those imposed by the detective form but also applicable to romance and historical fiction – which make it an attractive arena for innovation and experimentation, this chapter gives particular emphasis to writers who challenge or appropriate standard forms but also sketches out a wider context in which to understand the flourishing of women writers within genre fiction.

The most dominant area of growth in Scottish women's genre fiction has been the detective novel, in keeping with the genre's popularity in Scotland from the 1980s onwards. As Gill Plain suggests, the alienated figure of the detective was one well-suited to articulating opposition to Thatcherism: from this, crime fiction developed into one of the most significant forms for investigating the state of Scotland and continued to flourish within a post-devolution world.[7] Acknowledging possibilities of the move into the popular initiated by McIlvanney, building on the increasingly political writing of Rankin, and with an internationally recognised home-grown innovator of the form in Val McDermid, writers such as Manda Scott, Louise Welsh, Denise

Mina, Alex Gray, Lin Anderson and Karen Campbell represent a feminis-
ing of 'Tartan Noir'. Their dark and urban fictions assume an underbelly of
criminal activity through which their detectives – most often, although not
always, women – move through the challenges of a predominantly masculine
world.

At the same time, echoing the success of Alexander McCall Smith in
a more recognisably British tradition of crime fiction, a number of women
writers concentrate on localised contexts – small town and rural Scottish
life – with a more individualised concern for the eradication of the damaged
and damaging. From the caricatures of highland life found in the highly
successful 'Hamish Macbeth' series by M. C. Beaton (Marion Chesney),
through to the more nuanced depictions of Shetland life in the work of
Ann Cleeves, writers favouring the detective tradition of Agatha Christie
are attracted to the enclosed nature of Scottish rural communities, creating
milieus in which regional specificity is key. Signature locations reinforce the
careful delineation of fixed contexts in which plot events and character shifts
can reverberate. Regional identity is foregrounded as a point of entry in the
process of detection: the figure of the detective either uses local knowledge
to understand patterns less obvious to the reader, as in the Hamish Macbeth
series (written by Glasgow-born Chesney), or the detective's distance from
the community allows him or her to discern significance to which insiders are
oblivious. Ann Cleeves (who is not Scottish but lived for some time on Fair
Isle) demonstrates the latter in her series of novels set in Shetland. If Beaton's
Hamish Macbeth draws on the Neil Munro, Compton Mackenzie and 'local
hero' commonplaces of the 'knowing' native, Cleeves presents nuanced local
differences – her detective Jimmy Perez comes from Fair Isle and his ancestor
was a shipwrecked sailor in the Spanish Armada – as the key to understanding the dynamics of a small world from both within and outside. Catriona
McPherson's 'Dandy Gilver' historical murder mystery series, set after the
First World War, greeted as an example of 'Tartan Tweed', centres on an
amateur detective who, because of her sex, class status and wit, can move in
and out of a range of rural contexts, again deploying a specific kind of knowledge to uncover patterns in closed communities.[8] While this group of novels
may appear to have a concern with alternative forms of knowledge – which
might be read in the gendered terms that Christie's Miss Marple has been[9]
– their underlying concern is more obviously with the continuation of community and a conventional restoration of order, however, temporary, than
with the state of the nation or with addressing a specifically Scottish agenda.

Plain suggests that while both Rankin and McCall Smith 'valorise detective figures at odds with hegemonic masculinity', and focus on community
and government, McCall Smith offers a fantasy of communal coherence and
simple resolution rather than the world of increasing complexity explored

by Rankin.[10] Women writers who share the generic format of Christie or of McCall Smith may question dominant masculinities, and occasionally suggest a peripheral unease about movement towards resolution and reconciliation, but their fiction rarely demands that it be read in a context outside itself. For those writers who follow the steps of Rebus into a noir world, there are differing degrees to which they share his engagement with complexity and corruption.

Rankin, as Plain notes, remains pessimistic about imagining alternative modes of detection 'suggesting that women's entry into patriarchal structures can only end in corruption or marginalisation'.[11] Not all writers take up this challenge to extend the boundaries of the form. Alex Gray's fiction, while appealing to a taste for social realism, is ultimately conventional in its attribution of guilt and enactment of justice. Lin Anderson is more adventurous in her creation of forensic investigator Rhona Macleod, attempting to develop a narrative around the personal negotiations of a woman with the medical and criminal institutions in which her career takes shape. As the series develops, Anderson traces personal and psychological changes in both her central character and those in her immediate network. Manda Scott, by contrast, adheres to a world which in itself is on the peripheries of the social order: her lesbian characters possess sophisticated professional and technological resources but remain opposed to the repressive normative as represented (with sly reference to McIlvanney) by Inspector Laidlaw. With Scott's fiction, alternative perspectives are articulated by clever use of unvoiced replies in conversation, followed by the more conventional response in speech marks, which serves to undermine dominant discourses. Karen Campbell, although fixing her character very firmly within the police, presents a complicated take on the institution, drawing on her own experiences of working for the police force and Glasgow City Council.

Although (as demonstrated by Rankin)[12] the figure of the policeman has increasingly come to occupy the position of outsider, Campbell's central character, Anna Cameron, is ambitious for a career within the police. Her detective, at times as bitter and dysfunctional as Rebus, is shown in a range of situations often unacknowledged in more conventional fiction or that with a more masculine gaze; a striking example is when Anna has to strip-search a menstruating prisoner: 'The stink was rank: menstrual blood, a smorgasbord of semen and rotting, rotting – tobacco.'[13] As Campbell dissects the sexual and power politics of the police force, she situates her heroine in a complex web of relationships, not only exploring the familiar tensions between career and personal happiness but wider family dynamics, as in Anna's complicated relationship with her mother.[14]

Campbell's second novel, *After the Fire*, presents the greatest challenge to genre conventions by concentrating less on Anna than on her ex-lover and police officer, Jamie, imprisoned for murder through a firearm misuse incident, and his wife Cath, left with the children. The novel is structured to sustain a focus on the victim of the shooting and her life but the appalling incident becomes central to a wider network of questions around victimhood, justice, the police and prison service. Anna realises she 'had never thought beyond the jailing of neds. [. . .] Never once had she considered [. . .] what his wife was feeling, or if his kids were scared [. . .] And never ever, had she thought about asking why they'd done it in the first place. She would search for motives, yes, but reasons?'[15] Campbell's novels offer a sophisticated analysis of women's position within a particularly forceful career politics, a world in which physicality and physical force is a consistent issue and decisions about ways of being are constantly demanded. In their explorations of characters on the edges of society and of corruption, bullying and breakdown within forces of authority, her fiction demonstrates detective fiction in a post-devolution world continuing to engage with the health of the body politic.

Denise Mina, too, reconfigures ideas of authority, criminality and justice. Her first set of novels within the crime genre began with a character on the edges of society: a former psychiatric inpatient, suspected of murder, herself the victim of abuse but increasingly a woman who seeks vengeance in unconventional and dangerous ways. In the 'Garnethill Trilogy' Maureen O'Donnell raises questions around concepts of victimhood and agency, as well as challenging conventions of female identity. Maureen's adoption of some characteristics of the dysfunctional male detective – drinking too much, unstable in relationships, frequently saying the wrong thing – is uncomfortably juxtaposed with an emphasis on her physical femaleness, with her vulnerability and her shifts of mood between certainty and doubt. A conversation with her friend Leslie near the opening of Garnethill sets its agenda, as they discuss whether her relationship with Douglas, a colleague of her psychiatrist, is by its very nature, abuse:

> 'Oh, I dunno, Leslie, everything can't be abuse, you know? I mean, I wanted it. I was as much part of it as he was.'
> 'Yeah', she said adamantly. 'Everything can't be abuse but that was.' (p. 15)

The extent to which collusion with the systems of social order – the police, the law, the state – reproduces the structures of abuse or could offer possibilities of agency and change is a continuing question for Mina.

Mina's next group of novels, The Field of Blood, The Dead Hour and The Last Breath apparently attribute more obvious agency to their central character, in that Paddy Meehan, as a journalist, is closer to the investigative role of the conventional detective. The fact that the novels are set in the 1980s and the journalist shares her name with Patrick Meehan, victim of a controversial miscarriage of justice in Scotland following a murder in 1969, who later claimed intelligence services' involvement in his case, makes her a more ambiguous and proactive figure, exploring a world of outsiders, of police corruption and journalistic cynicism. Again they interrogate justice, the legal systems and normative moralities. Mina's next series, which began with *Still Midnight* (2009), complicates matters further by having her central character 'cross sides' into the police force. But moral codes are again questioned through DS Alex Morrow, who – as the dust-jacket claims – 'knows the difference between good and bad. She's just not sure which she prefers anymore.'[16] In Mina's tale of a Glasgow Asian family, whose suburban security is abruptly violated, she exposes centre/peripheries distinctions and appears even less keen to enforce simple retributive justice. Mina's most recent novel, *The End of the Wasp Season* (2011), again with Morrow as its centre, follows Rankin's *A Question of Blood* (2003), using the device of a public school set in Scotland as a means of widening out her sphere of exploration: in this instance into the world of bankers and corruption. This allows her to contextualise Glasgow in a different way, although the dynamics of police and public remain much the same. Making Morrow pregnant with twins also expands the potential intersections between private and professional lives: interviewing a suspect, her attention is turned inwards: 'She watched him until a tiny heel, no bigger than her thumb, karate-kicked her heart and stole her away from the world.'[17] But the insistence underpinning the novel is still on retributive justice and a belief in morality: Morrow mourns the inability of her superiors to believe that police officers 'might have an innate sense of the rightness of certain things' (p. 307), and the novel's plot conclusion reinforces the message of justice.

Established as a writer with an interest in metanarrative and fiction games, Kate Atkinson's crime writing perhaps challenges the genre most of all. Like her earlier novels, with their interest in 'history, family and identity within a postmodern aesthetic',[18] Atkinson's first 'detective' novel *Case Histories* (2004) is driven by a dynamic between pattern-making and the convergence of random forces into the tragedies and triumphs of individual lives. Weaving though this tale, epitomising both, is the figure of Jackson Brodie who, in subsequent novels, *When Will There Be Good News?*, *One Good Turn* and *Started Early, Took My Dog*, fulfils the role of detective but increasingly acts as catalyst for what appears as a series of unfortunate adventures. Atkinson, like Mina, is interested in the complexities of retribution and justice, but again explores the possibility that the most 'moral' resolutions for the victimised are at odds with the forces of law and order. Creating plot narratives in which most of the main characters have personal tragedy or trauma in their past or present, Atkinson offers new navigations of the public spheres of criminal investigation and legal justice in relation to the private and psychological.

If Atkinson's *Behind the Scenes at the Museum* plays with ideas of emplotment – 'the way by which a sequence of events fashioned into a story is gradually revealed to be a story of a particular kind'[19] – the four novels in the Brodie series (with its wry reference to that other J. Brodie, also created by an author obsessed with the power of plotting, Muriel Spark) consistently challenge readers into re-evaluating the kind of story they are reading. This re-evaluation, as with Campbell and Mina, develops across a number of texts: this is both characteristic of the formula of genre fiction, with its emphasis on repetition and, in each case, a cunning exploitation of its conventions. The challenge Campbell presents, between a traditional emphasis on motive and a new interest in underlying social structures which, the more they are explored the more conventional notions of victim, perpetrator and crime break down, is echoed in Mina and Atkinson: all three write fictions which are still fuelled by a desire for justice but in the social rather than legal or conventionally moral sense.

From the early interest of Naomi Mitchison to the later work of Margaret Elphinstone, Scottish women writers in the twentieth century have also been drawn to historical fiction. Like Mitchison, Elphinstone deploys early history to express contemporary concerns, in her case around ecology and identity.[20] Neither writer, however, could be described as producing 'genre' fiction in the conventional sense, in that their fictions represent experiments in location, explicitly articulate social agendas, and move between different periods without the element of formula that conventionally characterises genre writing.

A rather different kind of historical writing can be found in the work of Dorothy Dunnett (1923–2001), one of the most interesting but also under-rated Scottish writers in the second half of the twentieth century.[21] Dunnett produced two long and highly successful series of historical romances – the Lymond Chronicles and the House of Niccolò series. Dunnett may initially appear to belong with the post-Scott school of writers, described as keeping within the confines of a genre that desires to transcend rather than accurately represent history.[22] Certainly the plots of her novels, set in the sixteenth century in the case of Lymond and in fifteenth for Niccolò, as Colin Milton observes, play with the facts of history.[23] Milton suggests their plots of conspiracy and power shifts between strong nations could be read as enacting dynamics from the Cold War period in which they emerged. They are also conventional perhaps in the trajectory of each series, as a disaffected or marginal individual adopts social and political responsibilities.[24] The character of Francis Crawford (Lymond) moves from an apparently cynical recklessness in his military and sexual endeavours, to take up his role within Scotland, and finally with a wife, while Niccolò rises from illegitimate apprentice into the developing world of European trading empires, again playing a significant role in the development of Scotland. To trace these patterns in Dunnett's fiction is, however, to give only a small sense of their flavour and attraction for large numbers of readers.[25] In creating Lymond Dunnett presents us with a character of masculine prowess, intellectually superior to most around him, but a figure who in his wit, charm and beauty, his power to attract both men and women, offers a cross-gendered identification. His move from initial resistance to the social order into a transformative role within it suggests possibilities for the empowerment of feminine, as well as more conventionally masculine, virtues. Niccolò, because of his association with the comedic, his class position of outsider, and the emphasised gentleness of his responses to situations in which status is threatened, also offers an alternative to normative masculinity and point of feminised identification. At the same time, he bears many of the attributes of generic hero: an extraordinary facility with languages and the acquisition of new skills, the prowess of a great lover, cunning and foresight which consistently places his knowledge and interpretation of events several stages ahead of anyone else, including the reader.

Indeed, knowledge becomes the driving force and most complex dynamic within Dunnett's fiction. Stylistically, her novels are far from being formulaic or easily accessible: with a wit, erudition and flair for language which, with its interlacing of classical, medieval and Renaissance quotation, is at times almost baffling, they take the reader into a world of textual jouissance, a delight in artifice and artificers which might be seen as postmodernist.[26] The detailed historical research underpinning the novels, in which fantasy characters intersect with key historical moments and real figures, is equally overpowering and allows the reader an assumption of historical mastery and cultural knowledge, which again offers a seductive sense of empowerment. Little is explained but the assumption is, for example, that we will recognise the Florentine sculptor, who is neither Brunelleschi or Ghiberti, as Donatello (*The Spring of the Ram*) without his name ever being mentioned.[27] As Cleo Kearns suggests, the historical novel as a genre offers 'a seductive interplay between the freedom of fiction and the force of fact, or, better put, between the polyvalence of fantasy and what Roland Barthes calls the "reality effect", that constitutes at once this form's appeal and its faint uneasiness'.[28]

Much of the criticism on Dunnett focuses on the interplay of historical past and political present: Milton identifies the Cold War atmosphere inhabiting her international conspiracies; Hopkins suggests Dunnett responds to feminism in the Niccolò series; Kearns notes that, in addition to the grasp of economic and the force of material conditions, there is 'a love of country that does not fall into nationalist nostalgia and an insistence on a grasp of international forces that nevertheless retains a concern for justice, tolerance, freedom and cultural particularity at the local level as well'.[29] What none of these critics fully address is the significance of knowledge and of desire in Dunnett's fiction, the ways in which they become linguistic and political forces. Her second novel in the Lymond Chronicles begins with the bald statement: 'She wanted Crawford of Lymond.'[30] As the scene goes on to reveal, the Dowager Queen of Scotland seeks Lymond as a secret ally within France when she visits its court, but that initial assertion defines both the responses of half the characters in the novels – whether they want him for themselves or want to destroy him – and the reader's response. Lymond is insistently represented as a highly desirable character, because of his own wit, erudition and (although at times hidden) political acumen but also for the fluidity of his identity formations. Both Lymond and Niccolò traverse countries and roles as classic shape shifters: in each case their ability to disguise themselves, to speak other languages, to adapt to different people and situations, is key to their success. While the novels may ultimately drive towards a conservative settling down to responsibility, in the process, they also present a powerful fantasy of multiple selves and the power to escape fixed social situations. At the same time they offer an equally seductive fantasy of the mastery of knowledge, the possibility of a comprehensive understanding: Dunnett's novels, like those of Mina and Atkinson, are powered by the desire of the reader to make sense not just of the complex web of allusion, the sophistication of language, the intricacies of geographic detail, the extent to which the author is representing or inventing history, but also of the import of each novel itself.

While Mina, Atkinson and Dunnett appear to be moving their respective genres in new directions, playing with notions of heroes and victims, justice and crime, their most radical challenge lies in their deployment of the forms' most conventional feature: the drive towards knowledge.[31] All three writers create in their readers a powerful desire to understand, a desire which is ever only partially gratified by the closure of any one novel. Hence, Mina's series of grouped novels in which events play out over a changing dynamic; Atkinson's creation of Jackson Brodie as the point to link the apparently random events of four novels; Dunnett's working out of her larger designs in six or eight volume series. All three open their fictions with scenes or situations that are baffling and resistant to interpretation; all suggest that understanding is possible but also defer that gratification.

Dunnett, Mina and Atkinson capitalise on the 'serial' dimension of genre fiction: the constituent component of commercial success which pushes readers forward into another book, in their writing acquires interpretative significance. All three consistently engage with metanarratives – around national and gendered identity, justice, the play of society and history – and all suggest that the fictional forms in which they operate cannot contain these bigger questions. It is no coincidence that each has embarked on the development of their form over various series of novels. They refuse fictions that simply satisfy, which offer easy answers, instead demanding from their readers a complexity of investigation which can only be played out over multiple texts. In so doing they both challenge the boundaries of genre fiction and draw their energy from its constituent elements.

CHAPTER FOURTEEN

Twentieth-Century Poetry

Rhona Brown

Poetry by Scottish women in the twentieth century is a fertile seam of the Scottish literary tradition, yet to be fully mined. Often truly innovative, this poetry is simultaneously aware of enduring literary, cultural and linguistic traditions. While sharing wider poetic concerns with human experience – homeland, love, family, life and death – twentieth-century Scottish women's poetry often calls on a more localised vocabulary not only in its language and form but in its references to shared experiences and memories, traditions and archetypes. This twin poetic concern with the general and localised familiar is clearly seen in the work of three very different female poets from three very different parts of Scotland, writing at different points in the twentieth century. Marion Angus (1865–1946), Liz Lochhead (b. 1947) and Kathleen Jamie (b. 1962) are deeply exercised by questions of their own modernity. But it is in engagement with the past that we see their work at its most effective and affecting.

Angus is a poet often associated with past traditions. Perhaps because of this, she has received little critical notice: Katherine Gordon states that 'her "humble place" in Scottish poetry [. . .] has until recently manifested itself as more of an absence than a presence in Scottish letters'.[1] Lochhead, by contrast, enjoys a secure and popular place in Scottish literary culture as a poet and dramatist who, according to Matt McGuire, is 'generally considered to have laid the foundations for a generation of female writers that would follow in her wake'.[2] In her prose writing and poetry, Jamie insists, as Helen Boden notes, 'that universalisation can work alongside a prioritising of local cultural specificities, rather than erasing or homogenising them'.[3] This simultaneous push forward and pull back, far from engendering inertia, gives these writers' work its verve.

All three poets are especially concerned with memory and childhood. Sometimes joyful and sometimes bittersweet, memories of an earlier life are ubiquitous in their writing. In 'The Lilt', Angus's protagonist, 'Jean Gordon', busy at her weaving in 'the sma, sma rain', recalls a more temperate time of youthful love and beauty:

Aye, she minds o' a simmer's nicht
Afore the waning o' the licht –
Bairnies chanting in Lover's lane
The sang that comes ower an' ower again,
And a young lass stealin' awa' to the hill,
In the sma, sma rain.[4]

Here, and in Angus's work more generally, song acts as a bridge to the past: an evocative reminder of an earlier life. Here, as Jean weaves – an act in itself associated with the singing of old songs and with woman as 'tradition-bearer' – she overhears the 'tune o' the bairns at play' which, in turn, prompts her to recollect her own adolescence and 'stealing awa'' to youthful love trysts. Remembrance of her former beauty, when her 'lips were flamin' reid' and her 'hert was singin' a sang o' its ain', demonstrates the gentle collision of the general and the specifically familiar. The children's song is the same, even after 'a' the years that's bye and gane', but her own heart's is, we can infer, different: in youth's passion, her song was her own, particular to experience. In old age Jean no longer creates her own song, but passively overhears the time-less, unchanging song of her young neighbours. In 'The Lilt', a shared Scottish song vocabulary is alluded to and celebrated as enduring. However, song is not merely collective, but tailored to individual experience. Clearly influenced by Scottish ballad tradition,[5] Angus draws on their archetypal qualities but also the way in which they can be localised and specified by each singer. Her work thus breathes new literary life into an inherited form. As Angus states:

> I should like to write of fairies, not the identical fairies of the old days, but the elusive glamour of the universe; and, above all, I would fain give voice to Scotland's great adventure of the soul.[6]

Angus's work is not 'identical' to that of 'the old days'; it concerns itself with 'the universe' in addition to specific Scottish and, arguably, modern female experiences.

As well as recollecting the complex emotions of adolescence, Angus memorialises the innocence of childhood. In 'Gathering Shells', Angus uti-lises the plain, unaffected speech of infancy as she remembers her 'Grannie's sister', whom she 'likit' 'rael weel'.[7] This great-aunt, who hailed from a 'fisher toon' and 'carried the fisher creel', has a close and mysterious relationship with the sea which her young acquaintance is keen to understand and repli-cate. There is something essential and enduring in this relationship, not only with the elemental force of the sea, but with the primordial force of song. Unlike the complex relationships with older women portrayed by Lochhead and Jamie, Angus demonstrates admiration for the strong, solid simplicity of her foremothers. This reliance on the matriarch figure is reinforced by the contemporary experience of war, with its absent men and present, resilient women, also reflected in the work of Angus's near-contemporary, Willa Muir, in *Women in Scotland* and *Mrs Grundy in Scotland* (both 1936).

In 'Poem for my Sister', an often read and often anthologised piece, Liz Lochhead takes the opposite perspective to Angus's 'Gathering Shells'. Lochhead's narrator is an older sister, looking with admiration but also pro- tectiveness at her 'little sister', who 'likes to try my shoes'.[8] Although she 'wobbles' in the high heels of adulthood, she is proficient in the customary games of childhood:

> I like to watch my little sister
> playing hopscotch,
> admire the neat hops-and-skips of her,
> their quick peck,
> never-missing their mark, not
> over-stepping the line.
> She is competent at peever.

Gazing at the child, the adult marvels at her 'neat' footwork at games. But the little sister does not embody traditional notions of childhood's wildness and lack of control; rather her feet always hit 'their mark'. Showing her 'compe- tence' at 'peever' she is controlled and disciplined, never 'over-stepping the line' both in the game itself and, arguably, in life. When at her games, she is neatly contained in childhood; her experience and behaviour do not, in contrast to when she wears her elder sister's shoes, spill over into or antici- pate the complexities of adolescence or adulthood. Here, Lochhead's narrator wishes not for the innocence of childhood to continue, but for its discipline and confident knowledge of an admittedly limited world. Childhood is, for Lochhead's narrator, 'sure-footed': sensible and controlled. In what appears to be a poem on the universalities of growing up, Lochhead is also concerned with the local – here, the sisters refer to hopscotch in Scots vernacular as 'peever', replicating the language of the playground. 'Poem for my Sister' deals with universals and simultaneously with specifics, but it also upturns our expectations: it is childhood, rather than adulthood, which is associated with control and, as such, something to be envied.

Elsewhere in Lochhead's corpus, warnings are issued to young characters. Sometimes, as in 'The Lilt', these are given to a younger version of the nar- rative persona and at others, as in 'Poem for my Sister', to a younger relative. In Lochhead's 'Girl's Song', the narrator's memories of childhood are trig- gered by a letter from her father.[9] As in 'Poem for my Sister', childhood is associated with preciseness but also joy – 'I'm seven, I'm/over the moon./I've a brand new coat of bright red stuff' – while adulthood is associated with going 'over the score'. Whereas the narrator in 'Poem to my Sister' wished for her to remain 'sure-footed', the patriarch of 'Girl's Song' 'would warn of the danger', checking if the red coat is warm enough and if his daughter has enough money to get by. In 'Revelation', childhood is associated with fear in a farmyard setting.[10] The 'black bull', humanised and nicknamed 'Bob', is nevertheless a 'monster' whose 'Black Mass' makes him akin to the 'Anti-Christ'. 'Bob's' resistance to the characteristic control of childhood is key to his threat: his 'big bulk' and 'rage' are anathema to the hens' 'eggs, well-rounded, self-contained –/and the placidity of milk'. In the childish persona's mindset, 'Bob's' threat makes her rush 'past the big boys in the farm lane': they are connected to Bob in a way that is scarcely understood. As with the high-heeled shoes of 'Poem for my Sister', 'Bob's' straining, animal wildness in 'Girl's Song' upsets the order of childhood. It is tempting to read 'Bob' as a symbol of the threat of maleness to the naive persona's future life as a woman. According to Anne Varty, 'Revelation' tells 'with great economy of [the narrator's] own fertility to come, and the social role she will be expected to play even in the face of male threat'.[11] However, Lochhead argues otherwise: 'It was about small versus large, human versus animal: but it wasn't about male versus female, not consciously anyway.'[12]

Although the threat contained in 'Revelation' could be associated with maleness, femaleness is also a danger in Lochhead's world of childhood memory. In 'The Choosing', the female narrator shares 'first equal' with 'Mary'.[13] While both are initially 'First equal, equally proud', any notion of equality dissolves as the poem progresses. In her schooldays, the narrator possesses a 'terrible fear/ of her superiority at sums', but a meeting with Mary in adulthood only makes her 'wonder when the choices got made/ we don't remember making'. The female rival also has her effect on the 'self-contained' preciseness of childhood.

In 'Bonaly', Kathleen Jamie deals with childhood friendships and rivalries.[14] Far from constituting a threat, 'Fiona Murray' is entirely attuned to Jamie's narrator, their victorious performance at the three-legged race demonstrating their 'neat fit' and sheer compatibility: while Fiona possesses 'the practiced/ step of a sword-dance medallist', the narrator 'was sensible, possessed/ a Girl Guide uniform' adorned with 'badges'. Lochhead's view of the controlled proficiency of childhood is revisited here. Although their classmates are uncontrolled and 'shrieking' in wonder, the two girls 'pound' past them, dealing with the job in hand; proving their 'competence', all for the greater good of their house, 'Bonaly', which is 'denoted/ by a red sash and named for a loch/ somewhere high in the Pentlands'. Although 'Bonaly' is a place Jamie's girls can 'scarcely imagine' from their 'Wimpey scheme in Midlothian', they are, like Angus's and Lochhead's girls, quietly disciplined and knowledgeable: they know the extent of their limited childhood world and remain untouched by the chaotic complexity of adulthood.

Elsewhere, Jamie resurrects a lost world of childhood, dissimilar from but comparable to the world of memory in Angus's 'The Lilt'. In 'Song of Sunday', Jamie remembers the Sabbath as 'A dreich day, and nothing to do/ bar watch starlings fluchter.'[15] However, childhood inactivity is contrasted with the bustle of womanhood 'in the kitchen', as they tend the 'brisket lashed in string, tatties/ peeled lovelessly, blinded/ pale and drowned'. After-dinner pursuits, including 'African leopards on TV/ and *Songs of Praise*' as well as the careful preparation of a stamp collection, are concerned with knowledge and learning; they are, like 'Bonaly', symbols of an unknown but alluring wider world. They represent the archetypal 'pull towards home and away from it',[16] which both universalises human experience and, at the same time, grounds it in a specific place.

This complex concept is revisited in 'The Graduates', in which Jamie's narrator wishes for her children to 'know/ stories of the old country, the place/ we never left'.[17] There is a collision here between nostalgic, expatriate language and the register of the native: although the narrator 'never left', there is a sense that some aspects of Scotland have been lost even to her. Those lost aspects are inextricably linked with the domestic world presented in 'Song of Sunday', encapsulated in the narrator's memories of 'china milk-maids/on a mantelpiece', 'brass kilted pipers', 'coal-pits, fevers' and visits to 'the shows'. Icons of kitsch Scottish domesticity but also social realities, these are presented as dying traditions, only preserved in token gestures: 'emigrants of no farewell', 'keep our bit language/ in jokes and quotes'. The new genera-tion of Scots use their vernacular in a couthy, limited way; it is either associ-ated with humour, or replicates the words of others. But 'The Graduates' is not a pessimistic poem: as in 'Gathering Shells', matriarchs are 'tradition-bearers', capable of imparting knowledge to the community's cultural fabric. The very act of sharing memories with 'children' constitutes a pledge for the endurance of certain cultural traditions.

Angus, Lochhead and Jamie all demonstrate concern for the cultural and linguistic traditions of Scotland: in their use of the Scots vernacular and aspects of the Scottish literary tradition, they engage with them in complex and revealing ways. An interest in the Scottish ballads unites all three.[18] Herbert Grierson and J. C. Smith describe Angus as 'the sweetest singer of them all [with] that touch of natural magic, and that tragical undertone which, rightly or wrongly, we associate with Celtic blood'.[19] Her work, in turn, often utilises the ballads' tone, imagery and language. In the early 1980s, Lochhead had a great interest in 'the Border Ballads which were among the only poems I had liked at secondary school'.[20] Similarly, Jamie states that she is 'very fond of the Scottish Ballads. Sometimes, when I'm working in English – when I'm writing lyric poetry in English – I miss the sense of robust, demotic tradition that comes from the ballads', while admiring their 'strong, defiant heroines'.[21]

For Catherine Kerrigan, balladry 'is one of the most readily identifiable areas of literary performance by women'[22] and therefore a ripe genre for continuing development.

In poems such as 'By Candle Light',[23] 'The Graceless Loon'[24] and 'The Tinker's Road',[25] Angus utilises the incremental repetition, theme and style of the ballads. But in 'Heritage', their influence is something stronger, more practical and more elemental, as she declares that: 'The ancient folk are waking./ They beat on my heart and brain'.[26] As she walks the moorland, 'Their eyes are watching'; 'I hear their cry': they are a keenly felt presence. The link with the 'ancient folk' is made more concrete when the narrator comes on 'Lost and gone and forgotten,/ Old tracks by the bracken sown', as well as 'an altar shaped from stone' which tells of 'Mystical rites by the cold star lights'. Angus's 'heritage' poem revives the dead, but also draws attention to their physical monuments. Indeed, as Whyte argues, Angus 'achieves extremely complex effects using the simplest means. In her work folk poetry undergoes a change of narrative function to inner psychological vocabulary.'[27]

Although Angus wrote much of her poetry in Scots, it is not the only tradition on which she draws in her writing. In 'George Gordon, Lord Byron', Scottish tradition collides with notions of English Romanticism.[28] In this piece, set in 'Aberdeen, 1924', an 'auld grey wife' in the 'auld grey toon' is 'biddin her bairns hame'. Another, unknown boy appears in the street:

> Yon bairn he weers the Gordon plaid
> An' his een's the eagle's een.
> He sings as he gangs
> By the Collidge Croon,
> He fustles it ower the faem,
> A queer auld rune
> Til a gey auld tune,
> I'm thinkin' my bairn's won hame.

Here Byron, a giant of the English Romantic tradition and a poet about whom Angus knew much, is remembered as a child and wrapped in the 'Gordon plaid', physically and metaphorically.[29] Traditions collide but here Scots and English are not mutually exclusive, and the refrain and imagery of the ballad ignite a living memory of an icon of Romanticism.

In 'Tam Lin's Lady', Lochhead engages directly with one of the many and varied ballad sources for 'Tam Lin'.[30] But rather than replicate the imagery and idioms of the ballads, she provides a characteristically down-to-earth, no-nonsense, modern response to the idea of fairy enchantment. Working within a feminist tradition of appropriating myth and fairy tale and deploying, as Robert Crawford notes, the idiom of ordinary speech, Lochhead's narrator engages in conversation with Janet, the girl bewitched by Tam in the original song.[31] The narrator questions, 'So you met him in a magic place?/ OK/ But that's a bit airy fairy for me./ I go for the specific.' The magical world of Carterhaugh is brought into the contemporary realm, with Janet and Tam portrayed as teenage lovers who enjoy 'a coffee/ before he stuck you on the last bus'. The speaker rejects any idea of mystic enchantment: 'tell me how charmed you were/ when he wrote both your names and a heart in spilt coffee –/ anything except that he carved them on the eldern tree'. Depicting Janet as a love-struck teenager, Lochhead's narrator is exasperated with her idealising of her beau: if, as she says, 'he took you by the milkwhite hand & by the grassgreen sleeve/ & laid you on the bonnie bank & asked of you no leave,/ well, so what?/ You're not the first to fall for it'. In Lochhead's transformation, Tam becomes a knowingly handsome seducer, exploiting Janet's eager naivety, asking her to suffer 'what he was honest enough to admit in advance/ would be hell and highwater for you'. Alluding to the original ballad's portrayal of Janet holding Tam Lin as he goes through a series of terrifying transformations, Janet 'did/ hang on, hang on tight'. At the end of the poem, however, Lochhead's narrator questions Janet's motivation: 'now the drama's over', she asks, 'what about you?/ How do you think Tam Lin will take/ all the changes you go through?' Transplanting an enduring ballad tale into the modern world sacrifices none of its inherent power, but questions traditional gender stereotypes. In Lochhead's hands, Janet's story gains allegorical potency as a cautionary tale which demonstrates the dangers of falling under the spell of a handsome and complicated seducer.

In 'Meadowsweet', Jamie emphasises the enduring nature of ancient Scottish poetry by women.[32] Less directly allusive than Lochhead's take on the ballads, Jamie nevertheless provides a motto which outlines the poem's inspiration: 'Tradition suggests that certain of the Gaelic women poets were buried face down.' Their communities do so, 'not knowing the liquid/ trickling from her lips/ would seek its way down' into the earth, sowing seeds of

    meadowsweet, bastard balm,
    tokens of honesty, already
    beginning their crawl

    toward the light, so showing her,
    when the time came,
    how to dig herself out –

    to surface and greet them,
    mouth young, and full again
    of dirt, and spit, and poetry.

The image of the face-down corpse becomes a symbol of resurrection and rebirth or, at the very least, the cycles of life.[33] Not only does the poet's presence in the earth cultivate flowers, it also cultivates an enduring tradition: it makes the poet – and, by extension, her poetry – young again. Akin to Wordsworth's 'Lucy', 'rolled round in earth's diurnal course with rocks, and stones, and trees', the Gaelic woman poet is elemental; a force of nature.

Lochhead and Jamie are particularly noteworthy on the subject of Scots vernacular and Scottish culture more generally. Angus writes in a tuneful and nuanced Scots vernacular in much of her corpus and, as 'Heritage' shows, demonstrates an acute awareness of the influence of her ancestors. Lochhead and Jamie, in their post-war and post-devolution positions, use Scots to differing and powerful effects. Lochhead describes her language as 'Scots English', although her writing is 'sometimes actually in Scots'.[34] Jamie states that she is 'acutely aware of having Scots and English available to me, and try to keep both about me. If I work in one, I miss the other.'[35] In Lochhead's case, Scots adds potency and vibrancy to reported speech in her poetry. The Scots of 'Fetch on the First of January', is jaunty and comic as its narrator explores the pleasures and pitfalls of a Scottish Hogmanay[36] but is also, according to Aileen Christianson, used 'to enact and satirise difference between men and women, or women and women, connecting with class, gender and individuals.'[37] After shutting the windows 'some clown had thrown wide', the narrator admonishes her new year visitor for disturbing the peace:

> This some kinuffa Huntigowk for Hogmanay?
> Hell-mend-ye, ye're
> a bad penny, Jimmy –
> Mister Ne'erdy Ne'er-do-Weel
> sae chitterin' ill-clad for the caul'
> sae drawn an' pale,
> oh, wi' the black bun burnin' a hole
> in yir poackit an' the coal
> a Live Coal.

In a humorous mode of vituperation which resembles the ancient Scottish method of flyting, Lochhead's narrator refers to the icons of Scottish new year celebrations. She transplants 'Huntigowk', the Scots term for the trickster's search for a victim on April Fool's Day, into 'Hogmanay', suggesting that the narrator feels put-upon and somewhat humiliated by the presence of 'yir bare face, Jim Fetch'. Utilising Scots colloquialisms alongside the traditional tools for Hogmanay first footers – including a slab of black bun and a hunk of coal – Lochhead conjures a complex relationship in which the intimate acquaintance is warned away and the stranger welcomed: 'Come away in, stranger. Happy new year.' With high cultural specificity, the poem uses a snapshot of Hogmanay interchanges in which the narrator, although she knows she 'should shake a stick or ma fist', welcomes him in. It also echoes Angus's 'Hogmanay',[38] in which the speaker is visited by a younger version of herself who is invited to 'Come ben, come ben, tho' ye're deid lang syne.'[39]

Like Angus in 'George Gordon, Lord Byron', Lochhead draws on a larger poetic tradition. In 'The People's Poet', Lochhead memorialises Edwin Morgan, a writer whose role as Scotland's Makar she inherited in 2011. Morgan is depicted as having been plucked from a cosy domestic sphere to an ill-attended poetry reading: the narrator questions 'encouraging him to/ leave his Antartex and his looseleaf/ in the anteroom'. There is humour in this reading – 'Certainly there is fun in it –/ didn't the six/ particle poems tickle us pink?' – but there is also a seriousness which is inspirational. Alluding to Morgan's work throughout, Lochhead's narrator concludes that 'this winter city won't/ stay locked shut/ and that's what he sings about'. Glasgow, the generalised city, is, as it was for Morgan, an essential component of Lochhead's literary landscape. But Morgan's example is more than merely literary: 'the poem is becoming more miraculous/ more clear'. Although Morgan is, for Lochhead, 'the people's poet', he is also 'the poet's poet', offering inspiration and guidance, but also a tradition in which others can work. For Dorothy McMillan, 'The People's Poet' shows Lochhead's literary 'confidence that enables her to present Edwin Morgan and herself and their fellow writers as actors in a larger story, both private people and public poets'.[40]

Jamie's use of Scots and Scots tradition is similarly nuanced. In her celebrated and often-read 'Mr and Mrs Scotland are Dead', she revisits the domestic imagery of 'The Graduates' to make points about Scottish nationhood, past and present.[41] Depicting the man-and-wife personifications of Scotland as a recently deceased elderly couple, Jamie's narrator is among their bereaved offspring, faced with the task of retaining or dumping their lives' belongings. Poised at 'the civic amenity landfill site,/ the coup', 'old ladies' bags' bulge with old postcards 'in 1960: Peebles, Largs, the rock-gardens / of Carnoustie'. Their worldly goods are sad, antiquated and small – 'Dictionary for Mothers' and 'Mr Scotland's John Bull Puncture Repair Kit' – but demand decision: as the narrator asks, 'Do we take them?' This ambivalent attitude towards Mr and Mrs Scotland's domesticity is not, however, one of ridicule. The narrator is aware of the fact that, one day, 'that person' will enter her own house, opening 'kitchen drawers', and performing 'for us this perfunctory rite:/ the sweeping up, the turning out'. There is a sense of futility here, and of the smallness of life, but it is perfectly natural; perfectly 'perfunctory'. Whether or not to retain the keepsakes of 'Mr and Mrs Scotland' is left undecided, and the importance of keeping 'the old country', as it is known in 'The Graduates', alive is left to the reader. Yet, the possibility of preservation remains; as Boden states: 'What is important is that they (definitions, and postcards from the past) should enter the public sphere, to be re-read; re-written; recycled rather than binned.'[42]

In another celebrated piece, Jamie depicts and questions some of the more limited attitudes of Scots. 'The Queen of Sheba' imagines the day when the eponymous character arrives via 'first camel/ of a swaying caravan' across 'the Pentland hills' to the National Library of Scotland to face her Scottish audience.[43] Summoned by the fact that her name as been taken in vain 'just once too often/ in your Presbyterian living rooms', she is an exotic presence 'among the Masons and the elders and the police'. Invoking the Scottish insult, traditionally aimed at uppity young women – 'Who do you think you are, the Queen of Sheba?' – Jamie's cultural curiosity is based on the pursuit of knowledge, much in the vein of 'Song of Sunday's' nature documentaries and stamp collections. Here, knowledge of the Queen's 'fruity hemispheres –/ yellow Yemen, Red Sea, *Ethiopia*' leads a motherly voice to encourage her child:

> Stick in
> with the homework and you'll be
> cliver like yer faither,
> but no too cliver,
> no *above yersel*.

Although instructed to understand her and her location, Scottish girls are not to be like the Queen of Sheba; they are to impose a glass ceiling on their cleverness in order to not get 'above themselves'. However, in the context of the poem, the 'thousand laughing girls' reclaim the insult so often aimed at them when they respond to a narrow-minded comment from the Queen's audience: 'from the back of the crowd/ someone growls/ *whae do you think y'ur?*' In their 'shout' of '*the queen of sheba!*' the girls are triumphant, railing against the limitations placed on them. This reaction to Scottish narrow-mindedness is revisited in 'Wee Wifey', an account of the narrator's battles with her 'demon' of the same name.[44] A traditional Scottish term for a married woman or housewife, 'wee wifey' is at once pejorative and positive: 'she was out to do me ill' and yet, despite 'dividing/ land from sea, sea from sky,/ my own self from WEE WIFEY', distancing evokes 'mourning': 'For she and I are angry/cry/ because we love each other dearly.' As with the simultaneous movement from Scotland and pull towards it, the moniker of 'Wee Wifey' is one to which, despite resistance, the narrator has affinity.

In 'Arraheids', however, women are given back some power through the utilisation of Scots vernacular.[45] Exhibited arrowheads not in fact what they seem: 'The museums of Scotland are wrang.' Rather, the 'arraheids' are 'grannies' tongues,/ the hard tongues o' grannies/ aa deid an gaun'. In contrast to

Angus's awe-struck empowerment by the 'ancient folk' in 'Heritage', Jamie imagines their voices as admonishing, 'muttering/ *ye arenae here tae wonder,/ hae dae ye think ye ur?*' Much like the gruff heckler of 'The Queen of Sheba', the granny's voice beats out a reminder to be aware of limitations: the narrator should not get 'above herself'. In these poems, voices and reminders of the past are resolutely Scottish. They may need to be struggled against or wrestled with, but once mastered, reclaimed and digested, they are recycled for a new generation. In this reclamation, as Boden suggests, Jamie 'rewrites the narrative of the nation'.[46]

Jamie's concern with the voices of 'grannies' points to another major preoccupation of all three writers. Like Jamie, Angus and Lochhead are often engaged with images of archetypal or legendary women. In 'In a Mirror', Angus introduces the language of the fairy tale: 'Mirror, mirror, on the wall,/ Shadows rise and shadows fall,/ Who will answer when I call?'[47] not only dramatising divination rituals here but also adopting the terminology of Snow White, a tale thought to have existed in oral culture since the Middle Ages. (Angus may have known the version published by the Grimm brothers, to whom Lochhead also refers in her collection, *The Grimm Sisters*.) While 'In a Mirror' deals with archetypal views of female behaviour and beauty, 'Alas! Poor Queen'[48] revivifies a real historical personage in Mary, Queen of Scots, much as Lochhead does in her play, *Mary Queen of Scots Got her Head Chopped Off* (1987). Mary is portrayed by Angus as a woman fascinated by 'little things', like 'little dogs/ And parrots/ And red-legged partridges'; she is of 'soft and kind' words, in sharp contrast to John Knox. While, according to Gordon, 'Angus draws attention to the conflicting needs of both a political and a human, *female* body',[49] she also creates a portrait of a woman who was either 'Aware or unaware' of 'The net she herself had woven'. Although there is admiration for Mary, she emerges as a weak and unthinking creature, obsessed by small baubles. Lochhead's depiction would be very different indeed.

Images of archetypal women are also poetic fodder for Lochhead. In a collection entitled 'The Furies', Lochhead explores the personalities of three female 'types' in 'Harridan',[50] 'Spinster'[51] and 'Bawd'.[52] As with Jamie's 'Queen of Sheba' and 'Wee Wifey', 'Spinster's' speaker reclaims the title with humour: 'Get wise. Accept. Be/ a spinster of this parish./ My life's in shards./ I will keep fit in leotards.' With witty retorts to limiting female stereotypes, Lochhead's 'Furies' provide nuanced responses to the roles which women are expected to play. In 'Three Twists',[53] too, Lochhead plays with the roles and types found in fairy tales, thus interrogating traditional gender roles and questioning the constructions of masculinity and femininity fed to us since early childhood.

Jamie's work is also engaged in cross-examining female archetype. In 'The

Creel', 'The world began with a woman,/ shawl-happed, stooped under a creel', and expresses the fear that 'if ever she put it down/ the world would go out like a light'.[54] This view of woman as eternal legend climaxes in Jamie's 'Bolus'.[55] Here, woman is mother-poet of the world, passing words like 'the bolus/ of chewed bread/ a woman presses with her tongue/ into the gorgeous open mouth of her infant'. Jamie's archetypal women hold the weight of the world and keep it going. Thus, her work both questions and reinforces feminine archetypes.

The works by Angus, Lochhead and Jamie are not simply about Scottish experience, or even about women's experience: for Jamie, 'you're inevitably Scottish, like you're inevitably female, but there are other things more essential'.[56] Yet in their exploration of memory and childhood, Scots vernacular and culture and archetypes of femininity, the specifics of a Scottish childhood or literary tradition become universal. Cultural traditions, at times resisted and rejected and at others appropriated, celebrated and triumphantly reclaimed, are key to each writer's work. Angus, Lochhead and Jamie are far from revivalist poets but their engagement with the past adds both light and shade to their corpora. If 'Scottishness, like gender, turns out to be more a matter of the imagination than logic'[57] in their work it remains a powerful animating force.

CHAPTER FIFTEEN

Contemporary Fiction

Monica Germanà

To surface and greet them,
Mouth young, and full again
Of dirt, and spit, and poetry.
Kathleen Jamie[1]

The body of a Gaelic female poet digs herself out, ready to speak again, subverting the silencing ritual of her burial. Resurrecting the silenced body of female poetry from oblivion, Kathleen Jamie's 'Meadowsweet' enforces a critical departure from its cultural roots. This chapter argues that this paradoxical overlapping of figurative burials and exhumations, belonging and uprooting, spectrality and visibility found in Jamie's poetry, informs the emergence of new women's writing in Scotland. Focusing on four key figures, Janice Galloway, Jackie Kay, A. L. Kennedy, and Ali Smith, the chapter also traces the shared trajectories of a new generation of contemporary writers.

While the works of Muriel Spark – and particularly *The Ballad of Peckham Rye* (1960) and *The Prime of Miss Jean Brodie* (1961) – established solid (if geographically distant) foundations for twentieth-century Scottish women's writing, the climate of rejuvenation that followed the first decade of the 'second Scottish Renaissance' of the 1980s saw the consolidation of female literary voices: the works of Liz Lochhead, Kathleen Jamie and Emma Tennant foreshadowed investigations of gender and national identity explored later by Galloway, Kay, Kennedy, and Smith. The problematic notion of belonging, the ambivalent position of women within small nations and a particularly Scottish sense of alienation emerge in Galloway's *The Trick is To Keep Breathing* (1989) and Kay's *The Adoption Papers* (1991). Simultaneously, these authors' works manifest a prolific heterogeneity in women's writing. Widening the speculative scope of their investigation beyond immediate questions of gender and national identity, in the 1990s the contributions of these authors represented the coming of age of a new constellation of writers, whose works reflected on contemporary questions of homeland and exile, love and disaffection, apathy and mental health, family and individualism.

With the exception of Galloway's *Foreign Parts* (1994), all the novels discussed in this chapter – Kennedy's *Looking for the Possible Dance* (1993), Smith's *Like* (1997) and Kay's *Trumpet* (1998) – are first published novels, representing a sense of new beginning for the authors. While this chapter outlines the emergence of new women writers in the 1990s, offering some sense of shared themes and issues, its focus is on the distinctive vibrancy and resistance to categorisation of this new generation of Scottish women's writing. Nevertheless, the novels all engage with problematic notions of belonging, through interrogation of the boundaries separating private/public spaces, but also of centre/margins dichotomies, proposing models of identity which deviate from stable readings of home (lands) and roots. Thematically they register an emphatic – and at times self-conscious – shift to gendered writing, bringing the feminine self, women's desire and peripheral status into the foreground. Likewise, the non-linear structure and experimental use of language, particularly in Galloway's and Smith's works, appears representative of a deliberate attempt to break with conventions and engage with notions of *écriture féminine*. While a sense of absence from the centre underpins, in varying levels, the four novels, the texts also develop dynamic paradigms for reading identity in relation to nation and gender.

Movement, expressed through two principal metaphors – the dance and the journey – is the subtext underlying Kennedy's *Looking for the Possible Dance*. The narrative disrupts chronological conventions to accommodate the account of Margaret's memories and repressed traumas in an '"expandable" temporal framework', in which, as Sarah Dunnigan asserts, 'the instability of tense [. . .] renders the past and present lives of characters in intimate proximity'.[2] The train journey 'down south', which frames the narrative, acquires a wider significance, supporting the apparently disjointed memories that constitute a second narrative level. As Kennedy acknowledges: 'It's all tied together by a journey rather than a plot. It creates the illusion of arriving at the end of a story but actually you just arrive at the end of a railway line.'[3] Evocatively anticipated by the image of a train carrying all worries away used by Margaret's father when she was a child (p. 102), the purpose of this journey away from home is to decode the cryptic meaning of her life: 'Even now it seems so unclear. Why she is leaving Glasgow and possibly staying away; there must be a reason for that.'[4] Accompanying Margaret is a young cerebral-palsy sufferer, James Watt, whose name, significantly draws attention to the nation's heritage but who also, in his state of emotional neglect and isolation, represents 'Scotland's culture of self-denial' and 'the conditioned solipsism that Margaret is finally shaking off in reclaiming her Scottishness'.[5]

Parallel to the 'real' trip is the metaphorical journey through Margaret's memories, flashbacks that prompt the reader to piece her story together. Such recollections trace the pattern of Margaret's difficult self-development, situated within two sets of marginalities outlined by her gender and national identity. Margaret's job at the Community Link Centre, which she starts after university, exposes her to the uncomfortable threat of sexual harassment from the unpleasant manager, Mr Lawrence. But, the dysfunctional Centre also discloses the wider impact of social and political changes on gender during the late 1980s:

> Margaret ran the Young People's Theatre and the Women's Group, until the Women said they'd rather go to College and learn about cake decoration and the maintenance of cars. There was money in that. No offence. (p. 26)

This shift in the women's attitude toward employment clashes with Margaret's lack of assertiveness and anxieties about her social position. As a graduate at a time of economic downturn in a nation doomed by rising unemployment, her career prospects are stalled; her unmarried status makes her condition doubly peripheral:

> She was a single woman when a woman should never be single, but looking for a man, or for the right man, or marrying a man, or living with a man, or thinking about living with or marrying a man, or leading several men on a merry dance, or seducing a man, or deserting a man, or trying to understand, reform, divorce, encourage, murder, castrate or like a man. (p. 54)

In relation to national identity, Margaret's marginality is, the narrative suggests, the result of a distinctly Scottish education – 'THE SCOTTISH METHOD (FOR THE PERFECTION OF CHILDREN)' – which stipulates, that '[t]he chosen and male shall go forth unto professions while the chosen and female shall be homely, fecund, docile and slightly artistic' (p. 15). Her national culture, then, is held – partially, at least – responsible for the patriarchal structure that supports her marginal identity through the systematic enforcement of gender binarisms.

Women's decentred position is accentuated by the culture of self-denial, which affects Scotland overall. As the 'Method' summarises '[t]he history, language and culture of Scotland do not exist. If they did, they would be of no importance and might as well not' (p. 15), thus evoking a traditional Scottish education aimed at castrating positive self-assertiveness, at both individual and collective levels. While the encouragement of a rigid adherence to social norms clashes with her upbringing by a single father, Margaret's psyche suffers from an exclusive attachment to the paternal figure: her inability to establish other stable relationships points to a resistance to change.

Margaret's emotional ineptitude is firstly shaken by her relationship with Colin, her first boyfriend and sexual partner. With Colin, she finally feels – as she previously had only with her father – a strong sense of belonging, outlin-

ing a notion of identity centred around the strength of authentic human relationships. While dancing, which, as the title suggests, functions as the second
dominant metaphor throughout the story, Margaret feels her position shifting
from observer to observed; she now longs for being in the centre:

> They had moved the way that she and her father never could and Margaret had
> wanted to be watched, not watching; dancing, not sitting to the side. She had
> been part of two people, sometimes brushing the other dancers, but always miles
> above them and away. (p. 30)

As Helen Stoddart observes, '[t]he dance metaphor [. . .] works to conjure
up an imaginary fullness of communication between individuals or groups
who are otherwise uncertain or alienated'.[6] After university, the relationship
with Colin fades and back in Scotland Margaret's disaffected apathy – the
Scottish malaise – grows heavier, preventing her from joining 'students of
another generation' rejoicing over the end of Thatcher's mandate. She is
unable to

> dance across that distance, couldn't dance away that deathly fucking place. But
> still, she wanted to. Sometimes [. . .] she would find herself becoming desperate;
> looking for the possible dance, the step, the move to beat them all. (p. 40)

The dance metaphor also underpins the darkest episode in the novel, as the
ceilidh becomes a central plot event, leading to the death of Mrs Lawrence
and Margaret's (unfair) dismissal. Paradoxically, the Scottish dance, meant
to act as social glue, exposes the cracks in the community. As Graham, one
of the theatre workers at the Centre, sarcastically reflects, the choreography
of a ceilidh conceals the ambiguous core of the Scottish psyche:

> As every languageless, stateless, selfless nation has one last twisted image of its
> worst and best, we have the ceilidh. Here we pretend we are Highland, pretend
> we have mysteries in our work, pretend we have work. We forget our record of
> atrocities wherever we have been made masters and become servants again. Our
> present and our past creep in to change each other and we feel angry and sad
> and Scottish. Perhaps we feel free. (p. 146)

The novel shatters illusions about Scotland as an 'imagined community',[7]
united by collective feelings of national identity, shared history and patriotic
belonging. As a strategy aimed at maintaining complacency through popular
manifestations of Scottish culture, the ceilidh becomes the expression of
the delusional simulacrum of identity Scotland is left with in the late 1980s.
Rather than allowing people freedom to move, the ceilidh, in this context,
brings only death and loss.

The novel presents Scotland as a corrupt, sick, community, ready to exploit poverty and unemployment for personal gain. Margaret suffers the bullying tactics and sexual harassment of a corrupt manager who eventually fires her; having publicly accused a group of loan sharks operating on the fringes of the Centre, Colin is abducted and brutally attacked. His 'crucifixion' is the novel's climactic event, his sacrificial body representative of the nation's wounded body. This focus on the vulnerable male body returns in Kennedy's later works, including *So I Am Glad* (1995) and *On Bullfighting* (1999). Paradoxically, while symbolising social paralysis, the crucifixion is the critical incident to shake Margaret's emotional apathy. Her reunion with Colin – clearly the antithesis of the Glaswegian 'hard man' archetype – signifies a movement away from conventional gender roles. Offering a trajectory traced by other female authors concerned with the role of women in patriarchal relationships – such as Jane Eyre and the nameless narrator of Daphne Du Maurier's *Rebecca* (1938) – it is the death of the father and/or figurative (and, at times, physical) emasculation of the male character that enables the heroine to take a more active role in the relationship. When the train journey reaches its final destination at London Euston, Margaret's life takes a different turn; although the train may be still, the final line suggests that her future will be far from static: 'Margaret walks to one door and sinks into brilliant air, becoming first a moving shadow, then a curve, a dancing line' (p. 250).

Travelling and the confrontation of one's (gendered) national identity also emerge as important themes in Galloway's second novel. *Foreign Parts* unfolds as a series of travel notes, which, as in Kennedy's novel, avoid a linear chronology. Interwoven with the main narrative – the story of Cassie and Rona's trip to Normandy – are Cassie's recollections from other journeys with former boyfriends. The main narrative is mostly narrated in the third person, though occasionally the first persons 'I' and 'we' slip in, while previous memories (sometimes prompted by holiday photographs) are narrated in the first person. The text of this section is also graphically set aside from the main narrative through indentation: typographic borders frame other fictional extracts from travel guides. Elsewhere,[8] typographic conventions are altered to accommodate prose passages laid out in the fashion of concrete poetry, a major tool deployed by another important exponent of the second Scottish Renaissance, Edwin Morgan.[9] The disrupted typeface of Galloway's novel – something successfully experimented with in *The Trick is To Keep Breathing* (1989) – reveals the subversive anarchy inherent in her writing. More than a stream of consciousness, *Foreign Parts* deliberately ignores the conventions of plot and textuality to produce a narrative that openly resists the rules of the symbolic order and – by implication – patriarchy: 'while both texts are obviously dealing with states of brokenness in their themes', Glenda

Norquay suggests that Galloway's first two novels 'could also be described as "deconstructive texts" with a specific agenda in exposing and undermining the language, textual practices and discourses we live by'.[10]

The novel revolves largely around the notion of being 'foreign', of experiencing one's own otherness while travelling away from home. The journey abroad accentuates the limits of one's existence, drawing attention to the norms and constrictions to which life in the homeland is bound. Travelling throws light on Cassie and Rona's peripheral status and uncategorisable experience. The various episodes recounted in the novel point to the unsettling awareness of being outsiders, exposed and vulnerable, if not endangered. The encounter with a different culture reflects back on the limits of one's appreciation of other cultures, as poignantly expressed in the terrified response to an excited crowd in Saumur: 'Maybe it was football. God knew. Whatever, it was alien. Outside Cassie's ken' (p. 141). Conversely, interspersed with the journey into the foreign land is the nostalgia for the familiar sounds of home – Radio 4, The Archers, a weather forecast for their own country (p. 72) – and the surprising awareness that certain kinds of touristy locations, such as Chartres and Edinburgh, resemble each other (p. 77). Overall, however, the travel notes lead to Cassie's realisation that being Scottish is to be other, particularly in relation to England. While she is resigned to the idea that 'they always thought you were English' (p. 23) in France, an earlier trip to Turkey raises more pressing questions of home and belonging. Cassie's comment on Chris pretending to be English, talking of London as the capital – 'It's Edinburgh his bloody capital only he didn't want to risk saying that and have them think he was less important than they thought' (p. 179) – exposes the problematic marginality of Scotland as a dependent nation. As the Turkish experience draws the couple apart, the break-up has significant repercussions on Cassie's sense of belonging and how she might define 'home'.

A deep preoccupation with gender underlies all the journeying anecdotes. The novel points to the pervasiveness of the male gaze and the disruptive function of the female body within Western culture; while this is true of Scotland, where Cassie's body causes a stir simply by walking through male territory – 'The real men outside Mario's not needing to be worried about because you were past' (p. 000) – in the unfamiliar space of foreign lands, such friction escalates to generate a sense of dangerous trespassing. Such tensions are signalled in the narratives by apparently incidental observations such as the smell of '[m]ale urine. Bacteria-infested testosterone' (p. 3) on the ferry to France, which foreshadows the uncomfortable exposure to the male gaze faced by women travellers. While the self-conscious discomfort experienced in different places and modalities – pornography in London (p. 10), sexual harassment in Istanbul (p. 139) – is a latent motif in Carrie's memories from past journeys, her awareness of being other/female surfaces most

poignantly in France. This becomes apparent when Cassie and Rona, significantly locked out of their booked accommodation, request the help of some
local men: 'Men and women who did not know each other or speak the same
language shook hands outside a broken-down hotel after one in the morning.
Roles were reliably in place' (p. 87). Then, Cassie's imperfect French exposes
the vacuum of understanding, not just in relation to foreign languages, but
to a more complex set of foreignness: women's ostracised, vulnerable position
becomes intensely exposed through a confrontation with foreign men, but
also, more widely, the foreignness of the symbolic order, the language that
attempts to censor the female subject.

Gender is the principal filter through which Cassie responds to the new
places, bringing them closer to a universe of familiar things and simultaneously highlighting women's marginality in history, architecture, literature
and visual arts. More universally, women's peripheral status emerges from
Cassie's appreciation of the clash between a notion of official history,
endorsed by travel books and monuments, and the untold stories behind
them, evoked in Cassie's reflections on war cemeteries: 'Rows of dead people.
Dead men. Dead boys. There was nothing to understand but sheer, grind-
ing misery: women getting those wee letters Rona's grandmother had got
with the rubbish about gallantry' (p. 50). Reading about French history also
prompts reflection on the limited notions of Scottish history learnt at school,
revealing, again, a dichotomy between official history and the 'real' history
of a nation's people:

> Macbeth. St Columba. Your own country's medieval life restricted to an
> English play and a Velcro shape off the felt table at Sunday school. Robert the
> Bruce. Kings and generals, Men of letters. Of the mass of people, less than
> nothing. Women didn't come into the reckoning at all. (p. 165)

In highlighting the conspicuous absence of women from accounts of Scottish
and European history, the novel testifies to Cassie's emancipation from being
defined by her relationships with male partners. Instead, her relationship
with Rona – which presents hints of sexual tension, but never unfolds as a
lesbian affair – becomes a means of subversion. The strong bond between
Cassie and Rona exceeds the boundaries of lesbian romance to accommodate
a model of companionship based on the mutual acceptance of the other.
Simultaneously, the dynamic juxtaposition of Cassie, 'paralysed by thinking,
by uncertainty, by a sense of chaos and meaninglessness',[11] and the more
practical Rona allows the narrative to resist any crystallised and homogenous
definitions of gender. Ultimately, the journey into the foreign land becomes
a journey into female foreignness, an appreciation of each other's otherness,
despite not knowing one's place on the map: 'We stand on either side of this
car I cannot drive, Rona and Cassie, without cameras, not knowing our place

on the landscape, looking out over this field brim full with unexpected roses. And find it bearable. Bearable. Fine, fine, fine' (p. 192).

The spectral ontology – and hauntology – of lesbian desire and language pervades the twofold narrative of Smith's first novel, *Like*, presenting the parallel stories of former lovers Amy and Aisling (Ash). In this highly self-reflective debut, Smith demonstrates her deep engagement with language, developing its experimental potential in subsequent novels, *Hotel World* (2001) and *The Accidental* (2003). Language is the important subtext of *Like*, which begins with the story of Amy, once a successful academic and now unable to read, living on a caravan site, with her daughter, Kate. Occupying the second part of the novel, Ash's narrative simultaneously bleeds into Amy's story, inviting the reader to hunt for cross-references in their stories. In her narrative, Ash recalls a paper given by Amy at university, which prefigures later developments in Amy's life:

> I remember what she said. That language was meaningless, that words were just random noises. [. . .] Since language was only an act, a performance, since words were by nature all fiction, words could never express anything but the ghost of truth.[12]

This self-conscious reflection on the spectrality of language underpins the novel's main themes: identity and desire.

As language categories dissolve into simulacral shadows, so characters' identities are haunted by a pervasive sense of invisibility. Amy's life is daunted by her family name from the start of her narrative: 'Amy Shone. A surname like that will haunt all your life' (p. 4). As Amy's promising academic career fades rather than shines the irony behind her name is not lost; it highlights the fragility of identity and displaces the stability of the symbolic. Conversely, lacking a birth certificate, Kate's identity is placed outside the official structures that codify being. Far from implying self-annihilation, Kate's namelessness signifies an act of resistance to the symbolic order, leaving her identity loosely unattached to family, affiliation or place. The playfulness attached to Ash's name, too, discloses a sense of semantic and ontological instability. Short for 'Aisling', a noun for a 'dream poem' in the Gaelic tradition, 'Ash', is also evocative of the remains of death rituals – all that is left when Amy destroys all her books in the most cathartic moment of her life. Amy's letter, which we read in Ash's story, becomes a poetic inter-pretation of her friend's name and the redemptive manifesto celebrating the regenerative energy of language.

Memory, simultaneously shaped by mourning and desire, haunts Amy's narrative until the end. Just before the ceremonial burning of her diary, Amy's admission that 'Ash [is] all over her [Kate]' (p. 151) indicates the

lingering presence of Ash in Amy's life through a resemblance that exceeds
the biological laws of genetics; on the other hand, Ash's fear that her name
may have been censored out of Amy's diary leaves their relationship in the
vague territory of unwritten memories. Textuality is identified with security:
'Write it in the sand and let the sea smooth it away. Write it on paper then
hold a match to the corner. Write it in a book and shut the cover. Bury it in
a garden or send it through the post to a place that doesn't exist' (p. 309).
Ostracised from Amy's journal as unwritten memory, the censored one,
perhaps, Ash's fantasised library fire symbolises revenge against the language
that denies her existence:

> Not a word, not a thought, not a syllable. Not once did I get the mention. I
> wasn't there, anywhere. She'd left me out.
>   Now I turned and saw the sky was lit up behind me. The sight of it. The smell
> on the wind. The charred pages. The historic place of burning. I'd done that,
> me.
>   That'd get into her diary, then, if nothing else did. (p. 305)

The language of centuries of tradition is destroyed, burnt and finally turned
into ash. Ash's vision significantly mirrors Amy's real gesture at the end of
her own narrative. In both, the real or imaginary cathartic burning of texts
signals a break with the past and the symbolic, and, simultaneously, the rise
of a new voice, or 'a tongue of fire' (p. 306).

Such assertive resolution, while reflective of Ash's new found self-
awareness and confidence, comes after the critical recognition of the spectrality that informs her identity. Mirroring the estrangement from the homeland
previously exposed in Galloway's novel, to Ash, Scotland is 'ghost-ridden'
(p. 338) and alienating: 'So I'm home, and I haven't a clue where I am'
(p. 155), her narrative states at the very beginning. The sense of dislocation
is directly linked to the memories of her past with Amy, simulacral images
that her present has somehow made redundant. Spectrality pervades also the
other locations linked to her relationship with Amy: the 'unrepresentability'
of lesbian sex has, traditionally, linked the spectral incorporeality of the
lesbian lover with her absence from the symbolic system.[13] In Ash's narrative, the (ghost) theatre, one of Michel Foucault's deviant 'other spaces',[14]
is where unauthorised haunting points to the more assertive notion of pos-
sessing, demanding legitimate ownership of one's place. While the peripheral
position occupied by all the main characters in the novel suggests Smith's
engagement with the discourse of exclusion from the centre of signification,
it is Ash's assertiveness that informs the subversive deconstruction of an
implied presence/absence dichotomy. In the (metafictional) words of Ash:
'But it's you and I who are the ghosts, she said. It's you and I who are haunting
it' (p. 255).

The politics of identity and belonging underpin Kay's first novel, *Trumpet*, published after a prolific and increasingly successful career as a poet and playwright. Like Kay's poetry, her novel addresses questions of origin, legitimacy and authenticity. As with the other novels examined in this chapter, *Trumpet* avoids a linear mode of narration; its polyphonic structure unfolds as a set of parallel narratives all informed by the recent trauma of Joss's death and the traumatic revelation of his life secret. Born Josephine Moore, Joss Moody has lived his adult life as a male trumpet player, husband to Millie MacFarlane. His secret, known only to Millie in his lifetime, comes as a shocking surprise to their adopted son, Colman. The novel records the collective responses of people involved in Joss's life (and death), including Millie and Colman, but also a doctor, the registrar, and Sophie Stone, Colman's ghost-writer.

As the truth about Joss's biological sex becomes public domain after his death, it shakes the foundations of identity construction, initially pointing to the erasure of private/public boundaries of Millie's and Colman's lives. Suddenly the focus of tabloid newspapers and paparazzi, Millie's inability to recognise herself in the newspaper photographs displaces her own identity,[15] questioning the legitimacy of her marriage. Her self-alienation has an impact on relational paradigms of identity: home and family. Their family house becomes an unfamiliar space, both because of Joss's death and because of the consequent intrusions of public interest into their private space. As with Kennedy's and Galloway's fiction, home is no longer a stable category of meaning: 'It is a new place, with a new chubb and yale. It is familiar the way a memory is familiar, and changed each time like a memory too' (p. 92).

Simultaneously, while questioning Joss's role as a husband and father, the posthumous revelations about his identity lead to a rethinking of kinship and belonging, which, in postcolonial terms, deviates from teleological and essentialist ways of reading lineage and roots. The final chapter in the novel, Joss's letter to Colman, poignantly exposes the fragile foundations of diasporic identity, reflecting on his history, a history beginning with his father's journey to Scotland. It is the story of Scotland's cold embrace of the black immigrant (p. 271), a story of opportunities – he becomes a painter – and name changes (p. 276). As in Smith's *Like*, the novel proposes a view of names, and language in general, that resists categorical definitions and replaces the concept of stable roots with a more fluid reading of one's identity: rather than determining one's destiny and essence, names become the unstable signifiers of changing selves.

Gender is, however, the category at the centre of the novel's exploration. The truth about his father's biological sex upsets Colman's understanding of gender; when he sees his father in the coffin, with his clothes on, all seems normal again, the biological secret covered, annihilated by the layers of clothing (p. 72). But Joss's death – and the unveiling of his lifetime secret – shakes everybody involved in 'processing' his death. Even the undertaker sees his attitude toward sex/gender changed:

> All his working life he has assumed that what made a man a man and a woman a woman was the differing sexual organs. Yet today, he had a woman who persuaded him, even dead, that he was a man, once he had his clothes on. (p. 115)

Similar professional crises are suffered by the doctor and the registrar, the latter confronted with the difficult task of recording the death of a woman's husband who was born a woman. Death, however, comes as a liberating force, for Joss. His soul – the voice in the chapter titled 'Music' – is disembodied at last and therefore free to give into the only thing, music, that truly informed his existence when he was alive. The transition into the afterlife signals this transcendent movement toward a realm where the cumbersome interaction of body and identity no longer produces essentialist identity: 'He is a girl. A man. Everything, nothing. He is sickness, health. The sun. The moon. Black, white. Nothing weighs him down. Not the past or the future' (p. 136).

Since their fictional debuts in the 1990s, the four novelists examined in this chapter have established themselves as key representatives of a new generation of Scottish writers. This chapter's opening image of the body of a Gaelic female poet digging herself out and ready to speak again, reminds us that this literary resurgence extends to important new work in Gaelic from the innovative imprint Ùr-sgeul. The most impressive of these to date – Norma NicLeòid's trilogy, Dìleas Donn (2006), Taingeil Toilichte (2008) and Suthainn Sìor ('Fair and Faithful', 'Calm and Contented', 'Forever Eternal', 2011) – boldly and convincingly re-imagines the roles of family, morality and religion in contemporary identities, personal and communal.[16] Their work too brings energetic engagement with buried identities.

While some critics note a departure from themes explicitly linked to Scotland and identity in recent works by this new generation,[17] others have identified emergent writing with an opening up of the nation's distinctive literary production, embracing a positive sense of its confident positioning within a wider, cosmopolitan scene.[18] The writing of Galloway, Kay, Kennedy, and Smith continues in fact to raise questions about contemporary paradigms of origin and identity construction, while their critical acclaim, in Scotland and abroad, ironically perhaps, challenges the marginal predicament of Scottish women's writing, which rapidly moves towards the centre. The second Scottish Renaissance owes much to the powerful resurgence of women's voices, 'full of dirt, and spit, and poetry'.

Endnotes

Introduction – Norquay

1. Mary Brunton, Journal entry 1815, included in Alexander Brunton (ed.), *Emmeline with some other pieces* (Edinburgh: Constable & Co, 1819). See discussion Norquay, 'Welcome, Oh Mine Own Rugged Scotland!: Gender and Landscape in Scottish Fiction', in Paul Hullah (ed.), *Romanticism in Wild Places* (Edinburgh: Quadriga Press, 1998).
2. Marion Angus, 'The Seaward Toon', *The Tinkler's Road and Other Verses* (Glasgow: Gowans and Gray, 1924), p. 10. See discussion in Katy Gordon, 'Women "Wha' Lauched and Lo'ed and Sinned": Women's Voices in the Work of Violet Jacob and Marion Angus', *Études Écossaises* 9 (2003–4), pp. 73–90.
3. Kathleen Jamie, *Waterlight* (Saint Paul, MN: Graywolf Press, 2007), p. 98.
4. Janice Galloway, *Foreign Parts* (London: Vintage, [1994] 1995), p. 227.
5. Richard Finlay, 'The History of Scotland Since 1918', in Ian Brown et al. (eds), *The Edinburgh History of Scottish Literature: Volume 3* (Edinburgh: Edinburgh University Press, 2007), p. 6.
6. Cairns Craig, 'The Study of Scottish Literature', in Ian Brown et al. (eds), *The Edinburgh History of Scottish Literature: Volume 1* (Edinburgh: Edinburgh University Press, 2007), p. 17.
7. Suzanne Hagemann, 'From Carswell to Kay: Aspects of Gender, the Novel and the Drama', in Ian Brown et al. (eds), *The Edinburgh History of Scottish Literature: Volume 3*, p. 215.
8. This includes a number of studies which explore masculinity in a Scottish context: see, for example, Carole Jones, *Disappearing Men* (Scottish Cultural Review of Language and Literature) (Amsterdam: Rodopi, 2009).
9. Douglas Gifford and Dorothy McMillan (eds), *A History of Scottish Women's Writing* (Edinburgh: Edinburgh University Press, 1997).
10. Carol Anderson and Aileen Christianson (eds), *Scottish Women's Fiction, 1920s to 1960s* (East Linton: Tuckwell Press, 2000); Aileen Christianson and Alison Lumsden (eds), *Contemporary Scottish Women Writers* (Edinburgh: Edinburgh University Press, 2000).

11. Christopher Whyte (ed.), *Gendering the Nation* (Edinburgh: Edinburgh University Press, 1995).

12. Duncan J. Petrie, *Contemporary Scottish Fictions* (Edinburgh: Edinburgh University Press, 2004); Alan Riach, *Representing Scotland in Literature, Popular Culture and Iconography* (London: Palgrave Macmillan, 2004); Carla Sassi, *Why Scottish Literature Matters* (Edinburgh: Saltire Society, 2005).

13. Schoene, Berthold (ed.), *The Edinburgh Companion to Contemporary Scottish Literature* (Edinburgh: Edinburgh University Press, 2007).

14. Douglas Gifford and Dorothy McMillan, 'Introduction', *A History of Scottish Women's Writing* (Edinburgh: Edinburgh University Press, 1997), p. ix.

15. Cairns Craig, 'The Study of Scottish Literature', in Ian Brown et al. (eds), *The Edinburgh History of Scottish Literature: Volume 1*, p. 18. See, for example, Hagemann, 'From Carswell to Kay: Aspects of Gender, the Novel and the Drama', in Ian Brown et al. (eds), *The Edinburgh History of Scottish Literature: Volume 3*, pp. 214–24.

16. See, for example, Hagemann, 'From Carswell to Kay'. See also Judith Butler, *Gender Trouble* (London: Routledge, 1990).

17. See Lauren Berlant, *The Female Complaint* (Durham, NC: Duke University Press, 2008); Kate Flint, *The Woman Reader* (Oxford: Oxford University Press, 1995).

18. Cairns Craig, 'The Study of Scottish Literature', in Ian Brown et al. (eds), *The Edinburgh History of Scottish Literature: Volume 1*, p. 18.

19. Suzanne Hagemann, *History* 3, p. 215.

20. Caroline Gonda, 'An Other Country: Mapping Scottish/Lesbian Writing', in Whyte, *Gendering the Nation*, p. 5.

21. Elizabeth Ewan, Sue Innes, Siân Reynolds and Rose Pipes (eds), *The Biographical Dictionary of Scottish Women* (Edinburgh: Edinburgh University Press, 2006).

22. Sonya Stephens, *A History of Women's Writing in France* (Cambridge: Cambridge University Press, 2000), p. 2.

23. Liz Lochhead, 'Women's Writing and the Millennium', in *Meantime: Looking Forward to the Millennium* (Edinburgh: Polygon, in association with *Woman*, [1991] 2000), p. 73.

24. Dale M. Bauer and Philip Gould (eds), *The Cambridge Companion to Nineteenth-century American Women's Writing* (Cambridge: Cambridge University Press, 2001), p. 2.

25. Ian Brown et al., *The Edinburgh History of Scottish Literature: Volume 1* (Edinburgh: Edinburgh University Press, 2007), p. 11.

26. Lynn Abrams, Eleanor Gordon, Deborah Simonton and Eileen Janes Yeo (eds), *Gender in Scottish History Since 1700* (Edinburgh: Edinburgh University Press, 2006), p. 7.

27. Alasdair Gray, *Lanark* (1981).

Chapter 1 – Dunnigan

1. Lilias Skene, 'Memoirs', in David Mullan (ed.), *Women's Life Writing in Early Modern Scotland* (Aldershot: Ashgate, 2003), p. 145. On Skene, who wrote poetry as well as prose, see Pamela B. Giles, 'Scottish Literary Women, 1560–1700', unpub. PhD dissertation, University of Saskatchewan, Saskatoon (2004); Gordon DesBrisay, 'Lilias Skene: a Quaker Poet and her "Cursed Self"', in Sarah M. Dunnigan, C. Marie Harker and Evelyn S. Newlyn (eds), *Woman and the Feminine in Medieval and Early Modern Scottish Writing* (Basingstoke: Palgrave Macmillan, 2004), pp. 162–77.

2. Skene, 'Memoirs', p. 145.

3. See Gilbert Markus, 'Saving Verse: Early Medieval Religious Poetry', in Ian Brown et al. (eds), *The Edinburgh History of Scottish Literature*, vol. 1 (Edinburgh: Edinburgh University Press, 2007), pp. 99–100; Audrey Beth Fitch, 'Power through Purity: The Virgin Martyrs and Women's Salvation in Pre-Reformation Scotland', in Elizabeth Ewan and Maureen M. Meikle (eds), *Women in Scotland, c.1100–1750* (East Linton: Tuckwell Press, 1999), pp. 16–28.

4. See Anne Frater, 'The Gaelic Tradition up to 1750', in Douglas Gifford and Dorothy McMillan (eds), *A History of Scottish Women's Writing* (Edinburgh: Edinburgh University Press, 1997), pp. 15–43. See also Frater, chapter 2.

5. Melville's poetic corpus has been substantially increased by Jamie Reid Baxter's recent discoveries, published in Jamie Reid Baxter (ed.), *Poems of Elizabeth Melville, Lady Culross* (Edinburgh: Solsequium, 2010); see Baxter, 'Elizabeth Melville, Lady Culross: 3500 New Lines of Verse', in Dunnigan et al. (eds), pp. 195–200.

6. See Colm Ó Baoill (ed.), *Sìleas na Ceapaich c.1660–c.1729 / Poems and Songs by Sìleas MacDonald* (Edinburgh: Scottish Academic Press, 1972).

7. See Mullan, *Women's Life Writing*; cf. Mullan, 'Mistress Rutherford's Narrative: A Scottish Puritan Autobiography', *Bunyan Studies*, 7 (1997), pp. 13–37; Giles, Chapter 4.

8. With evangelical prose writers, there is little evidence of mediation by a male scribe, as in most medieval female visionary writing; Sìleas's verse, in contrast, survived through oral tradition.

9. David Mullan, *Scottish Puritanism, 1590–1638* (Oxford: Oxford University Press, 2000); p. 143, citing Archibald Simson.

10. Ó Baoill (ed.), pp. 62–3, ll. 731–2.

11. Ó Baoill (ed.), pp. 14–15, l. 151; pp. 14–15, ll. 166–7.

12. For manuscript source of Mary's religious sonnets: Add.C.92, Bodleian Library, Oxford, ff. 22r, 22v and 24r. Robin Bell (ed.), *Bittersweet Within My Heart: The Poems of Mary Queen of Scots* (London: Pavilion, 1992; 1995) provides a modern translation.

13. Bell (ed.), pp. 80–1 (l. 8); see Dunnigan, 'Sacred Afterlives: Mary, Queen of

Scots, Elizabeth Melville, and the Politics of Sanctity', *Women's Writing* 10: 3 (2003), pp. 401–24.

14. See Sarah M. Dunnigan, 'Scottish Women Writers, c.1560–c.1650', in Gifford and McMillan (eds), p. 31.

15. On Melville's *Dreame*, see Deanna Delmar Evans, 'Holy Terror and Love Divine: The Passionate Voice in Elizabeth Melville's Ane Godlie Dreame', in Dunnigan et al. (eds), pp. 153–61, esp. p. 158.

16. See Mullan, *Narratives of the Religious Self in Early Modern Scotland* (Aldershot: Ashgate, 2010).

17. Mullan, *Women's Life Writing*, p. 94.

18. On the pattern of protestant conversion stories, see Mullan, *Scottish Puritanism*, p. 87ff; pp. 269–74.

19. Mullan, *Women's Life Writing*, p. 48.

20. Ibid., p. 53

21. Ibid., p. 49.

22. Ibid., p. 49.

23. Ibid., p. 56.

24. Mullan, *Scottish Puritanism*, pp. 52, 53; 161–2, Chapter 5.

25. Wilson MacLeod and Meg Bateman (eds), *Duanaire na Sracaire. Songbook of the Pillagers*, trans. Meg Bateman (Edinburgh: Birlinn, 2007), p. 175, ll 1–2.

26. Baxter (ed.), p. 35.

27. Baxter (ed.), p. 43.

28. Baxter (ed.), p. 48.

29. Mullan, *Women's Life Writing*, p. 145.

30. Ibid., p. 145.

31. Ibid., pp. 148, 149.

32. Ibid., p. 179.

33. Baxter (ed.), p. 11.

34. Mullan, *Women's Life Writing*, p. 409; Mullan, *Scottish Puritanism*, Chapter 7.

35. Baxter (ed.), p. 12.

36. Mullan, *Women's Life Writing*, p. 47.

37. Ibid., p. 47, fn 56.

38. Baxter (ed.), p. 56.

39. Ibid., pp. 23, 20.

40. Ibid., p. 33.

41. Mullan (ed.), *Women's Life Writing*, p. 370, and fn 42.

42. Ibid., pp. 387, 386, 387.

43. Ibid., pp. 145–6.

44. Mullan, *Scottish Puritanism*, pp. 39–41, and *Narratives*, pp. 102–4.

45. Baxter (ed.), pp. 23–34; Ó Baoill (ed.), pp. 118–19, ll 1389–92.

46. Domhnall Uilleam Stiùbhart, 'Women and Gender in the Early Modern Western Gaidhealtachd', in Ewan and Meikle, pp. 240–2.

47. Mullan (ed.), p. 161.
48. Mullan (ed.), p. 196.
49. Mullan (ed.), p. 198.
50. Ibid., p. 190.
51. Ibid., pp. 50, 97.
52. Quotations from Mackenzie of Rosehaugh, cited in Mullan, *Scottish Puritanism*, p. 371.
53. Mullan (ed.), pp. 137, 139, 141.
54. Mullan, *Scottish Puritanism*, p. 16ff; 21–2.
55. Baxter (ed.), p. 28.
56. Stiùbhart, p. 242.
57. Ó Baoill (ed.), pp. 100–1, ll. 1185–88.
58. Kate Aughterson, 'Livingstone, Helen, Countess of Linlithgow (d. 1627)', *Oxford Dictionary of National Biography* (Oxford University Press, September 2004) (http: //www.oxford.com/view/article/46909, accessed 16 August 2010).
59. Julian Goodare, 'Introduction', *The Scottish Witch-Hunt in Context* (Manchester: Manchester University Press, 2002), p. 7.
60. John Sinclair (ed.), *Statistical Account of Scotland*, 21 vols (Edinburgh, 1771–99), vol. 1, part 3, p. 234; vol. 2, part 1, p. 609; vol. 1, part 3.

Chapter 2 – Frater and Byrne

1. See Domhnall Uilleam Stiùbhart, 'Women and Gender in the Early Modern Western Gàidhealtachd', in E. Ewan and M. M. Meikle (eds), *Women in Scotland c.1100–c.1750* (East Linton: Tuckwell, 1999), pp. 233–49.
2. Martin MacGregor, 'The Statutes of Iona: Text and Context', *The Innes Review* 57: 2 (2006), pp. 175–6.
3. Alan Bruford, 'Workers, Weepers and Witches: the Status of the Female Singer in Gaelic society', *Scottish Gaelic Studies* vol. XVII (1996), p. 61.
4. See Wilson McLeod and Meg Bateman (eds), *Duanaire na Sracaire Songbook of the Pillagers* (Edinburgh: Birlinn, 2007), pp. 174–9.
5. McLeod and Bateman, *Duanaire*, pp. 286–91.
6. Tomás Ó Rathile, *Dánta Grádha, An Anthology of Irish Love Poetry* (Cork: Cork University Press, 1984 [1925]).
7. On the paucity of courtly love poetry from Gaelic Scotland compared to Ireland, and the highly patriarchal nature of Scottish Gaelic society of this period, see Stiùbhart, 'Women and Gender', pp. 233–4.
8. See Malcolm Maclean and Theo Dorgan (eds), *An Leabhar Mòr The Great Book of Gaelic* (Edinburgh: Canongate, 2002), p. 54.
9. Martin MacGregor, 'The view from Fortingall: the worlds of the *Book of the Dean of Lismore*', *Scottish Gaelic Studies* 22 (2006), p. 46. For discussion of this poem and clergy and women as thematic foci of *BDL*, see William Gillies,

'Gaelic Literature in the later Middle Ages: *The Book of the Dean* and Beyond', in Ian Brown et al. (eds), *The Edinburgh History of Scottish Literature, Vol. 1* (Edinburgh: Edinburgh University Press, 2007), p. 224.

10. Colm Ó Baoill (ed.), *Mairghread nighean Lachlainn song-maker of Mull* (Edinburgh: Scottish Gaelic Texts Society, 2009), pp. 72–85.

11. Frances Tolmie, *105 Songs of Occupation from the Western Isles of Scotland* (Ceredigion: Llanerch Press, 1997), pp. 216–17.

12. Colm Ó Baoill (ed.), *Màiri nighean Alasdair Ruaidh, Songmaker of Skye* (Edinburgh: Scottish Gaelic Texts Society, 2012).

13. Ibid., p. xiii.

14. John Mackenzie, *Sàr-obair nam Bàrd Gaelach* (Edinburgh: Keltia Publications, 2001 [1841]), p. 21.

15. Ó Baoill, *Mairghread*, pp. 28–32.

16. Colm Ó Baoill, *Bàrdachd Shìlis na Ceapaich* (Edinburgh: Scottish Gaelic Texts Society, 1972), pp. 78–9.

17. Ibid., p. lxii.

18. Colm Ó Baoill, '"Neither out Nor in": Scottish Gaelic Women Poets 1650–1750', in Sarah M. Dunnigan, C. Marie Harker and Evelyn S. Newlin, *Woman and the Feminine in Medieval and Early Modern Scottish Writing* (Basingstoke: Palgrave Macmillan, 2004), p. 146.

19. Ó Baoill, '"Neither out nor in"', p. 145.

20. Ibid., p. 70

21. Ibid., p. 108; Ibid., p. 50.

22. Bruford, 'Workers', p. 65.

23. Samuel Johnson, *A Journey to the Western Islands of Scotland* (Edinburgh: Canongate, 1998 [1775]), p. 54.

24. On division of labour in the early modern Gàidhealtachd see Stiùbhart, 'Women and Gender', pp. 234–5.

25. Because of the very late collecting and publishing of this material (late nine-teenth–twentieth century), the circumstances of composition of much of the 'waulking-song' corpus remains fascinatingly and frustratingly opaque. For a more cautious assessment of the extent of both extemporisation and compos-ite production in this corpus, in the context of recent study of the processes of orality, see William Gillies, 'Traditional Gaelic Women's Songs', in *Alba Literaria: A History of Scottish Literature*, ed. Marco Fazzini (Venezia Mestre: Amos Edizioni, 2005), pp. 165–78.

26. Ibid., pp. 112–21.

27. John MacInnes, 'The Oral Tradition in Scottish Gaelic Poetry', *Scottish Studies* 12: 1 (1968), pp. 29–43, 41.

28. Ó Baoill, 'Neither out Nor in', pp. 148, 141.

29. Alexander Maclean Sinclair, *The Gaelic Bards from 1715 to 1765* (Charlottetown, PEI, 1892), p. 150.

30. MacInnes, 'The Oral Tradition', p. 37. For associated song see J. L. Campbell

and Francis Collinson (eds), *Hebridean Folksongs* vol. III (Oxford: Clarendon Press, 1981), pp. 94–9.

31. John Mackenzie, *Sàr-obair nam Bàrd Gaelach* (Edinburgh: Keltia Publications, 2001 [1841]), p. 21.

32. Bruford, 'Workers', p. 66.

33. McLeod and Bateman, *Duanaire*, pp. 494–7.

34. Mary Mackellar, 'Unknown Lochaber Bards', *Transactions of the Gaelic Society of Inverness* 12 (1886 [1985–86]), p. 212.

35. Ibid., p. 212.

36. A. Maclean Sinclair, 'A Collection of Gaelic Poems', *Transactions of the Gaelic Society of Inverness*, 26 (1910 [1904–7]), p. 238.

37. Campbell and Collinson, *Hebridean Folksongs* II, p. 32. For the ascription see William Matheson, 'Notes on Mary Macleod', *Transactions of the Gaelic Society of Inverness* 41 (1953 [1951–52]), p. 20.

38. On this lack of stigma, see Stiùbhart, 'Women and Gender', p. 238.

39. J. L. Campbell (ed.), *Songs Remembered in Exile* (2nd edn, Edinburgh: Birlinn, 1999), pp. 124–7.

40. Ibid. pp. 125, 127.

41. *Gairm* 9, p. 47.

42. Ibid., p. 47.

43. K. C. Craig (ed.), *Òrain luaidh Màiri nighean Alasdair* (Glasgow: Alasdair Matheson 1949), p. 9.

44. Martin Martin, *A Description of the Western Isles of Scotland circa 1695* (Edinburgh: Birlinn, 1999 [1703]), p. 27.

45. Ibid., p. 67.

46. Ibid., p. 78. For a discussion of marital practice in the Highlands see W. D. H. Sellar, 'Marriage, Divorce and Concubinage in Gaelic Scotland', *Transactions of the Gaelic Society of Inverness* 51 (1981 [1979–80]), pp. 464–95.

47. Johnson, *Journey*, p. 52.

48. Ibid., p. 92.

49. Martin, *Description*, p. 79.

50. McLeod and Bateman, *Duanaire*, pp. 420–3.

51. Bruford, 'Workers', p. 66.

52. For examples see Donald E. Meek (ed.), *Caran an t-Saoghail/The Wiles of the World* (Edinburgh: Birlinn, 2003).

53. For one local suggestion of this see John Angus Macdonald (ed.), *Orain Dhòmhnaill Ailein Dhòmhnaill na Bainich / The Songs of Donald Allan MacDonald 1906–1992* (Benbecula: Comuinn Eachdraidh ann Eilean mu Dheas, 1999), p. 259.

54. Donald Meek specifically draws attention to the 'daringly erotic images [. . .] reminiscent of Gaelic folk-song' in Anna NicEalair's sole surviving hymn (*Caran*, 263); while Meg Bateman finds that an 'almost exclusively celebratory tone' marks out the women's spiritual songs from their male counterparts

('Women's Writing in Scottish Gaelic since 1750', in Douglas Gifford and Dorothy McMillan (eds), *A History of Scottish Women's Writing* (Edinburgh: Edinburgh University Press, 1997), p. 666).

55. For a further discussion of the waulking-song corpus see John MacInnes, 'Òrain luaidh and other work songs', in John Beech, Owen Hand, Mark Mulhern and Jeremy Weston (eds), *Oral Literature and Performance Culture* (Edinburgh: John Donald, 2007), pp. 412–26.

56. See Ronald Black (ed.), *An Lasair Anthology of 18th Century Scottish Gaelic Verse* (Edinburgh: Birlinn, 2001), pp. 278–81.

57. Marairead Cham'ron, *Orain Nuadh Ghaidhealach* (Dun-Eidin: D. MacPhatraic, 1785; reprint, Inbhirneis: E. Young, 1805). For MacGregor see Michel Byrne, 'A Window on the Late Eighteenth-century Scottish Highlands: The Songs of Mairearad Ghriogarach', in Erin Boon, Margaret Harrison, A. Joseph McMullen and Natasha Sumner (eds), *Proceedings of the Harvard Celtic Colloquium, 30: 2010* (Harvard, 2011), pp. 39–60.

58. See Mary Mackellar, *Poems and Songs Gaelic and English* (Edinburgh: Maclachlan & Stewart, 1880).

59. See Sheila M Kidd and Michel Byrne, 'Two 19th-century poetry collections and their subscribers', in Kidd and Byrne (eds), *Gaelic Networks* (Glasgow: University of Glasgow, forthcoming).

60. Màiri Nic-a-Phearsoin, *Dàin agus Orain Ghaidhlig* (Inbhirnis: A. agus U. MacCoinnich Macpherson, 1891). For a sample of her range, with translations, see Meek, *Caran*, songs 4, 20, 25, 59 (pp. 20–3, 120–5, 142–7, 366–73) and associated notes; and Donald E. Meek (ed.), *Tuath is Tighearna: Tenants and Landlords* (Edinburgh: Scottish Gaelic Texts Society, 1995), pp. 163–9, and associated translations.

61. See Dòmhnall MacAmhlaigh (ed.), *Nua-bhàrdachd Ghàidhlig: duanaire dà-theangach / Modern Scottish Gaelic Poems* (Edinburgh: Canongate, 1995).

62. Ciorstai NicLeòid, *An Sireadh* (Struibhle: Aonghas MacAoidh, 1952).

63. See Ronald Black (ed.), *An Tuil: anthology of 20th century Scottish Gaelic verse* (Edinburgh: Polygon, 1999), pp. 821–2. For a discussion of NicGill-Eain's one novella, see Moray Watson, *An Introduction to Gaelic Fiction* (Edinburgh: Edinburgh University Press, 2011), pp. 90–4.

64. Timothy Neat with John MacInnes (eds), *The Voice of the Bard* (Edinburgh: Canongate, 1999), p. 48. See also Black, *An Tuil*, pp. 438–45 and associated notes.

65. For examples see Dorothy McMillan and Michel Byrne (eds), *Modern Scottish Women Poets* (Edinburgh: Canongate, 2003), and Black, *An Tuil*.

66. See for example 'An Toll Dubh' (*Recovery*, Ridge Records, 1981).

67. So the Glasgow-based group Bannal, which has two recorded CDs to date, *Waulking Songs* and *Bho Dhòrn gu Dòrn* (Greentrax, 1996, 2006).

68. See Watson, *Gaelic Fiction*, pp. 81–2, 141–2.

69. Christopher Whyte (ed.), *An Aghaidh na Sìorraidheachd: Ochdnar Bhàrd*

Gàidhlig/ In the Face of Eternity: Eight Gaelic Poets (Edinburgh: Polygon, 1991).

70. Whyte, *An Aghaidh*, pp. 26–8, 156–9.
71. Bateman, 'Women's Writing', p. 659.
72. See Bateman, 'Women's Writing', p. 675.
73. For a discussion of NicGumaraid's fiction, see Watson, *Gaelic Fiction*, pp. 83–4, 109–11.

Chapter 3 – Gilbert

1. Tricia Lootens, *Lost Saints: Gender and Victorian Literary Canonization* (Charlottesville, Virginia: University of Virginia Press, 1996) traces the word 'artless' through the reception of Christina Rossetti's poetry.
2. *The Oxford English Dictionary*, 2nd edn, 20 vols (Oxford: Clarendon, 1989).
3. John Dryden, 'Prologue to *Julius Caeser*', in *The Works of John Dryden*, ed. Vinton A. Dearing (Berkeley: University of California Press, 2002), p. 535.
4. References to ballads give in brackets numbers assigned by Francis J. Child in *The English and Scottish Popular Ballads* (Boston: Houghton Mifflin Harcourt, 1882–1898; rpt. New York: Cooper Square, 1965). Letters following indicate variants.
5. Thomas Percy, *Reliques of Ancient English Poetry*, ed. H.B. Wheatley, 3 vols (1886; rpt. New York: Dover, 1966 [1765]), vol. 1, p. 112.
6. Hugh Blair, 'Lecture XXXVIII. Nature of Poetry [. . .] its Origin and Progress [. . .] Versification', *Lectures on Rhetoric and Belles Lettres* (Philadelphia: Porter, 1873), p. 247.
7. 'Mr. Gosse on "The Poetry of Women"', *The Critic* (January 1893), pp. 37–8.
8. A. Mary F. Robinson, *The Collected Poems Lyrical and Narrative* (London: T. Fisher Unwin, 1902), p. x.
9. Virginia Woolf, *A Room of One's Own* (San Diego: Harcourt Brace, 1981), p. 63.
10. Ibid., p. 49.
11. Catherine Kerrigan (ed.), *An Anthology of Scottish Women Poets* (Edinburgh: Edinburgh University Press, 1991), p. 2.
12. Ibid.
13. Alan Bold, *The Ballad* (London: Methuen, 1979), p. 39.
14. Ibid.
15. Ibid., p. 40.
16. David Buchan, *The Ballad and the Folk* (London and Boston: Routledge, 1972), p. 66.
17. Quoted in Buchan, *The Ballad*.

18. Francis J. Child, 'Old Ballads: Professor Child's Appeal', 'Notes and Queries', *The Nation*, 12 (1873); quoted in Mary Ellen Brown, 'Old Singing Women and the Canons of Scottish Balladry and Song', in Clifford and McMillan (eds) *A History of Scottish Women's Writing*, ed. Douglas Gifford and Dorothy McMillan (Edinburgh: Edinburgh University Press, 1997), p. 47.

19. See Kirsteen McCue, 'Women and Song 1750–1850', in *A History of Scottish Women's Writing*, pp. 58–70; and Sarah Tytler and J. L. Watson (eds), *The Songstresses of Scotland*, 2 vols (London: Strahan & Co., 1871).

20. Bold, *The Ballad*, p. 40.

21. See Brown, 'Old Singing Women and the Canons of Scottish Balladry and Song'; and Dianne Dugaw, *Warrior Women and Popular Balladry, 1650–1850* (Cambridge University Press, 1989).

22. Hugh Blair, 'Lecture XXXVIII. Nature of Poetry [. . .] its Origin and Progress [. . .] Versification', p. 247.

23. Walter Scott, *Minstrelsy of the Scottish Border*, ed. T. F. Henderson, 2nd edn, 3 vols (Edinburgh: Oliver, 1932), vol. 1, p. 7.

24. Scott, *Minstrelsy of the Scottish Border*, vol. 1, p. 10.

25. J. G. Lockhart, *The Life of Sir Walter Scott, Bart* (London, 1893), p. 98.

26. Bertrand Bronson, 'Mrs Brown and the Ballad', *The Ballad as Song* (Berkeley: University of California Press, 1969), p. 76.

27. J. W. Hales and F. J. Furnivall, 'Introduction', *Bishop Percy's Folio Manuscript*, 4 vols (London, 1867–68), vol. 1, p. xvi.

28. Mary Ellen Brown, *William Motherwell's Cultural Politics* (Lexington: University Press of Kentucky, 2001), pp. 91, 85.

29. Buchan, *The Ballad and the Folk*, p. 72.

30. Albert B. Friedman, *The Ballad Revival* (Chicago: University of Chicago Press, 1961), p. 57; David C. Fowler, *A Literary History of the Popular Ballad* (Durham, North Carolina: Duke University Press, 1968), p. 294.

31. Child, *The English and Scottish Popular Ballads*, vol. 1, p. vii.

32. The three Brown manuscripts include: the Jamieson-Brown manuscript in the David Laing Papers, University of Edinburgh Library (1783); William Tytler's Brown manuscript (1783); Alexander Fraser Tytler-Brown manuscript (1800). Joseph Ritson's copy of William Tytler's manuscript is in the Harvard Library.

33. Fowler, p. 294.

34. Buchan, *The Ballad and the Folk*, pp. 63–4.

35. John Bowyer Nichols, *Illustrations of the Literary History of the Eighteenth Century*, 8 vols (London, 1898), vol. 7, pp. 178–9.

36. Nichols, vol. 7, pp. 89–90.

37. Buchan, *The Ballad and the Folk*, p. 64.

38. Ibid.

39. Ibid.

40. Nichols, vol. 7, pp. 89–90.

41. J. E. H. Thomson, *Memoir of the Ettrick Shepherd*, in *Domestic Manners*, by James Hogg (Stirling: Eneas Mackay, 1909), pp. 13–14.

42. *The Collected Letters of James Hogg*, ed. Gillian Hughes, 3 vols (Edinburgh: Edinburgh University Press, 2004–8), vol. 1, p. 15.

43. Elaine E. Petrie, 'James Hogg: A Study in the Transition from Folk Tradition to Literature' (unpublished doctoral thesis, University of Stirling, 1980), pp. 45–6.

44. Ibid., p. 36.

45. James Hogg, *Anecdotes of Scott*, edited by Jill Rubenstein (Edinburgh: Edinburgh University Press, 1999), p. 37.

46. Hogg, *Anecdotes of Scott*, p. 38.

47. Ibid.

48. James Porter and Herschel Gower, *Jeannie Robertson* (East Linton: Tuckwell Press), 1997.

49. James Porter, '(Ballad-)Singing and Transformativity', *The Stockholm Ballad Conference 1991*, ed. Bengt R. Jonsson (Stockholm: Svenskt Visarkiv, 1993), p. 179.

50. Porter and Gower, p. 87.

51. School of Scottish Studies, SA 1972/22/B; quoted in Elaine Petrie, '"What a Voice!" Women, Repertoire and Loss in the Singing Tradition', in *A History of Scottish Women's Writing*, pp. 262–73 (p. 268).

52. Ibid.

53. Ibid.

54. School of Scottish Studies SA 1985/214; quoted in Stephanie Smith, 'The Categorization and Performance Aesthetics of Narrative Song among Scottish Folk Revival Singers', *Arv: Nordic Yearbook of Folklore* 48 (1992), pp. 231–2.

55. Ibid., p. 234.

56. 'Karine Polwart on the traditional ballad and Seth Lakeman', BBC Radio 2, http://www.bbc.co.uk/blogs/folk/2008/07/karine-polwart-on-the-traditio.html (accessed 6 August 2011).

57. Muriel Spark, *Curriculum Vitae* (London: Penguin, 1992), p. 98.

Chapter 4 – Perkins

1. Eliza Fletcher, Unpublished Letter to Robert Anderson, 6 November 1801 (Edinburgh: National Library of Scotland, Adv. Ms. 22.4.11, ff. 253–4).

2. Roger L. Emerson, 'Women on the Edges of the Scottish Enlightenment', pp. 1–2. (Not yet published and cited by permission. I am grateful to Professor Emerson for permission to quote from his work in progress.)

3. Ibid. p. 3.

4. David Hume, *Selected Essays* (Oxford: Oxford University Press, 2008).

5. Edward Topham, *Letters from Edinburgh in 1774 and 1775* (Edinburgh: West Port Books, 2003), pp. 37–9, 52.

6. John Gibson Lockhart, *Peter's Letters to his Kinsfolk* (New York: C. S. Van Winkle, 1820), p. 172.

7. William Mure, *Selections from the Family Papers Preserved at Caldwell*, 3 vols (Glasgow: Maitland Club, 1854), vol. 1, p. 269.

8. They were, however, still being discussed some eighty years later. Alexander Campbell, writing in 1802, refers to them as 'a society of female literati' that offered proof of the 'great progress in the improvement of the mind' made by Scottish women of that time. See Alexander Campbell, *A Journey from Edinburgh through Parts of North Britain*, 2 vols (London: Longman and Rees, 1802), vol. 2, p. 327.

9. *An Account of the Fair Intellectual Club in Edinburgh* (Edinburgh: J. McEuen and Company, 1720), p. 10.

10. Ibid. p. 9.

11. Compare Vickery's comments about the dramatic increase in opportunities for public amusement and education in the north of England over the course of the eighteenth century: Amanda Vickery, *The Gentleman's Daughter* (New Haven: Yale University Press, 1998). The shift would have been even more dramatic in Scotland, particularly in the urban centres of Edinburgh and Glasgow. See also Emerson, 'Women on the Edges', pp. 6–12.

12. Moyra Haslett, *Pope to Burney, 1714–1779* (Basingstoke: Palgrave Macmillan, 2003), pp. 40, 51.

13. Benedetta Craveri, *Madame du Deffand and her World*, trans. Teresa Waugh (London: Peter Halban, 2002), p. 103.

14. William Wallace (ed.), *Robert Burns and Mrs. Dunlop*, 2 vols (New York: Dodd, Mead and Company, 1898), vol. 1, p. xiii.

15. Thomas Craig-Brown (ed.), *Letters and Memoir of her own Life, by Mrs. Alison Rutherford or Cockburn* (Edinburgh: David Douglas, 1900), p. xxvii.

16. Ibid. pp. xxxi–xxxii.

17. Ibid. p. 112.

18. Ibid. p. 162.

19. Wallace, *Robert Burns*, vol. 1, pp. 25, 26.

20. Hugh Miller, *My Schools and Schoolmasters* (Edinburgh: B&W Publishing, [1854] 1993), p. 432.

21. Ibid. p. 434.

22. See Kames' letter to Rose on the subject, printed in Cosmo Innes, *A Genealogical Deduction of the Family of Rose of Kilravock* (Edinburgh: T. Constable, 1848), p. 493.

23. Anne Grant, *Letters from the Mountains*, 3 vols (London: Longman, Hurst, Rees & Orme, 1807), vol. 3, p. 183.

24. Innes, *A Genealogical Deduction*, p. 470.

25. Henry Holland, Unpublished Letters to Peter Holland (Edinburgh, National Library of Scotland, Acc. 7515).

26. Köbel-Ebert, 'The Role of British and German Women', p. 161; see also Miller, *My Schools and Schoolmasters*, p. 433. Lady Gordon Cumming might have been less intimidated by literary pursuits than many women of her generation because of the example of her mother, Lady Charlotte Bury, a friend of Scott and the author of several novels, two collections of poetry, and two volumes of scandalous memoirs of her experiences in George IV's court.

27. Martha Somerville (ed.), *Personal Recollections, from Early Life to Old Age, of Mary Somerville* (Boston: Roberts Brothers, 1874), pp. 28, 88.

28. Innes, *A Genealogical Deduction*, p. 469.

Chapter 5 – McIntosh

1. Mary Cullinan, *Susan Ferrier* (Boston: Twayne Publishers, 1984), 'Preface'.

2. Ian Duncan, *Scott's Shadow* (Princeton: Princeton University Press, 2007), p. 79.

3. Peter Garside, James Raven and Rainer Schöwerling (eds), *The English Novel 1770–1829: A Bibliographical Survey of Prose Fiction Published in the British Isles*, Vol. II: 1800–1829 (Oxford: Oxford University Press, 2000), p. 79.

4. Cullinan, *Susan Ferrier*, p. 118.

5. Carol Anderson and Aileen M. Riddell, 'The Other Great Unknowns: Women Fiction Writers of the Early Nineteenth Century', in Douglas Gifford and Dorothy McMillan (eds), *A History of Scottish Women's Writing* (Edinburgh: Edinburgh University Press, 1997), pp. 180–1.

6. Gary Kelly, *English Fiction of the Romantic Period 1789–1830* (London and New York: Longman, 1989), p. 184.

7. Garside, Raven and Schöwerling, *The English Novel 1770–1829*, pp. 58–9.

8. Sarah W. R. Smith, 'Men, Women, and Money: The Case of Mary Brunton', in Mary Anne Schofield and Cecilia Macheski (eds), *Fetter'd or Free? British Women Novelists, 1670–1815* (Ohio: Ohio University Press, 1987), p. 41.

9. Anderson and Riddell, 'The Other Great Unknowns', p. 186.

10. Mary Brunton, *Discipline* (London: Pandora Press, 1986). All references are to this edition.

11. Douglas Gifford, 'Contemporary Fiction I: Tradition and Community', in *A History of Scottish Women's Writing*, p. 581; See also Anne K. Mellor, *Romanticism and Gender* (London: Routledge, 1993), pp. 40, 60.

12. Sharon Alker, 'The Business of Romance: Mary Brunton and the Virtue of Economy', *European Romantic Review*, vol. 13 (2002), p. 203.

13. Anderson and Riddell, 'The Other Great Unknowns', p. 187.

14. Isabelle Bour, 'Mary Brunton's Novels, or, the Twilight of Sensibility', *Scottish Literary Journal*, 24.2 (1997), p. 30.

15. Duncan, *Scott's Shadow*, pp. 81–2.

16. See Susan Ferrier, *The Inheritance* (Glasgow: Kennedy and Boyd, 2009), pp. 311–14.

17. Juliet Shields, *Sentimental Literature and Anglo-Scottish Identity, 1745–1820* (Cambridge: Cambridge University Press, 2010), pp. 136–7.

18. Loraine Fletcher, 'Great Expectations: Wealth and Inheritance in the Novels of Susan Ferrier', *Scottish Literary Journal* 16: 2 (1989), p. 60.

19. See Cullinan, *Susan Ferrier*, pp. 115–16.

20. Susan Ferrier, *Destiny* (London: Richard Bentley & Son, 1882). All references are to this edition.

21. Anne K. Mellor, *Romanticism and Gender*, p. 105.

22. Ibid., p. 103.

23. Vineta Colby, *Yesterday's Woman: Domestic Realism in the English Novel* (Princeton: Princeton University Press, 1974), pp. 100–1.

24. Fletcher, 'Great Expectations', p. 72; See also Mellor, *Romanticism and Gender*, p. 60.

25. Francis Russell Hart, *The Scottish Novel from Smollett to Spark* (Cambridge, MA: Harvard University Press, 1978), p. 67.

26. Shields, *Sentimental Literature and Anglo-Scottish Identity*, p. 135.

Chapter 6 – Boos

1. David Vincent, *The Rise of Mass Literacy* (Cambridge: Cambridge University Press, 2000), p. 10.

2. David Vincent, *Bread, Knowledge and Freedom: A Study of Nineteenth-Century Working-Class Autobiography* (London: Methuen, 1981), p. 203. For little-educated working-class poets, see Boos, *Working-Class Poets of Victorian Britain: An Anthology* (Peterborough, Ontario: Broadview, 2008), pp. 350–1.

3. Glasgow: Richard Stobbs, 1859. Brief memoirs also appeared in Ellen Johnston, *Autobiography, Poems and Songs* (Glasgow: W. Love, 1867 and 1869); Elizabeth Campbell, *Songs of My Pilgrimage* (Edinburgh: Andrew Elliott, 1875). Later nineteenth-century Scottish autobiographers and diarists included Jane Stevenson, *Homely Musings by a Rustic Maiden* (Kilmarnock, 1870), Janet Bathgate, *Aunt Janet's Legacy to Her Nieces* (Selkirk: G. Lewis, 1894), and the posthumously published *The Christian Watt Papers*, ed. and intro. David Fraser (Edinburgh: Paul Harris, 1983).

4. For reassessments of working-class Victorian Scottish poetry see: Valentina Bold, 'Beyond "The Empire of the Gentle Heart": Scottish Women Poets of the Nineteenth Century', in D. Gifford and D. McMillan (eds), *A History of Scottish Women's Writing* (Edinburgh: Edinburgh University Press, 1997), pp. 246–61; William Findlay, 'Reclaiming Local Literature: William Thom and Janet Hamilton', in D. Gifford (ed.), *The History of Scottish Literature: the Nineteenth Century* (Aberdeen: Aberdeen University Press, 1988),

pp. 353–75; Florence Boos, 'Janet Hamilton', in William Thesing (ed.), *Victorian Women Poets. Dictionary of Literary Biography* (Columbia, SC).

5. James Boswell, *The Life of Dr. Johnson* (London: Charles Dilly), vol. 1, pp. 205–6.

6. 'Opinions of the Press', Hamilton, *Poems* (Glasgow: James Maclehose, 1870), p. 397.

7. See autobiographical sketch in the second edition of her 1863 *Poems and Essays* (Glasgow: Murray); prefaces by George Gilfillan and Alexander Wallace to the *Poems, Essays and Sketches of Janet Hamilton*, ed. James Hamilton (Glasgow: Maclehose, 1880), hereafter *PES*; and John Young, *Pictures in Prose and Verse; or, Personal Recollections of the Late Janet Hamilton, Langloan* (Glasgow: George Gallie, 1877).

8. John Whitelaw was the subject of Hamilton's 'Lines Sacred to the Memory of Mr. John Whitelaw' and 'Ballad of the New Monkland Martyr', *PES*, pp. 56–7, 212–15.

9. *Poems* (1870), p. ix.

10. *Poems* (1870), pp. ix–x.

11. See memoirs of Campbell; Bathgate; Hannah Mitchell's *The Hard Way Up* (1968); Peig Sayers's *Peig* (1938). See Boos, 'The Hard Way Up: Victorian Women and the Education Acts', in Teresa Mangum (ed.), *Berg Cultural History of Women on the Age of Empire* (Oxford: Berg, 2012).

12. *Poems* (1870), p. viii.

13. Two hundred of these were for *The Working Man's Friend*: when this inspired Cassell to commission two supplementary volumes of *The Literature of Working Men*, six hundred more poured in. See Boos, 'The Homely Muse in her Diurnal Setting: The Periodical Poems of "Marie", Janet Hamilton and Fanny Forrester', *Victorian Poetry* 39: 2 (2001), pp. 262–9, 282–3.

14. Cassell published a second poem, 'Summer Voices', in *The Working-Man's Friend*, 1853, n. s. 3., and 'Lines on the Calder', in his temperance publication, *The Quiver*, 18 July 1863.

15. The nomenclature is confusing. Her first (1863) volume reprinted 'Sketches of a Scottish Roadside Village Sixty Years Ago'; the 1865 volume included 'Sketches of Scottish Peasant Life and Character in Days of Auld Langsyne' as a separate piece, along with three 'Local Sketches' and seven 'Sketches of Village Life and Character', of which one, 'Local Changes', is more properly characterised as an essay. In the posthumous *Poems, Essays and Sketches*, the category 'Sketches of Village Life and Character, and other Essays' includes nineteen instances of prose.

16. *Social Science: Being Selections from John Cassell's Prize Essays, by Working Men* (London: Cassell, 1861); 'Social Science Essay – On Self-Education' in the 1863 volume. Since Cassell's other volumes based on these competitions have apparently not survived, it is impossible to tell whether Hamilton won others.

17. Benjamin Parsons, sub-editor for *The Literature of Working Men* (London: Cassell, 1850, vol. 1) wrote *The Mental and Moral Education of Women* (London, 1842), an appeal for equal education of women at all levels.
18. *Poems*, p. 304.
19. Elliott (1781–1849): volumes by the 'Corn Law Rhymer' were widely publicised in the working-class press: *Corn Law Rhymes* (1831) and *The Poetical Works of Ebenezer Elliot: The Corn-Law Rhymer* (1840).
20. The first Working Men's College was founded in London in 1854; a Working Women's College ten years later.
21. See Brian Harrison, *Drink and the Victorians* (London: Faber, 1971); Elspeth King, *Scotland Sober and Free* (Glasgow: Glasgow Museums and Art Galleries, 1979).
22. See Boos, 'The Homely Muse', p. 282.
23. King, pp. 10–12.
24. Brian Maidment, *Poorhouse Fugitives* (Manchester: Carcanet Press, 1987).
25. 'Sketches of a Scottish Roadside Village Sixty Years Since' appeared in *The Literature of Working Men* (1851); nine more followed in *Poems and Purpose and Sketches of Scottish Peasant Life and Character in Auld Langsyne* (1865); three were reprinted in *Poems* (1870); all but 'Maggie Gibson' were included in the posthumous *Poems, Essays and Sketches* (1880).
26. MacNeill (1746–1818): *Scotland's Skaith, or the History of Will and Jean* (1795), gained him a wide reputation, with 14 editions in its first year. A 1796 sequel, 'The Waes of War', was also popular.

Chapter 7 – Christianson

1. See Chapters 9 and 10 for discussion of Oliphant's work in other contexts.
2. For discussion of Somerville in relation to intellectual circles, see Perkins, Chapter 4.
3. On Ferrier's fiction see McIntosh, Chapter 5.
4. Karina Williamson, 'The Emergence of Privacy: Letters, Journals and Domestic Writing' in Ian Brown et al. (eds), *The Edinburgh History of Scottish Literature. Volume 2* (Edinburgh: Edinburgh University Press, 2007), p. 57.
5. Elizabeth Grant, *Memoirs of a Highland Lady*, vol. 1, ed. Lady Strachey (Edinburgh: Canongate, 1988), 2 vols; p. 134.
6. Ibid., preface and p. 225.
7. Williamson, p. 58.
8. Jane Welsh Carlyle and Thomas Carlyle, *The Collected Letters of Thomas and Jane Welsh Carlyle*, 1849, vol. 24, ed. C. R. Sanders, K. J. Fielding, I. Campbell, A. Christianson et al. (Durham: Duke University Press, 1970–2011), p. 272.
9. Dorothy McMillan, 'Selves and Others: Non-fiction Writing in the Eighteenth and Early Nineteenth Centuries', in Douglas Gifford and

Dorothy McMillan (eds), *A History of Scottish Women's Writing* (Edinburgh: Edinburgh University Press, 1997), pp. 72, 74.

10. Williamson, p. 65.
11. Harriet Martineau, *Autobiography*, vol. 1 (London: Virago, 1983), pp. 3–4.
12. Welsh Carlyle, 1843, vol. 16, p. 35.
13. Welsh Carlyle, 1858, vol. 34, p. 49.
14. Welsh Carlyle, 1859, vol. 35, p. 248.
15. Welsh Carlyle, 'Budget *of a Femme incomprise*', 1855, vol. 29, p. 251.
16. Ibid., p. 257.
17. Ibid., p. 259.
18. Welsh Carlyle, 'Much ado about Nothing', 1849, vol. 24, pp. 159–71, 214, 171.
19. Welsh Carlyle, '*The simple Story* of my own first Love', 1852 vol. 30, p. 194.
20. Carlyle, 1866, vol. 30, p. 184.
21. Williamson, p. 69; T. Carlyle, *Reminiscences*, eds. K. J. Fielding and Ian Campbell (Oxford: Oxford University Press, [1881] 1997).
22. For a discussion of the way that Carlyle laid claim to his place in her life in his *Reminiscences* while acknowledging but containing her talents, see Aileen Christianson, 'Jane Welsh Carlyle's "Private Writing Career"', in Gifford and McMillan (eds), *A History of Scottish Women's Writing*, pp. 232–3.
23. For further discussion, see A. Christianson, *Jane Welsh Carlyle, Biography and Biographers* (Edinburgh: Carlyle Society, 2008); James Anthony Froude (ed.), *Letters and Memorials of Jane Welsh Carlyle, Prepared for Publication by Thomas Carlyle*, 3 vols (London: Longmans, Green, 1883).
24. Elizabeth Grant, *Memoirs of a Highland Lady*, ed. Lady Strachey (Edinburgh: R & R Clark, 1897); for a later edition, see, for example, Elizabeth Grant, *Memoirs of a Highland Lady* (London: John Murray, 1928).
25. Susan Ferrier, *Memoir and Correspondence*, ed. John A. Doyle (London: Eveleigh Nash & Grayson, [1898] 1929), vol. 4 of *The Works of Susan Ferrier*.
26. Ferrier, 1929, vol. 4, p. 68.
27. Cited by Rosemary Ashton, 'Introduction', Susan Ferrier, *Marriage* (London: Virago, 1986), p. x.
28. Ferrier, 1929, vol. 4, p. vii.
29. Peter D. Butter, 'Elizabeth Grant', in *A History of Scottish Women's Writing*, p. 210.
30. Grant, 1988, vol. 1, p. 34.
31. Ibid., p. 130.
32. Ibid., p. 1.
33. Mary Somerville, *Queen of Science: Personal Recollections of Mary Somerville*, ed. Dorothy McMillan (Edinburgh: Canongate, 2001), p. 1.
34. *Personal Recollections, from Early Life to Old Age, of Mary Somerville* (London: John Murray, 1873).
35. McMillan, 'Introduction', Somerville, 2001, p. xx.

36. Somerville, 2001, p. 299.

37. Ellen Johnston, *Autobiography, Poems and Songs of Ellen Johnston, the 'Factory Girl'* (Glasgow: William Love, 1867).

38. Johnston, 'Autobiography' in Dorothy McMillan (ed.), *The Scotswoman at Home and Abroad* (Glasgow: ASLS, 1999), pp. 255, 258.

39. McMillan, 'Selves and Others', 1997, p. 83.

40. See A. Christianson, 'Jane Welsh Carlyle: imaginary letters and ghost publications', *Women's Writing* 10: 3 (2003), pp. 459–72.

41. Welsh Carlyle, 1822, vol. 2, pp. 165–8; see also Christianson, 'Jane Welsh Carlyle's travel narratives: portable perspectives', in David R. Sorensen and Rodger L. Tarr (eds), *The Carlyles at Home and Abroad* (Aldershot: Ashgate, 2004), pp. 208–12.

42. Welsh Carlyle, 1850, vol. 25, p. 221.

43. Oliphant, 'Mrs. Carlyle', *Contemporary Review* 43 (1883), p. 611.

44. Oliphant, 'Thomas Carlyle', *McMillan Magazine* 43 (1881), pp. 482, 483.

45. Oliphant, 'Mrs Carlyle', p. 609.

46. Oliphant, *Autobiography and Letters of Mrs Margaret Oliphant*, ed. Mrs Harry Coghill (Leicester: Leicester University Press, [1899] 1974).

47. Elisabeth Jay, 'Introduction', *The Autobiography of Margaret Oliphant* (Oxford: Oxford University Press, 1990), p. xv. See also Jay, 'Freed by Necessity', in D. J. Trela (ed.), *Margaret Oliphant: Critical Essays on a Gentle Subversive* (Slensgrove and London: Susquehanna University Press and Associated University Press, 1995), pp. 135–46; Laurie Langbauer, 'Absolute Commonplaces: Oliphant's Theory of Autobiography', Trela (ed.), pp. 124–34.

48. Oliphant, 1990, p. 17.

49. W. Robertson Nicoll, 'Mrs. Oliphant's Autobiography', *The Bookman* (June 1899), pp. 67, 68.

50. Oliphant, [1899] 1974, p. 4; 1990, p. 14.

51. McMillan, 'Selves and Others', 1997, p. 73.

Chapter 8 – Sutherland

1. Elizabeth Jay (ed.), *The Autobiography of Margaret Oliphant* (Peterborough, Ontario; Ormskirk: Broadview Press, 2002), 'Introduction', p. 8.

2. Oliphant, *Katie Stewart* in *Blackwood's Edinburgh Magazine*, vol. 72 (July–November 1852).

3. Oliphant, *Annals of a Publishing House*, 3 vols (Edinburgh: Blackwood, 1897). The first two volumes by Oliphant; volume 3 by Mary Porter.

4. David Finkelstein, *The House of Blackwood* (Pennsylvania: Pennsylvania State University Press, 2002), p. 101.

5. Laurel Brake, *Print in Transition 1850–1910* (Basingstoke: Palgrave, 2001), p. 4.

6. Finkelstein, *The House of Blackwood*, pp. 16, 17–18.

7. Oliphant, *Autobiography*, pp. 66–7.

8. Julianne Smith, 'Private Practice: Thomas de Quincey, Margaret Oliphant and the Construction of Women's Rhetoric in the Victorian Periodical Press', *Rhetoric Review*, vol. 23, no. 1 (2004), p. 52.

9. Elizabeth Jay, *Mrs Oliphant: 'A Fiction to Herself'* (Oxford: Clarendon Press, 1995), p. 15.

10. Virginia Woolf suggested that Oliphant 'sold her brain, her very admirable brain, prostituted her culture and enslaved her intellectual liberty in order that she might earn her living and educate her children'. *Three Guineas, A Room of One's Own and Three Guineas* (London: Penguin, 1993), p. 217.

11. Valerie Sanders, *Eve's Renegades* (Basingstoke: Macmillan, 1996).

12. Oliphant, 'The Laws Concerning Women', *Blackwood's Edinburgh Magazine*, vol. 79 (April 1856), pp. 379–87.

13. Ibid., p. 379.

14. Ibid., p. 380.

15. Ibid., p. 382.

16. Ibid., p. 382.

17. Ibid., p. 381.

18. R. Thicknesse, 'New Legal Position of Married Women', *Blackwood's Edinburgh Magazine*, vol. 133 (1883), pp. 207–20.

19. Oliphant, 'The Great Unrepresented', *Blackwood's Edinburgh Magazine*, vol. 100 (1866), pp. 367–79, 367.

20. Ibid., p. 370.

21. Ibid., p. 374.

22. Ibid., p. 379.

23. Jay, 'A Fiction to Herself', p. 292.

24. Oliphant, *The Autobiography and Letters of Mrs M. O. W. Oliphant*, ed. Mrs Harry Coghill (Edinburgh and London: William Blackwood, 1899), p. 160.

25. 'The Old Saloon', *Blackwood's Edinburgh Magazine* vol. 146 (August 1889), pp. 254–75. This was a regular feature in *Blackwood's* at this time.

26. Ibid. pp. 256–62.

27. Ibid., p. 257.

28. 'The Grievances of Women', *Fraser's Magazine*, vol. 605 (May 1880), p. 699.

29. Ibid., p. 700.

30. Ibid., p. 701.

31. Ibid., p. 707.

32. Ibid., p. 708.

33. Ibid., p. 710.

34. Jay, 'A Fiction to Herself', p. 249

35. Ibid., p. 276.

36. Brake, *Print in Transition*, pp. 9–10.

37. Finkelstein, *The House of Blackwood*, p. 11.

38. Ibid. p. 57.

39. Kelly J. Mays, 'The Disease of Reading and Victorian Periodicals', in John O. Jordan and Robert L. Patten (eds), *Literature in the Marketplace* (Cambridge: Cambridge University Press, 1995), p. 169.

40. Jay, 'A *Fiction to Herself'*, p. 25.

Chapter 9 – Macdonald

1. Julia Kristeva, *Revolution in Poetic Language*, trans. Margaret Waller (New York: Columbia University Press, [1974] 1984).

2. Ibid., p. 28.

3. Ibid., p. 70.

4. Stories collected in: Margaret Oliphant, *A Beleaguered City and Other Tales of the Seen and Unseen* (Edinburgh: Canongate Classics, 2000).

5. Richard and Vineta Colby, 'Mrs. Oliphant's Scotland: The Romance of Reality', in Ian Campbell (ed.), *Nineteenth-Century Scottish Fiction* (Manchester: Carcanet Press, 1979), p. 90: 'Not herself drawn to superstition or spiritualism, she nevertheless was fascinated by Scottish folklore and legends.' See the argument that Oliphant was influenced by an older brand of 'Celtic Christianity', accommodating myth and folklore, in Anne Scriven, *A Scotswoman in the Text: Margaret Oliphant's Literary Negotiations with National Identity* (unpublished doctoral thesis, University of Strathclyde, 2004) 'Chapter One: Seer and Seannachaidh'.

6. On her journalism see Joanne Shattock, 'Work for Women: Margaret Oliphant's Journalism', in Laurel Brake, Bill Bell, and David Finkelstein (eds), *Nineteenth-Century Media and the Construction of Identities* (New York: Palgrave, 2000), pp. 165–77; Barbara Onslow, *Women of the Press in Nineteenth-Century Britain* (London: Macmillan, 2000), pp. 183–99; Sutherland, Chapter 8.

7. 'Mrs. Oliphant's Scotland', p. 93.

8. Margarete Rubik, *The Novels of Mrs. Oliphant* (New York: Peter Lang, 1994), p. 285.

9. See Sandra M. Gilbert and Susan Gubar, *The Madwoman in the Attic* (New Haven: Yale University Press, 1979); Elaine Showalter, *The Female Malady* (London: Virago, 1987).

10. June Sturrock, 'Mr. Sludge and Mrs. Oliphant: Victorian Negotiations with the Dead', *The Victorian Newsletter* 101 (Spring 2002), p. 4.

11. Critics have described the tale as 'a flawless piece of work' (Merryn Williams, *Margaret Oliphant* (Basingstoke: Macmillan, 1986), p. 178), and 'among the best in the English language' (Jenni Calder, introduction to *A Beleaguered City and Other Tales of the Seen and the Unseen by Margaret Oliphant* (Edinburgh: Canongate, 2000), p. vii).

12. Penny Fielding, *Writing and Orality* (Oxford: Oxford University Press, 1996), p. 210.

13. 'Library Window', *A Beleaguered City and Other Tales of the Seen and Unseen*, p. 380.

14. John Gibson Lockhart, *Memoirs of the Life of Sir Walter Scott* (7 vols, Edinburgh: Robert Cadell, 1837), vol. 3, pp. 128–9.

15. 'Library Window', p. 399.

16. Ibid., p. 402.

17. R. D. Laing, *The Politics of Experience and the Bird of Paradise* (Harmondsworth: Penguin, 1967), p. 110.

18. The anthropological theory of Diffusionism is apparent in key Scottish texts of the early twentieth-century Renaissance period. For writers such as Lewis Grassic Gibbon and Neil Gunn, Diffusionism suggested that history was not progression but regression away from a hunter-gatherer, community-based ideal. The development of 'civilisation' and even Capitalism had, for Diffusionists, resulted in a loss of aspects of humanity rooted in the communal.

19. 'Waater o' Dye', collected in *Voices from Their Ain Countrie: The Poems of Marion Angus and Violet Jacob*, ed. Katherine Gordon (Glasgow: ASLS, 2006), p. 90.

20. See Christopher Whyte, 'Marion Angus and the Boundaries of Self', in D. Gifford and D. McMillan (eds), *A History of Scottish Women's Writing*; Katherine Gordon, *Voices from Their Ain Countrie*, p. 21.

21. Naomi Mitchison, *Five Men and a Swan* (London: Allen & Unwin, 1957).

22. Ibid., p. 93.

23. Ibid., p. 96.

24. For detailed analysis of Mitchison's use of the supernatural see Moira Burgess, *Mitchison's Ghosts* (Glasgow: Humming Earth, 2008).

25. Naomi Mitchison, *Among You Taking Notes*, ed. Dorothy Sheridan (Oxford: Oxford Paperbacks, 1986), p. 172.

26. A. L. Kennedy, *So I Am Glad* (London: Jonathan Cape, 1995), p. 95.

27. See Tzvetan Todorov, *The Fantastic: A Structural Approach to a Literary Genre*, trans. Richard Howard (New York: Cornell University Press, [1970] 1975).

28. Kennedy, *So I Am Glad*, p. 222.

29. Ibid., p. 76.

30. Ibid., p. 217.

31. Ibid., p. 59.

32. Ibid., p. 280.

33. For analysis of the supernatural in Ali Smith's novel 2001 *Hotel World*, see Macdonald, 'Against Realism: Contemporary Scottish Literature and the Supernatural' in Berthold Schoene (ed.), *The Edinburgh Companion to*

Contemporary Scottish Literature (Edinburgh: Edinburgh University Press, 2007), pp. 328–35.

Chapter 10 – McCulloch

1. Virginia Woolf, 'Character in Fiction', in A. Neillie (ed.), *The Essays of Virginia Woolf* vol. III (London: Hogarth Press, 1988), p. 421.
2. Dora Marsden, 'Bondwomen', *Freewoman* 1: 1 (23 November 1911), p. 1.
3. Glenda Norquay (ed.), The *Collected Works of Lorna Moon* (Edinburgh: Black & White Publishing, 2002)
4. Marsden, 'Commentary on Bondwomen', *Freewoman*, 1: 2 (30 November 1911), p. 22.
5. Catherine Carswell, *The Savage Pilgrimage* (Cambridge: Cambridge University Press, [1932] 1981), p. 4; see also 'Fanciful titles: D. H. Lawrence, *The White Peacock*', *Glasgow Herald*, 18 March 1911, p. 12.
6. Lawrence, letter to Carswell 16 April 1916, James T. Boulton (ed.), *The Letters of D. H. Lawrence*, vol. II (Cambridge: Cambridge University Press, 1979–2000), pp. 594–5.
7. Carswell, *Open the Door!* (London: Virago, [1920] 1986), p. 34.
8. See Liz Heron (ed.), *Streets of Desire* (London: Virago, 1993).
9. Alfred Tennyson, 'Mariana', *Poetical Works of Alfred Lord Tennyson* (London: Macmillan, 1899), p. 7.
10. Carswell, letter to F. Marian McNeill, 27 January 1926, *Lying Awake*, ed. John Carswell (Edinburgh: Canongate, [1950] 1997), p. 195.
11. Carswell, *The Camomile* (London: Virago, [1922] 1987), pp. 250–1.
12. Carswell, *Open the Door*, p. 327.
13. Lorna Moon, *Dark Star* ([1929] 2002); Nan Shepherd, *The Quarry Wood* (Edinburgh: Canongate, [1928] 1987).
14. Nancy Brysson Morrison, *The Gowk Storm* (Edinburgh: Canongate, [1933] 1988), p. 115.
15. Muir, *Imagined Corners, Mrs Ritchie* and *Mrs Grundy in Scotland* in Kirsty Allan (ed.), *Imagined Selves* (Edinburgh: Canongate, [1931, 1933, 1936] 1996), p. 3.
16. Ibid., p. 50.
17. Ibid., p. 115.
18. Muir, letter to F. Marion McNeill, in Margery Palmer McCulloch (ed.), *Modernism and Nationalism* (Glasgow: ASLS, 2004), p. 209.
19. Muir, *Belonging* (London: Hogarth Press, 1968), p. 163.
20. Carswell, 'The Grundy Women', *Spectator* (May 1936), p. 946.
21. Muir, *Belonging*, p. 172.
22. Jenni Calder, *The Nine Lives of Naomi Mitchison* (London: Virago, 1997), p. xi
23. Ibid., p. 61.

24. Naomi Mitchison, *The Bull Calves* (Glasgow: Richard Drew Publishing, [1947] 1985), p. 77.

25. Mitchison, 'Pages from a Russian Diary', *Modernism and Nationalism*, p. 210.

26. Virginia Woolf, 'Women and Fiction' (1929) in David Bradshaw (ed.), *Virginia Woolf: Selected Essays* (Oxford: Oxford University Press, 2008), pp. 136–7.

27. Dot Allan, *Makeshift and Hunger March: Two Novels by Dot Allan*, ed. Moira Burgess (Glasgow: ASLS, [1928, 1934] 2010).

28. Liz Lochhead, quoted by Colin Nicholson in 'Knucklebones of Irony: Liz Lochhead' in *Poem, Purpose and Place* (Edinburgh: Polygon, 1992), p. 223.

Chapter 11 – Anderson

1. Margaret Oliphant, *Kirsteen* (Glasgow: ASLS, 2010), ed. Anne M. Scriven, p. 26. Further references are to this edition.

2. Karen R. Lawrence, *Penelope Voyages* (Ithaca and London: Cornell University Press, 1994), p. 23.

3. Henri Lefebvre, *The Production of Space*, trans. Donald Nicholson-Smith (Oxford: Blackwell Publishing, [1991] 2010), p. 154.

4. Doreen Massey, *Space, Place and Gender* (Cambridge: Polity Press, [1994] 2007), pp. 2, 264.

5. See Alison Blunt and Gillian Rose, 'Introduction', Alison Blunt and Gillian Rose (eds), *Writing Women and Space* (New York and London: Guilford Press, 1994), pp. 1–25.

6. Andrew Thacker, *Moving through Modernity* (Manchester: Manchester University Press, [2003] 2009), p. 13. Space is frequently associated with 'movement' and place with 'location', but geographers use these terms in varying, often conflicting ways. The idea of place as 'rootedness' is emphasised by the philosopher Heidegger.

7. Wendy Parkins, *Mobility and Modernity in Women's Novels 1850s–1930s* (Basingstoke: Palgrave Macmillan, 2009), p. 9.

8. Massey, *Space, Place and Gender*, p. 11.

9. In Dorothy McMillan (ed.), *The Scotswoman at Home and Abroad* (Glasgow: ASLS, 1999), pp. 252, 253.

10. Lila Marz Harper, *Solitary Travelers* (Madison-Teaneck, NJ: Fairleigh Dickinson University Press and London: Associated University Press, 2001), p. 144, pp. 152–3.

11. Lefebvre, *The Production of Space*, p. 25.

12. Thacker, *Moving Through Modernity*, p. 3.

13. Laura Doyle and Laura Winkiel, *Geomodernisms* (Bloomington: Indiana University Press, 2005), p. 1.

14. Lawrence, *Penelope Voyages*, pp. 17, 19.
15. James Joyce, *Dubliners* (London: Penguin, [1992] 2000), p. 190.
16. *The Lum Hat*, in Violet Jacob, *Flemington and Tales from Angus* (Edinburgh: Canongate, 1998), ed. Carol Anderson, pp. 159–217, 159. All references are to this edition.
17. Lefebvre in *The Production of Space*, referring to early church architecture, remarks 'the verticality and political arrogance of towers' (p. 261); 'the phallic formant' is a space symbolising 'force, male fertility, masculine violence' (pp. 286–7).
18. Cairns Craig, *The Modern Scottish Novel: Narrative and the National Imagination* (Edinburgh: Edinburgh University Press, 1999), pp. 37–74.
19. Catherine Carswell, *The Camomile* (Glasgow: Kennedy & Boyd, [1922] 2007), p. 36. All references are to this edition.
20. Deborah L. Parsons, *Streetwalking the Metropolis: Women, the City and Modernity* (Oxford: Oxford University Press, 2000).
21. Ibid., p. 15.
22. Ana Parejo Vadillo, 'Phenomena in Flux: The Aesthetics and Politics of Traveling in Modernity', in Ann L. Ardis and Leslie W. Lewis (eds), *Women's Experience of Modernity, 1875–1945* (Baltimore: Johns Hopkins University Press, 2003), pp. 205–20, 212.
23. Rita Felski, *The Gender of Modernity* (Cambridge, MA and London: Harvard University Press, 1995), pp. 61–2.
24. Parsons, *Streetwalking the Metropolis*, pp. 101–2.
25. Dennis Smith (ed.), *The Third Statistical Account of Scotland vol. xxix, The County of Kincardine* (Edinburgh: Scottish Academic Press, 1988), p. 288.
26. Nan Shepherd, *A Pass in the Grampians* in *The Grampian Quartet*, ed. Roderick Watson (Edinburgh: Canongate, 1996), pp. 7–8. All page references are to this edition.
27. Barbara Green, 'The New Woman's Appetite for "Riotous Living": Rebecca West, Modernist Feminism and the Everyday', in Ardis and Lewis (eds), *Women's Experience of Modernity* (pp. 221–36), pp. 223, 232.
28. 'Robert Macfarlane, "I walk therefore I am"', *The Guardian*, 30 August 2008, and online (accessed 4 February 2011).
29. *Ord's Bothy Songs and Ballads of Aberdeen, Banff & Moray, Angus and the Mearns* (Edinburgh: John Donald, [1930] 1995), include 'Cairn-o-Mount' and 'The Maiden of Drumdurno'.
30. Parkins, *Mobility and Modernity*, p. 9.

Chapter 12 – Bell

1. See McCulloch, Chapter 10.
2. Jenni Calder, *The Nine Lives of Naomi Mitchison* (London: Virago Press, 1997), p. 94.

3. Moira Burgess begins to explore Mitchison's complex relationship with the writers of the Scottish Literary Renaissance movement in *Mitchison's Ghosts* (Glasgow: Zeticula, 2008). Burgess writes: 'In spite of differences and discontents, Mitchison warmly welcomes and praises the Scottish Literary Renaissance movement in her poem "The Scottish Renaissance in Glasgow: 1935" and includes the poem in her 1978 collection *The Cleansing of the Knife*', p. 7.

4. Naomi Mitchison, *Saltire Self-Portrait 2* (Edinburgh: Saltire Society, 1986), p. 9.

5. See Gill Benton, *Naomi Mitchison* (London: Pandora Press, 1990): 'Naomi's retreat into the Scottish Highlands gradually ended in the 1950s when she began to worry over the wider world. She was particularly concerned about hydrogen bombs as NATO installations proliferated in Scotland. In 1959 [. . .] was a major speaker at a mass Nuclear Disarmament rally, and in 1961 in Glasgow she helped lead a march of 10000 people against the Polaris missile base planned for the Holy Loch' (p. 144).

6. Despite not being a scientist herself, the book nonetheless received praise in scientific journals. In his review in the *New Scientist* Professor Ritchie Calder commented that: 'As a new map of knowledge it achieves its purpose. It is a series of outlines but it will encourage many to travel farther. [. . .] as editor Naomi Mitchison has made a good selection of authorities, who certainly write more intelligently than most of their predecessors, while she, intervening as commentator, helps the whole thing to hang together' (*New Scientist*, no 309, 18 October 1962, p. 170).

7. *The Scotsman*, 3 August 1963.

8. Edwin Morgan 'The Young Writer in Scotland' in *Edinburgh International Festival 1962: 'The Novel Today': International Writers' Conference: 20th–24th August, McEwan Hall, Edinburgh: programme and notes* (Edinburgh: Edinburgh International Festival, 1962), p. 37.

9. 'Yet it Shall be Tempest Tost', NLS Acc.10461/21.

10. See Calder, *The Nine Lives of Naomi Mitchison*.

11. Valentina Poggi, 'Vision and Space in Elspeth Davie's Fiction' in Douglas Gifford and Dorothy McMillan (eds), *A History of Scottish Women's Writing* (Edinburgh: Edinburgh University Press, 1997), p. 527.

12. Ann Jefferson, *The Nouveau Roman and the Poetics of Fiction* (Cambridge: Cambridge University Press, 1980), p. 16.

13. 'The claustrophobic atmosphere suggested by her long enumerations of objects of all kinds, whether hand-made or mass-produced, suggests that identity and sanity are liable to be deranged by the multiplying of possessions like a stream banked up by boulders and mud'. Poggi, 'Vision and Space in Elspeth Davie's Fiction', p. 530.

14. John Calder, *Pursuit: The Uncensored Memoirs of John Calder* (London: Calder, 2001), p. 379.

15. Peter Todd and Benjamin Cook (eds), *Subjects and Sequences: A Margaret Tait Reader* (London: Lux, 2004), pp. 9–10.
16. 'And I asked Christopher [Hugh MacDiarmid was the pseudonym of Christopher Murray Grieve] if he thought he could walk along as if he was balancing Earth, making the Earth turn round with his own foot, and he thought he could do that [. . .]' (quoted in *Subjects and Sequences*, p. 80).
17. Margaret Tait, *The Hen and the Bees* (Glasgow: The University Press, 1960), p. 44.
18. Kristin Prevallet (ed.), *A Helen Adam Reader* (Orono: National Poetry Foundation, 2007), p. 218.
19. Prevallet, *A Helen Adam Reader*, p. 24.

Chapter 13 – Norquay

1. Carla Sassi, *Why Scottish Literature Matters* (Edinburgh: Saltire Society, 2005), p. 168.
2. Isla Dewar is the best example of a Scottish writer working within romantic 'chicklit' fiction, with a humorous emphasis on the domestic. Science fiction underpins much of Margaret Elphinstone's work; Sian Hayton is another notable figure in the field.
3. Johannes Willem Bertens and Theo d'Haen, *Contemporary American Crime Fiction* (London: Palgrave Macmillan, 2001), p. 67.
4. Gill Plain, *Twentieth Century Crime Fiction* (Edinburgh: Edinburgh University Press, 2001).
5. Kate Flint, *The Woman Reader 1837–1914* (Oxford: Oxford University Press, 1995).
6. Janice A. Radway, *Reading the Romance*, 2nd edn (Carolina: University of North Carolina Press, 1991).
7. Plain, 'Concepts of Corruption: Crime Fiction and the Scottish "State"' in Berthold Schoene (ed.), *The Edinburgh Companion to Contemporary Scottish Literature* (Edinburgh: Edinburgh University Press, 2007), pp. 132–40.
8. '"Tartan noir has reigned unopposed for too long. Tartan tweed might give it a run for its dirty money." *Scottish Daily Mail*', from *The Armistice Ball*, cover (London: Constable, 2005).
9. Marian Shaw, *Reflecting on Miss Marple* (London: Routledge, 1991).
10. Gill Plain, 'Concepts of Corruption: Crime Fiction and the Scottish "State"'.
11. Ibid., p. 137.
12. Ibid.
13. Karen Campbell, *The Twilight Time* (London: Hodder, 2009), p. 111.
14. See particularly, *Shadowplay* (London: Hodder, 2010).
15. Campbell, *After the Fire* (London: Hodder, 2009), pp. 334–5.
16. Denise Mina, *Still Midnight* (London: Reagan Arthur Books, 2009).

17. Mina, *The End of the Wasp Season* (London: Orion, 2011), p. 128.
18. Fiona Tolan '"Everyone has left something here": The Storyteller-Historian in Kate Atkinson's *Behind the Scenes at the Museum*', *Critique* 50: 3 (2009), pp. 275–90, 276.
19. Tolan, p. 279, quoting from Hayden White, *Metahistory* (Baltimore: Johns Hopkins University Press, 1973).
20. Naomi Mitchison early novels *The Conquered* (1923) and *Cloud Cuckoo Land* (1925) were set in the first and fifth century BC respectively. *The Corn King and the Spring Queen* (1931) is located in historical and fictive primitive cultures. *The Bull Calves* (1947) covers the Jacobite Rising. Novels by Margaret Elphinstone include *The Gathering Light* (2001), set in the Mesolithic period; *Sea Road* (2001) about Viking explorations in the North Atlantic; and *Light* (2007), set in the 1830s.
21. Dunnett is not mentioned in Ian Brown and Alan Riach (eds), *The Edinburgh Companion to Twentieth-Century Scottish Literature* (Edinburgh: Edinburgh University Press, 2009).
22. Mariadele Boccardi, 'Pedlars of their Nations Past: Douglas Galbraith, James Robertson, and the New Historical Novel', in Schoene (ed.), *The Edinburgh Companion to Contemporary Scottish Literature*, pp. 97–105, also quoting Craig, *The Modern Scottish Novel* (1999), p. 97.
23. Colin Milton, 'Past and Present: Modern Scottish Historical Fiction', in Ian Brown et al. (eds), *The Edinburgh History of Scottish Literature* vol. 3 (Edinburgh: Edinburgh University Press, 2007), pp. 114–29.
24. Helen Hughes, *The Historical Romance* (London: Routledge, 1993).
25. For internet activity see: http://www.dorothydunnett.co.uk/ and: marzipan@yahoo.groups.com.
26. Milton, 'Past and Present: Modern Scottish Historical Fiction'.
27. See Lisa Hopkins, ' Dorothy Dunnett's Lymond and Niccolò series: History versus Experience', *Working Papers on the Web*: http://extra.shu.ac.uk/wpw/historicising/HopkinsL.htm.
28. Cleo McNelly Kearns, 'Dubious Pleasures: Dorothy Dunnett and the Historical Novel', *Critical Quarterly* 32: 1 (1990), p. 38.
29. See Milton; Hopkins; Kearns, 'Dubious Pleasures', p. 47.
30. Dunnett, *Queen's Play* (1964) (London: Arrow Books, 1986), p. 17.
31. Dunnett in fact worked in both genres, publishing, as Dorothy Halliday, the 'Dolly' series of detective fiction in the 1960s and 1970s.

Chapter 14 – Brown

1. Katherine Gordon (ed.), *Voices from their Ain Countrie: The Poems of Marion Angus and Violet Jacob* (Glasgow: ASLS, 2006), p. 3.
2. Matt McGuire, *Contemporary Scottish Literature* (Basingstoke: Palgrave Macmillan, 2009), p. 65.

3. Helen Boden, 'Kathleen Jamie's Semiotic of Scotlands', in Aileen Christianson and Alison Lumsden (eds), *Contemporary Scottish Women Writers* (Edinburgh: Edinburgh University Press, 2000), p. 39.

4. Gordon (ed.), *Voices from their Ain Countrie*, p. 63.

5. Christopher Whyte suggests that 'echoes of the ballads' 'can be heard throughout her verse'. 'Marion Angus and the Poetry of Self' in Douglas Gifford and Dorothy McMillan (eds), *A History of Scottish Women's Writing* (Edinburgh: Edinburgh University Press, 1997), p. 383.

6. Marion Angus, 'Scottish Poetry Old and New' in *The Scottish Association for the Speaking of Verse: Its Work for the Year 1927–1928* (Edinburgh: Constable, 1928), p. 29.

7. Gordon (ed.), *Voices from their Ain Countrie*, p. 157.

8. Liz Lochhead, *Dreaming Frankenstein and Collected Poems, 1967–1984* (1984; reprinted Edinburgh: Polygon, 2003), p. 113.

9. Lochhead, *Dreaming Frankenstein*, p. 116.

10. Lochhead, *Dreaming Frankenstein*, p. 147.

11. Anne Varty, 'The Mirror and the Vamp: Liz Lochhead', in Gifford and McMillan (eds), *A History of Scottish Women's Writing*, p. 644.

12. Lochhead, quoted in Colin Nicholson, *Poem, Purpose and Place: Shaping Identity in Contemporary Scottish Verse* (Edinburgh: Polygon, 1992), p. 208.

13. Lochhead, *Dreaming Frankenstein*, pp. 185–6.

14. Kathleen Jamie, *Waterlight: Selected Poems* (Saint Paul, MN: Graywolf Press, 2007), p. 59.

15. Ibid., p. 64.

16. 'Kathleen Jamie' in The Poetry Archive (http://www.poetryarchive.org/poetryarchive/singlePoet.do?poetId=190).

17. Jamie, *Waterlight*, p. 41.

18. See also Gilbert, Chapter 3.

19. Herbert Grierson and J. C. Smith, quoted in Whyte, 'Marion Angus and the Boundaries of Self', p. 386.

20. Lochhead in Nicholson, *Poem, Purpose and Place*, p. 211.

21. Kathleen Jamie in Atilla Dósa, *Beyond Identity: New Horizons in Modern Scottish Poetry* (Amsterdam: Rodopi, 2009), p. 144.

22. Catherine Kerrigan, *An Anthology of Scottish Women Poets* (Edinburgh: Edinburgh University Press, 1991), p. 2.

23. Gordon (ed.), *Voices from their Ain Countrie*, p. 55.

24. Ibid., p. 66.

25. Ibid., p. 67.

26. Ibid., p. 108.

27. Whyte, 'Marion Angus and the Boundaries of Self', p. 383.

28. Ibid., p. 72.

29. Angus's refrain is taken from 'The Lyke Wake Dirge'. See Gordon, p. 307.

30. Lochhead, *Dreaming Frankenstein*, p. 93.

31. Robert Crawford, 'The Two-Faced Language of Lochhead's Poetry', in Robert Crawford and Anne Varty (eds), *Liz Lochhead's Voices* (Edinburgh: Edinburgh University Press, 1993), p. 61.
32. Jamie, *Waterlight*, p. 79.
33. See discussion Germanà, Chapter 15.
34. Lochhead, in Rebecca E. Wilson, *Sleeping with Monsters* (Edinburgh: Polygon, 1990), p. 10.
35. Jamie, in Dósa, *Beyond Identity*, p. 144.
36. Lochhead, *Dreaming Frankenstein*, p. 72.
37. Aileen Christianson, 'Liz Lochhead's Poetry and Drama: Forging Ironies', in Christianson and Lumsden (eds), *Contemporary Scottish Women Writers*, p. 44.
38. Gordon (ed.), *Voices from their Ain Countrie*, p. 117.
39. Lochhead, *Dreaming Frankenstein*, p. 14.
40. Dorothy McMillan, 'Liz Lochhead and the Ungentle Art of Clyping', in Crawford and Varty (eds), *Liz Lochhead's Voices*, p. 35.
41. Jamie, *Waterlight*, p. 96.
42. Helen Boden, 'Kathleen Jamie's Semiotic of Scotlands', p. 31.
43. Jamie, *Waterlight*, p. 85.
44. Ibid., p. 92.
45. Ibid., p. 98.
46. Boden, 'Kathleen Jamie's Semiotics of Scotlands', p. 30.
47. Gordon (ed.), *Voices from their Ain Countrie*, p. 73.
48. Ibid., p. 83.
49. Ibid., p. 311.
50. Lochhead, *Dreaming Frankenstein*, p. 84.
51. Ibid., p. 85.
52. Ibid., p. 85.
53. Ibid., pp. 89–92.
54. Jamie, *Waterlight*, p. 31.
55. Ibid., p. 77.
56. Jamie, in Wilson, *Sleeping with Monsters*, p. 94.
57. Douglas Gifford and Dorothy McMillan, 'Introduction' to A *History of Scottish Women's Writing*, p. xx.

Chapter 15 – Germanà

1. Kathleen Jamie, 'Meadowsweet', *Jizzen* (London: Picador, 1999), p. 49. On the 'silencing' burial of two Early Modern Hebridean poets, see p. 26 and associated endnote 27.
2. Sarah M. Dunnigan, 'A. L. Kennedy's Longer Fiction: Articulate Grace', in Aileen Christianson and Alison Lumsden (eds), *Contemporary Scottish Women Writers* (Edinburgh: Edinburgh University Press, 2000), p. 145.

3. Christie Leigh March, 'Interview with A.L. Kennedy' (17 March 1999), *Edinburgh Review* 101 (1999), p. 100.

4. A. L. Kennedy, *Looking for the Possible Dance* (London: Minerva, [1993] 1994), p. 71. All page references are to this edition.

5. Dominic Head, *The Cambridge Introduction to Modern British Fiction, 1950–2000* (Cambridge: Cambridge University Press, 2002), pp. 153, 154.

6. Helen Stoddart, '"Tongues of Bone": A. L. Kennedy and the Problems of Articulation', in Nick Bentley (ed.), *British Fiction of the 1990s* (London: Routledge, 2005), p. 142.

7. Benedict Anderson, *Imagined Communities* (London: Verso, [1983] 1991), p. 6.

8. Janice Galloway, *Foreign Parts* (London: Vintage, [1994] 1995), p. 120.

9. Edwin Morgan, *Collected Poems* (Manchester: Carcanet, 1990).

10. Glenda Norquay, 'Janice Galloway's Novels: Fraudulent Mooching', in Christianson and Lumsden, *Contemporary Scottish Women Writers*, p. 131.

11. Norquay, 'The Fiction of Janice Galloway', p. 328.

12. Ali Smith, *Like* (London: Virago, 1997), p. 269.

13. Terry Castle, *The Apparitional Lesbian* (New York: Columbia University Press, 1993), p. 60.

14. Michel Foucault, 'Of Other Spaces', *Diacritics* 16: 1 (Spring 1986), pp. 22–7 (p. 25).

15. Jackie Kay, *Trumpet* (London: Picador, [1998] 1999), p. 1.

16. See also works by Mairi E. NicLeòid, Alison Lang, Catriona Lexy Chaimbeul and Mairi Anna NicDhomhnaill.

17. Richard Bradford, *The Novel Now* (Oxford: Blackwell, 2007), p. 172.

18. Head, *The Cambridge Introduction to Modern British Fiction*, pp. 118–55.

Further Reading

General

Abrams, Lynn, Eleanor Gordon, Deborah Simonton and Eileen Janes Yeo (eds), *Gender in Scottish History Since 1700* (Edinburgh: Edinburgh University Press, 2006).

Anderson, Carol and Aileen Christianson (eds), *Scottish Women's Fiction, 1920s to 1960s: Journeys into Being* (East Linton: Tuckwell Press, 2000).

Black, Ronald (ed.), *An Tuil: Anthology of 20th Century Scottish Gaelic Verse* (Edinburgh: Polygon, 1999).

Black, Ronald (ed.), *An Lasair Anthology of 18th Century Scottish Gaelic Verse* (Edinburgh: Birlinn, 2001).

Brown, Ian, Thomas Owen Clancy, Susan Manning and Murray Pittock (eds), *The Edinburgh History of Scottish Literature*, 3 vols (Edinburgh: Edinburgh University Press, 2007).

Christianson, Aileen and Alison Lumsden (eds), *Contemporary Scottish Women Writers* (Edinburgh: Edinburgh University Press, 2000).

Ewan, Elizabeth, Sue Innes, Siân Reynolds and Rose Pipes (eds), *The Biographical Dictionary of Scottish Women* (Edinburgh: Edinburgh University Press, 2006).

Gifford, Douglas and Dorothy McMillan (eds), *A History of Scottish Women's Writing* (Edinburgh: Edinburgh University Press, 1997).

McLeod, Wilson and Meg Bateman (eds), *Duanaire na Sracaire Songbook of the Pillagers: Anthology of Scotland's Gaelic Verse to 1600* (Edinburgh: Birlinn, 2007).

Meek, Donald E. (ed.), *Caran an t-Saoghail / The Wiles of the World: Anthology of nineteenth century Scottish Gaelic Verse* (Edinburgh: Birlinn, 2003).

Ó Baoill, Colm (ed.) and Meg Bateman (trans.), *Gàir nan Clàrsach / The Harps' Cry: an Anthology of 17th century Gaelic Poetry* (Edinburgh: Birlinn, c.1994).

Sassi, Carla, *Why Scottish Literature Matters* (Edinburgh: Saltire Society, 2005).

Schoene, Berthold (ed.), *The Edinburgh Companion to Contemporary Scottish Literature* (Edinburgh: Edinburgh University Press, 2007).

Whyte, Christopher (ed.), *An Aghaidh na Sìorraidheachd: Ochdnar Bhàrd Gàidhlig / In the Face of Eternity: Eight Gaelic Poets* (Edinburgh: Polygon, 1991).

Whyte, Christopher (ed.), *Gendering the Nation* (Edinburgh: Edinburgh University Press, 1995).

Pre-1800

Benger, Elizabeth, *Memoirs of the Late Mrs Elizabeth Hamilton*, 2 vols (London: Longman, Hurst, Rees, Orme and Brown, 1818).

Bold, Alan, *The Ballad* (London: Methuen, 1979).

Brown, Mary Ellen, 'Old Singing Women and the Canons of Scottish Balladry and Song', in Gifford and McMillan (eds), *A History of Scottish Women's Writing*, pp. 44–57.

Bruford, Alan, 'Workers, weepers and witches: the status of the female singer in Gaelic society', *Scottish Gaelic Studies* vol. XVII (University of Aberdeen, 1996).

Buchan, David, *The Ballad and the Folk* (London and Boston: Routledge, 1972).

Clancy, Thomas and Murray Pittock (eds), *The Edinburgh History of Scottish Literature: Volume 1: From Columba to the Union* (Edinburgh: Edinburgh University Press, 2007).

Drescher, Horst W. (ed.), *Henry Mackenzie: Letters to Elizabeth Rose of Kilravock* (Edinburgh and London: Oliver and Boyd, 1967).

Dugaw, Dianne, *Warrior Women and Popular Balladry, 1650–1850* (Cambridge: Cambridge University Press, 1989).

Ewan, Elizabeth and Maureen M. Meikle (eds), *Women in Scotland, c.1100–1750* (East Linton: Tuckwell Press, 1999).

Ezell, Margaret J. M., *Social Authorship and the Advent of Print* (Baltimore: Johns Hopkins University Press, 1999).

Grant, John Peter (ed.), *Memoir and Correspondence of Mrs Grant of Laggan*, 3 vols (London: Longman, 1845).

Gribben, Crawford and David George Mullan (eds), *Literature and the Scottish Reformation* (Aldershot: Ashgate, 2009).

Guest, Harriet, 'Bluestocking Feminism', in *Huntington Library Quarterly* 65.1–2 (2002), pp. 59–80.

McCue, Kirsteen, 'Women and Song 1750–1850', in Gifford and McMillan (eds), *A History of Scottish Women's Writing* (Edinburgh: Edinburgh University Press, 1997), pp. 58–70.

Ó Baoill, Colm (ed.), *Bàrdachd Shìlis na Ceapaich* (Edinburgh: Scottish Gaelic Texts Society, 1972).

Ó Baoill, Colm (ed.), *Mairghread nighean Lachlainn song-maker of Mull* (Edinburgh: Scottish Gaelic Texts Society, 2009).

Petrie, Elaine, '"What a Voice!" Women, Repertoire and Loss in the Singing Tradition', in Gifford and McMillan (eds), *A History of Scottish Women's Writing* (Edinburgh: Edinburgh University Press, 1997), pp. 262–73.

Ryrie, Alec, *The Origins of the Scottish Reformation* (Manchester: Manchester University Press, 2006).

Schellenberg, Betty, *The Professionalization of Women Writers in Eighteenth-Century Britain* (Cambridge: Cambridge University Press, 2005).

Shields, Juliet, *Sentimental Literature and Anglo-Scottish Identity, 1745–1820* (Cambridge: Cambridge University Press, 2010).

Todd, Margo, *The Culture of Protestantism in Early Modern Scotland* (New Haven: Yale University Press, 2002).

Watson, J. C., *The Gaelic Songs of Mary Macleod* (Edinburgh: Scottish Gaelic Texts Society, 1982).

Post-1800

Alker, Sharon, 'The Business of Romance: Mary Brunton and the Virtue of Economy', *European Romantic Review*, vol. 13 (2002), pp. 199–205.

Anderson, Carol (ed.), *Opening the Doors: The Achievement of Catherine Carswell* (Edinburgh: Ramsay Head Press, 2001).

Ardis, Ann L. and Leslie W. Lewis (eds), *Women's Experience of Modernity 1875–1945* (Baltimore: Johns Hopkins University Press, 2003).

Bateman, Meg, 'Women's Writing in Scottish Gaelic Since 1750', in Douglas Gifford and Dorothy McMillan (eds), *A History of Scottish Women's Writing* (Edinburgh: Edinburgh University Press, 1997), pp. 659–76.

Blunt, Alison and Gillian Rose (eds), *Writing Women and Space* (New York and London: Guilford Press).

Bold, Valentina, 'Beyond "The Empire of the Gentle Heart": Scottish Women Poets of the Nineteenth Century', in Gifford and McMillan (eds), *A History of Scottish Women's Writing*, pp. 246–61.

Boos, Florence, 'The Homely Muse in Her Diurnal Setting: The Periodical Poems of "Marie", Janet Hamilton and Fanny Forrester', *Victorian Poetry* 39: 2 (2001), pp. 255–85.

Boos, Florence, *Working-Class Women Poets of Victorian Britain: An Anthology* (Peterborough, Ontario: Broadview, 2008).

Borthwick, David, 'A. L. Kennedy's Dysphoric Fictions', in Berthold Schoene (ed.), *The Edinburgh Companion to Contemporary Scottish Literature* (Edinburgh: Edinburgh University Press, 2007), pp. 264–71.

Burgess, Moira, *Mitchison's Ghosts* (Glasgow: Humming Earth, 2008).

Calder, Jenni, *The Nine Lives of Naomi Mitchison* (London: Virago Press, 1997).

Carter, Gillian, '"Domestic Geography" and the Politics of Scottish Landscape in Nan Shepherd's *The Living Mountain*', *Gender, Place and Culture: A Journal of Feminist Geography* 8: 1 (2001), pp. 25–36.

Christianson, Aileen, *Jane Welsh Carlyle, Biography and Biographers* (Edinburgh: Carlyle Society, 2008).

Christianson, Aileen, 'Jane Welsh Carlyle's "Private Writing Career"', in Gifford and McMillan (eds), *A History of Scottish Women's Writing*, pp. 232–45.

Christianson, Aileen, *Moving in Circles: Willa Muir's Writings* (Edinburgh: Word Power Books, 2007).

Corcoran Neil (ed.), *The Cambridge Companion to 20th Century English Poetry* (Cambridge: Cambridge University Press, 2007).

Crawford, Robert and Anne Varty (eds), *Liz Lochhead's Voices* (Edinburgh: Edinburgh University Press, 1993).

Cruickshank, Helen B., *Collected Poems* (Edinburgh: Reprographia, 1971).

Cruickshank, Helen B., *Octobiography* (Montrose: Standard Press, 1976).

Doyle, Laura and Laura Winkiel, *Geomodernisms: Race, Modernism, Modernity* (Bloomington: Indiana University Press, 2005).

Duncan, Ian, *Scott's Shadow* (Princeton: Princeton University Press, 2007).

Gordon, Katherine (ed.), *Voices from their Ain Countrie: The Poems of Marion Angus and Violet Jacob* (Glasgow: ASLS, 2006).

Jefferson, Ann, *The Nouveau Roman and the Poetics of Fiction* (Cambridge: Cambridge University Press, 1980).

Jones, Carole, 'Burying the Man that was: Janice Galloway and Gender Disorientation', in Schoene (ed.), *The Edinburgh Companion to Contemporary Scottish Literature* (Edinburgh: Edinburgh University Press, 2007), pp. 210–18.

Jones, Carole, *Disappearing Men: Gender Disorientation in Scottish Fiction 1979–1999* (Amsterdam: Rodopi, 2009).

King, Elspeth, *Scotland Sober and Free: The Temperance Movement 1829–1979* (Glasgow: Glasgow Museums and Art Galleries, 1979).

Lumsden, Alison, 'Jackie Kay's Poetry and Prose', in Christianson and Lumsden, *Contemporary Scottish Women Writers* (Edinburgh: Edinburgh University Press, 2000), pp. 79–91.

Maidment, Brian (ed.), *The Poorhouse Fugitives: Self-Taught Poets and Poetry in Victorian Britain* (Manchester: Carcanet, 1987).

March, Christie L. *Rewriting Scotland: Welsh, McLean, Warner, Banks, Galloway, and Kennedy* (Manchester: Manchester University Press, 2002).

Massey, Doreen, *Space, Place and Gender* (Cambridge: Polity Press, [1994] 2007).

McGuire, Matt, *Contemporary Scottish Literature* (Basingstoke: Palgrave MacMillan, 2009).

McMillan, Dorothy, 'Selves and Others: Non-fiction Writing in the Eighteenth and Early Nineteenth Centuries', in Gifford and McMillan (eds), *A History of Scottish Women's Writing* (Edinburgh: Edinburgh University Press, 1997), pp. 71–91.

McMillan, Dorothy (ed.), *The Scotswoman at Home and Abroad: Non-Fiction Writing 1700–1900* (Glasgow: ASLS, 1999).

McCulloch, Margery Palmer (ed.), *Modernism and Nationalism: Literature and Society in Scotland 1918–1939: Source Documents for the Scottish Renaissance* (Glasgow: ASLS, 2004).

McCulloch, Margery Palmer (ed.), 'Women, Modernism and the Modern World', in *Scottish Modernism and its Contexts* (Edinburgh: Edinburgh University Press, 2009), pp. 68–90.

Mellor, Anne K., *Romanticism and Gender* (New York and London: Routledge, 1993).

McNeill, F. Marian, *The Road Home: A Novel* (London: Maclehose, 1932).

McNeill, F. Marian, *The Silver Bough: A Four-Volume Study of the National and Local Festivals of Scotland* (Glasgow: Maclellan, 1957–68).

McNeill, F. Marian, *The Scots Kitchen* (Edinburgh: Mercat Press, [1929] 1993).

Mermin, Dorothy, *Godiva's Ride: Women of Letters in England 1830–1880* (Bloomington and Indianapolis: Indiana University Press, 1993).

Murray Isobel (ed.), *Beyond This Limit: Selected Shorter Fiction of Naomi Mitchison* (Edinburgh: Scottish Academic Press, 1986).

Norquay, Glenda, 'The Fiction of Janice Galloway: "Weaving a Route Through Chaos"' in Glenda Norquay and G. Smyth (eds), *Space and Place: The Geographies of Literature* (Liverpool: John Moores University Press, 1997), pp. 323–30.

Norquay, Glenda, 'Janice Galloway's Novels: Fraudulent Mooching', in Christianson and Lumsden (eds), *Contemporary Scottish Women Writers* (Edinburgh: Edinburgh University Press, 2000), pp. 131–44.

Norquay, Glenda, 'Finding a Place: the Voice of Lorna Moon', *Études Écossaises* 9 (2003–4), pp. 91–104.

Porter, James and Herschel Gower, *Jeannie Robertson* (East Linton: Tuckwell Press, 1997).

Prevallet, Kristin (ed.), *A Helen Adam Reader* (Orono, ME: National Poetry Foundation, 2007).

Rubik, Margarete, *The Novels of Mrs Oliphant* (New York: Peter Lang, 1994).

Stirling, Kirsten, *Bella Caledonia: Woman, Nation, Text* (Amsterdam: Rodopi, 2008).

Todd, Peter and Benjamin Cook (eds), *Subjects and Sequences: A Margaret Tait Reader* (London: Lux, 2004).

Trela, D. J. (ed.), *Margaret Oliphant: Critical Essays on a Gentle Subversive* (Slensgrove and London: Susquehanna University Press and Associated University Press, 1995).

Vincent, David, *Bread, Knowledge and Freedom: A Study of Working-Class Autobiography* (London: Methuen, 1982).

Watson, Roderick (ed.), *MacCaig, Morgan, Lochhead: Three Scottish Poets* (Edinburgh: Canongate, 1992).

Williams, Merryn, *Margaret Oliphant* (Basingstoke: Macmillan, 1986).

Williamson, Karina, 'The Emergence of Privacy: Letters, Journals and Domestic Writing' in Ian Brown et al. (eds), *The Edinburgh History of Scottish Literature* (Edinburgh: Edinburgh University Press, 2007). Volume 2, pp. 57–70.

Young, John, *Pictures in Prose and Verse; or, Personal Recollections of the Late Janet Hamilton* (Langloan: George Gallie, 1977).

Notes on Contributors

Carol Anderson has written extensively on Scottish literature. She co-edited *Scottish Women's Fiction 1920s–1960s* (2000) with Aileen Christianson, and edited *Opening the Doors: The Achievement of Catherine Carswell* (2001). She currently tutors Creative Writing with the Open University, and has published prize-winning short stories.

Eleanor Bell is a lecturer in English Studies at the University of Strathclyde. She is author of *Questioning Scotland: Literature, Nationalism, Postmodernism* (2004). Her research interests are in twentieth-century Scottish literature and she is currently working on several projects relating to the 1960s in particular.

Florence S. Boos, a professor of English at the University of Iowa, has published monographs on the poetry of Dante G. Rossetti and William Morris and is the general editor of the Morris Online Edition (http://morrisedition. lib.uiowa.edu). She is the author of several articles on Victorian working-class women poets and the editor of *Working-Class Women Poets of Victorian Britain: An Anthology* (2008).

Rhona Brown is a lecturer in Scottish Literature at the University of Glasgow where she specialises in eighteenth-century Scottish literature. She is author of *Robert Fergusson and the Scottish Periodical Press* (2012). She is currently continuing work on Fergusson, Scottish magazine culture and the work of James Beattie.

Michel Byrne studied Gaelic at Edinburgh University, and has been teaching Gaelic literature at Glasgow University's Celtic and Gaelic section since 1997.

Aileen Christianson is a senior editor of *The Collected Letters of Thomas and Jane Welsh Carlyle* (1970–ongoing: vol. 40, 2012). She publishes on Jane

Welsh Carlyle, Muriel Spark, Liz Lochhead and others. Her most recent monograph is *Moving in Circles: Willa Muir's Writings* (2007). She is an honorary fellow of the School of Literatures, Languages and Cultures, Edinburgh University.

Sarah M. Dunnigan is senior lecturer in English Literature at Edinburgh University where she teaches Scottish and medieval literature. Currently completing a book on Scottish fairy tales, she has written about medieval and Renaissance Scottish writing, Burns, early modern and contemporary women writers, and traditional ballads.

Anne Frater was brought up in Pabail Uarach on the Isle of Lewis. After gaining an MA in Celtic and French, then a PhD in Celtic (Scottish Gaelic Women's Poetry up to 1750), from Glasgow University, she worked in the media before returning to Lewis in 1999 as a lecturer on the UHI Gaelic Degree courses based at Lews Castle College.

Monica Germanà is senior lecturer in English Literature and Creative Writing at the University of Westminster. Her research interests and publications concentrate on contemporary British literature, with a specific emphasis on the Gothic, women's writing and Scottish literature. Her first monograph, *Scottish Women's Gothic and Fantastic Writing*, was published in 2010.

Suzanne Gilbert, senior lecturer in English at Stirling University, publishes on eighteenth- and nineteenth-century Scottish literature, ballads, and chapbooks. She and Ian Duncan are general editors of the Stirling/South Carolina Research Edition of *The Collected Works of James Hogg* (Edinburgh University Press), for which she co-edited *Queen Hynde* (1998) and edited *The Mountain Bard* (2007).

Kirsty A. Macdonald is a lecturer in Scottish Cultural Studies at the University of the Highlands and Islands. Her research interests include Scottish Gothic and representations of the Highlands and Islands in literature and popular culture. She is currently working on a monograph on contemporary Highlands and Islands literature.

Ainsley McIntosh recently completed a year as Research Fellow on the planned Edinburgh Edition of the Poetry of Walter Scott at the University of Aberdeen. Her research interests lie in the poetry and fiction of the British Romantic period, and in particular she works, and has published, on Walter Scott.

Glenda Norquay is Professor of Scottish Literary Studies at Liverpool John Moores University. Her books include a monograph on *Robert Louis Stevenson and Theories of Reading*, the edited collection *Across the Margins* (with Gerry Smyth), and a number of essays and articles on Stevenson and on Scottish women writers. She edited *The Collected Works of Lorna Moon*, and two collections of women's suffrage fiction.

Margery Palmer McCulloch is currently senior research fellow in Scottish Literature at the University of Glasgow and co-edits *Scottish Literary Review*. Her books include monographs on Neil M. Gunn and Edwin Muir, an edited collection on Lewis Grassic Gibbon, *Modernism and Nationalism: Source Documents for the Scottish Renaissance*, and *Scottish Modernism and its Contexts 1918–1959*. With Scott Lyall, she co-edited the *Edinburgh Companion to Hugh MacDiarmid* (2011).

Pam Perkins teaches eighteenth-century and Romantic literature at the University of Manitoba. Her recent publications include a study of the professional careers of Elizabeth Hamilton, Anne Grant, and Christian Johnstone and an edition of Hamilton's *Cottagers of Glenburnie*. She is currently working on eighteenth- and early nineteenth-century Scottish travel writing.

Helen Sutherland teaches in Adult and Continuing Education at the University of Glasgow, and is editor of the *Journal of the Sylvia Townsend Warner Society*. Her doctoral thesis is on 'The Function of Fantasy in Victorian Literature, Art and Architecture' and she has published on James Hogg, Gothic literature, and the fantasy writing of Sylvia Townsend Warner.

Index